C.S. LEWIS AND THE ARTS

CREATIVITY in the SHADOWLANDS

"Even fifty years after his death, C.S. Lewis remains one the most popular and influential Christian writers and thinkers of the twentieth century. So much has been written about him, one wonders what else can possibly be said. But this book is a fascinating exploration of Lewis's thinking about the arts, making it a must read book for anyone who loves Lewis and loves the arts."

—Mary McCleary, Regents Professor Emeritus at Stephen F. Austin State University

"Helpful and worthwhile. Anyone seeking to understand Lewis's approach to the arts will profit from this array of interesting perspectives."

—Dr. Michael Ward, co-editor of *The Cambridge Companion to C.S. Lewis*

"I have found C.S. Lewis to have deep insights in the areas of theology, history, literature, education, mythology, and more. He has an unerring way of turning the world upside down so that it makes sense again. It is no different with his thoughts on the arts; he can help us to see through the fog of competing "isms" of the art world to find again what art always had: a *telos,* a reason for being."

—Matthew Clark, Artist, Art instructor

"This thought-provoking collection of essays refreshes and refocuses our understanding of C.S. Lewis's work. It does this by re-establishing the importance of the relationship of art and aesthetics to Lewis's moral and ethical writings while providing fresh insight into some of his own artistic endeavors. It is a brilliant book that needs to be on the shelf of every Lewis fan or scholar."

—Dr. Melody Green, Urbana Theological Seminary

"The essays in *C.S. Lewis and the Arts* reveal the complexity of Lewis's concepts of creativity. This is not the contemporary, mythical Lewis who is merely considered the author of simple, though entertaining allegorical fairy tales. This is the Lewis who wrote everything from poetry to apologetics, and who believed in the aesthetic necessity in both endeavors. This is the Lewis who knew that if it was worth doing, it was worth doing beautifully."

—Tyrus Clutter, art professor and the former director of Christians in the Visual Arts (CIVA)

"We need more books like this: books that not only celebrate and decipher Lewis's defense of the arts and of the ineradicable links between the Good, the True, and the Beautiful, but that wrestle alongside Lewis, extending and nuancing his arguments so that they will speak with direct and prophetic power to our modern and postmodern colleges and universities."

—Dr. Louis Markos, author of *Restoring Beauty: The Good, the True, and the Beautiful in the Writings of C.S. Lewis*

C.S. LEWIS AND THE ARTS

CREATIVITY in the SHADOWLANDS

Edited by Rod Miller

Foreword by Theodore Prescott

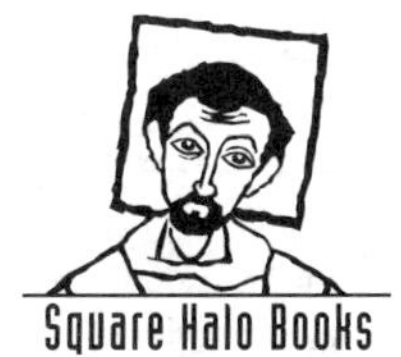

In Christian art, the square halo identified a living person presumed to be a saint. Square Halo Books is devoted to publishing works that present contextually sensitive biblical studies and practical instruction consistent with the Doctrines of the Reformation. The goal of Square Halo Books is to provide materials useful for encouraging and equipping the saints.

The artwork on the cover is "St. Jack" by Ned Bustard

First Edition 2013

P.O. Box 18954, Baltimore, MD 21206

ISBN 978-0-9785097-7-4

Library of Congress Control Number: 2013940013

Contents

Foreword: Using C.S. Lewis

THEODORE PRESCOTT

One of the most vexing distinctions concerning the arts is about their use. Unsurprisingly, judgments about the negative effects of use on art flowered during the rise of modern art, along with concepts like "art for art's sake." Surprisingly, if you think of C.S. Lewis as someone who did not march to the drum beat of modernity, it was an idea he endorsed.

In *How the Few and the Many Use Pictures and Music,* Lewis argued that "the many use art and the few receive it." The distinction rests on how a person engages an artwork. The many seek pleasure and confirmation of what they already know. The few engage art receptively, "in order to have something done" that might take them out of themselves. The many use art to "call out of you what is already there," while the few lay themselves open by "surrender" to the qualities in the work itself.[1] In this view, there is an inverse proportion between uses, and a work's ability to be perceived as art.

The distinctions Lewis described do exist, and as an artist I certainly prefer audiences that look closely, and are open to an experience unencumbered by viewer preconceptions. Lewis is right when he argues that fully engaging something requires a suspension of our immediate interests and knowledge. But I am not persuaded by his understanding of use. It parallels the modernist distinction between the Fine Arts and the useful arts, which is problematic in many ways. I'll briefly describe two problems.

The first is the overwhelming contradiction of the idea provided by history. We can get an inkling of this when we survey all of the useful objects—altar pieces, urns, monuments—in our great museums. We cannot experience these objects the way their makers and original cultures did. That possibility is closed to us. We relish them in the isolating context of the museum gallery, which is the ideal site for what philosopher Nicholas Wolterstorff called "perceptual contemplation." Wolterstorff saw this contemplation as modernism's dominant aesthetic paradigm.[2] (It should be noted that while "perceptual contemplation" and similar concepts still have currency within philosophical aesthetics, the artistic and critical communities that comprise "the art world" today are more accepting of uses and causes. Public art is one example of this, and art shaped by political or social ideologies is another.)

But surely those distant makers and users must have had some experience of the things themselves? Or, couldn't they at least have found harmony between their experiences of use, and a recognition of a works being, its inscape, apart from its use? It stretches credulity to think it is only modern people who have experienced such works by means of what Lewis called art's "real appreciation."[3]

This leads to my second problem, which doubts the existence of a special category for disinterested contemplation. The idea that art's audience should be disinterested emerged around the same time as the idea of uselessness, and was seen as a necessary condition for proper aesthetic appreciation. I do not question whether someone can be relatively disinterested—by putting aside personal appetites and desires—when one begins to see, read, or hear. One can certainly choose how to engage art. My concern is whether any such engagement is really so "useless."

The philosopher Roger Scruton, writing about beauty, speaks of "disinterested interest." It is his way of acknowledging the fact that we can be interested in things for their own sake, and yet still be personally involved. As he says, "To be disinterested in something is not necessarily to be uninterested in it, but to be interested in a certain way."[4] He never utters the word "use," but he does argue that works of art have a function. "They may fulfill this function in a rewarding way, offering food for thought and spiritual uplift, winning for themselves a loyal public that returns to them to be consoled or inspired."[5] Surely, it is splitting hairs to say these functions are not uses.

My purpose in broaching the topic of use is to encourage it. I believe that using the arts is natural, and properly a part of God's created order. I surely believe in using C.S. Lewis. While I find *How the Few and the Many Use Pictures and Music* problematic, there is much in my experience of Lewis's writings that justifies speaking of his usefulness. Generally his works not only provide me with contemplative delight—as artfully wrought forms—but also have given me useful insights into my vocations as an artist and a teacher.

As an example, Lewis identified the difficulty in discerning the meaning of modern works of art as being one of the frontiers between the modern era and those eras that came before. He described this new state of art in his 1954 inaugural lecture at Cambridge, *De Descriptione Temporum.* Lewis used a symposium about poetry to make his point. The seven participants, whose lives had been devoted to the study of poetry, could not agree on the meaning of T.S. Eliot's short poem, *Cooking Egg.* Lewis said that he was "not in the least concerned to decide whether this state of affairs is a good thing or a bad thing. I merely assert that it is a new thing."[6] Thus for Lewis, one of the hallmarks of modernity is discord about art, and a lack of cultural consensus about what it means. In a footnote Lewis made an aside that anticipates deconstruction and post modernism, and indicates, I think, his own sentiments about the affairs he has described. He muses, "Why, should there not come a period when the art of writing poetry stands lower than the art of reading it? Of course rival readings would then cease to be 'right' or 'wrong' and become more or less 'brilliant performances'."[7]

Lewis was prescient. What he imagined came to pass, and prompted George Steiner to write *Real Presences* in 1989. Steiner wanted to rescue the work of art from the critical tumors growing upon its body, which multiplied "readings" and "brilliant performances," but which obscured or deformed an experience of the work itself. So Lewis's conviction that a work of art actually means something, and might be grasped by a perceptive, literate, or sympathetic audience—without the intervention of professional expositors—has fortified me as I have grappled with the ascendency of critical theory, and a corresponding decline of concern about the general cultural intelligibility of the arts.

Apparently quite by chance, while writing this, I had a conversation with a student who had just finished reading Lewis's *Till We Have Faces.* She had been so moved by the book that she had retained some dialog, and proceeded to quote it. She vowed that she would read the book "at least eleven more times before I die." Lewis would approve—but not because of vanity. He thought Faces was his most mature and best work of literature. Further, he believed rereading the same work several times is a sign of how one engages literature for its *literary* merits, thus distinguishing the few from the many.

Clearly my friend loved the art of the book, and meant to enjoy what Scruton called arts function, by planning to return for further "rewards." What struck me was how useful she found Lewis's retelling of the Cupid and Psyche myth. The section that had moved her so forcefully was the dialog between Orual and the Fox where Orual is told that the gods are not just, because "what would become of us if they were?"[8] The concept of God's mercy was hardly unknown to my friend, but Lewis's telling of the long travails which culminated in Orual's recognition of a divine mercy illuminated something my friend hadn't really understood in that way. What Lewis gave her wasn't "information." Her knowing was only possible through the experience of that work of literature. Lewis had given her an aesthetic form that opened up and deepened something lying beyond concepts or ideas. For her, there was no conflict between her use of *Faces* and her love of its art.

The essays that follow here aspire to do something similar. They are reflecting on Lewis, sometimes critically, sometimes approvingly. But they all seek to illuminate aspects of Lewis's writings about the arts that may be useful for the artists, poets, musicians, and dramatists, as well as the art and Lewis lovers who pick this book up. With apologies to St. Augustine, please, "take and read"... and use.

Theodore Prescott
April 2013

ENDNOTES

1 C.S. Lewis. *An Experiment in Criticism* (Cambridge, Cambridge University Press, 1961), 19-21.

2 Nicholas Wolterstorff. *Art in Action* (Grand Rapids, William B. Eerdmans Publishing, 1980), 33-40.

3 Lewis, 18.

4 Roger Scruton. *Beauty* (Oxford, Oxford University Press, 2009), 28.

5 Scruton, 99.

6 C. S. Lewis. *Selected Literary Essays*. Ed by Walter Hooper (Cambridge, Cambridge University Press, 1969), 9.

7 Ibid.

8 C. S. Lewis. *Till We Have Faces* (Grand Rapids, William B. Eerdmans Publishing, 1966), 297.

Introduction

ROD MILLER

If a human believes he ought to spend his few short years on this earth exploring various issues of aesthetics, literature, artistic quality, beauty, and culture, he ought to have an answer as to why that is a worthy pursuit. For the theist, the one who believes the universe not a product of chance and that human existence is rich with teleological opportunity, the need for an explanation, or justification, is even more pressing. Are discussion and debate about literary theory more pressing than feeding the hungry, clothing the naked, and saving souls?

The essays in this volume explore various aspects of Lewis's thinking in regards to art, beauty, creativity, and their value for humans. It seeks to assist those who want to be faithful and discerning when encountering art and/or using their creative gifts to make art. The term arts is to be understood broadly as creative endeavors: the thoughtful and deliberative process of creating objects/performances/texts that manifest neither a temporal fad nor mere passing pleasure but, one may say, the splendor of wisdom.

David Downing's essay investigates Lewis's claims to an objective beauty by giving a closer reading to *The Abolition of Man.* With a bit more clarification into the actual incident with Coleridge and the waterfall, he seeks to pin down Lewis's understanding of beauty both in *The Abolition of Man* and other sources.

Bruce Hermann draws connections between Lewis's thinking regarding culture and that of linguist George Steiner and philosopher Hans Georg Gadamer. Looking at Lewis's book, *Experiment in Criticism,* he addresses Lewis as answering pragmatism, utilitarianism, and reductionism with the romantically influenced art for art's sake. From there he launches into how Steiner and Gadamer's concepts offer an alternative to the postmodern "free play of signifiers" in hopes of a genuine and hospitable welcoming of a text. But can this be accomplished during a time rife with transgressive art?

In "The Moral Aesthetic of Perelandra," Scott Key supports the idea that style acts as a cypher of human desire seeking an understanding of the good and the beautiful. Aiding his thesis that seeks to offer an answer to that desire is a review of notions of beauty in the post-Kantian west followed by an in-depth and inspiring examination of Lewis's novel, *Perelandra.*

When considering the lucid and successful prose of Lewis, Don King posits the need for an understanding of Lewis's original writing goal: to be a poet. King examines correspondence from Lewis to various friends, some of whom are poets, that evidence his struggle to write excellent poetry. Three versions of Lewis's poem, "As the Ruin Falls" are searched for a better grasp of how Lewis composed. King goes on to examine Lewis's search for greater understanding of prosody through several of his prose works.

Challenging some of Lewis's statements on the value of artistic endeavor, Rod Miller takes him to task for comments that have offered tepid support for creative enterprise and misunderstood beauty. Many of those claims have led to confusing, if not bizarre, conclusions. Miller finds that Lewis struggled with the long-standing problem of attempting to claim an objective status for the aesthetic.

Jerry Root examines the connections between Lewis's claims for objectivity and objective beauty. The argument Lewis makes in *The Abolition of Man* demands an object, one that lies outside of us and to which we may respond. Those responses may be correct or in error; Root continues to explore where Lewis applied this same thinking to beauty and the arts, finding arguments in Aquinas for objective beauty and its three conditions. Through Lewis's *The Personal Heresy,* Root finds a model for how one may consider objective beauty rightly.

Theory-driven criticism is problematic, finds David Rozema, and he posits a criticism, informed in part by Lewis's ideas from *An Experiment in Criticism,* to allow the actual text, the characters and plot, to speak for themselves. Rozema aspires to rehabilitate the art as primary and restore proper pleasure to reading, avoiding entirely the modern and post-modern passion for theory.

Peter Shakel delves into Lewis's musical interests. From youth onwards, Lewis had a profound interest in the pleasures of music; throughout his writings he uses examples of music and musical metaphors. Dance, also an activity Lewis liked to watch, but not perform, figures frequently as metaphor or social activity and is linked to profound notions of universal significance and ultimate delight.

Charlie Starr suggests Christians need smarter answers when seeking knowledge about art and culture and Lewis can be a guide. Exploring Lewis's answers to meaning, imagination, and myth, Starr links them to examples of contemporary film, lending new dimension to Lewis's thoughts. Indeed, meaning itself can only be through "hints, similies, and metaphors" that is, contends Starr, through particular experience.

Will Vaus starts with Lewis's comment that Christianity is not intended to replace human culture, but to direct it. Man is sub-creator and is to seek creative outlets and yet, can man truly create anything original? Vaus traces Lewis's thoughts on arts and creativity and uses them to explore compelling differences from ancient views on art to ones modern. Vaus concludes with a more detailed look at Lewis's "Christianity and Culture" essay and a look at specific areas of arts and enjoyment, church, and the Christian artist.

Variously have the arts been considered. Entertainment, therapy, distraction from death, vague statements about "knowing where we came from," or the "highest and best" have been offered as justification, or meaning. Sorting through often contradictory notions is challenging under the best of circumstances; making sense of creativity and cultural products when one is a Christian, during times when any intellectual exercise even smacking of faith is left outside, requires assistance. It is hoped that the thoughtful reflection of the essayists and the formidable wit of C.S. Lewis offers useful direction.

Rod Miller
Hendrix College
2013

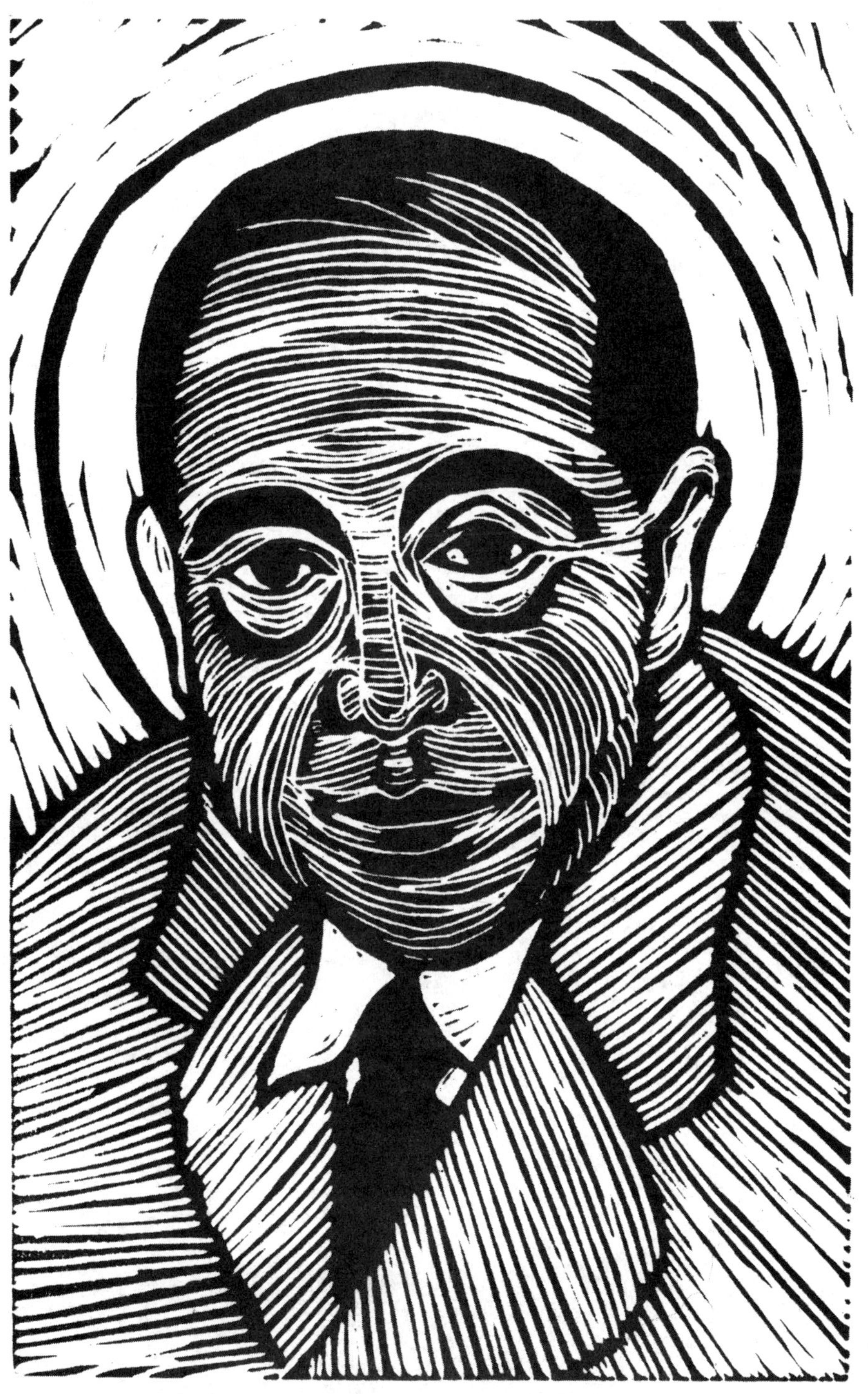

Beauty is in the "I" of the Beholder: A Critique of Lewis's Aesthetic Theories in *The Abolition of Man*

DAVID C. DOWNING

C.S. Lewis's *The Abolition of Man* (1947) is one of his most significant and influential works of cultural criticism. The book is rich in penetrating insights about moral relativism, misguided educational methods, and the abuses of technology. But for all its strengths as a study of ethical values, *The Abolition of Man* is not particularly helpful on the issue of aesthetic values. Lewis's opening example, an incident from the life of Coleridge, is particularly problematic in its assumptions about the nature of the Sublime.

The Abolition of Man is based on Lewis's Riddell Memorial Lectures, three presentations delivered on the evenings of February 24-26, 1943, at Newcastle-on-Tyne. In these lectures, Lewis forcefully argued that many foundational values cannot be deduced from reason nor can they be mere expressions of people's instincts. Despite his many cogent insights about ethical values, Lewis begins on a confusing note, using the term "values" to cover both ethical norms and aesthetic tastes. These are two different branches of philosophy, each with its history and its own problems of definition.

Lewis begins by summarizing from a textbook he calls "The Green Book" by authors "Gaius and Titius." (The book Lewis actually had in mind was *The Control of Language* [1940] by Alec King and Martin Ketley. The review copy sent to Lewis, now at the Wade Center in Wheaton, Illinois, did indeed have a green cover.) King and Ketley recount an incident which they believe illustrates the nature of aesthetic values:

> This is a story told by Coleridge: he was standing with a group of tourists beside a waterfall, and, after a silence, one of the men of the party said, "That is sublime." Coleridge felt that "sublime" was exactly the right word. And then one of the women in the party added "Yes, it is pretty," and Coleridge turned away in disgust, feeling that "pretty" was exactly the wrong word. [1]

King and Ketley use this incident to illustrate what they consider to be an important distinction between objective traits of the waterfall versus subjective responses in the minds of its viewers. They argue that if the waterfall had been described as "brown" or "blue," these would have referred, whether rightly or wrongly, to actual traits of the waterfall. But terms such as "sublime" or "pretty" have no objective referent, but only "emotive meaning," reporting subjective responses in the minds of different observers.[2]

In *The Abolition of Man,* Lewis strongly objects to King and Ketley's analysis: "The schoolboy who reads this passage . . . will believe two propositions: firstly, that all sentences containing a predicate of value are statements about the emotional state of the speaker, and, secondly, that all such statements are unimportant."[3] Some readers may find that summary too reductionist, creating a false dilemma that all values must be inherent or else they are trivial. But more problematically, Lewis chooses an incident involving *aesthetic* responses to nature when the central argument of his book is about *ethical* values, or Natural Law, found in all cultures, ancient and modern. However plausible it may be to argue for universal ethical norms (or at least a broad moral consensus), it is much more difficult to muster the evidence of universal aesthetic norms, standards of Beauty found in all cultures at all times.

The term Beauty itself is highly elastic. It is not possible to find any one set of traits that apply equally to lilacs, landscapes, lapis lazuli, or the loveliness of a human face. But Lewis's insistence that the waterfall is inherently sublime is not supported by the evidence of cultural history nor by Lewis's own writings in other contexts.

Lewis might have been even more annoyed with King and Ketley if he had checked their source and discovered how inaccurately they summarized the original incident. The story is not "by Coleridge," as they assert, but rather about Coleridge, as recorded in the diary of William Wordsworth's sister Dorothy. In her book *Recollections of a Tour in Scotland, A.D. 1803,* she recounts an episode that occurred at Cora Linn, near New Lanark, on August 21, 1803:

> We had different views of the Linn. We sat upon a bench, placed for the sake of one of these views, whence we looked down upon the waterfall, and over the open country ... A lady and gentleman, more expeditious tourists than ourselves, came to the spot; they left us at the seat, and we found them again at another station above the Falls. Coleridge, who is always good-natured enough to enter into conversation with anybody whom he meets in his way, began to talk with the gentleman, who observed that it was a majestic waterfall. Coleridge was delighted with the accuracy of the epithet, particularly as he had been settling in his own mind the precise meaning of the words grand, majestic, sublime, etc., and had discussed the subject with William at some length the day before. "Yes, sir," says Coleridge, "it is a majestic waterfall." "Sublime and beautiful," replied his friend. Poor Coleridge could make no answer, and, not very desirous to continue the conversation, came to us and related the story, laughing heartily.[4]

As can be seen, King and Ketley have taken several liberties in their retelling of the story. In the original version, it was the same tourist who used the term "majestic" first, which suited Coleridge, but then later used "beautiful," which didn't suit Coleridge. King and Ketley substitute "sublime" and "pretty" for "majestic" and "beautiful," and—perhaps on a sexist note, they depict a man choosing the right adjective and a woman choosing the wrong one. They also describe Coleridge as feeling "disgust" over the poor choice of words, when his response was actually closer to amusement. Coleridge found it laughable that the man should choose as synonyms two words that Coleridge would view as nearly opposites.

The word sublime derives from Latin *supra*, "above" + *limen*, "threshold," referring to anything above the threshold of everyday experience. In distinguishing specifically between the Beautiful and the Sublime, Coleridge must have certainly had in mind Edmund Burke's *Philosophical Inquiry into the Origin of our Ideas of the Sublime and Beautiful* (1756). Burke argues that the Beautiful evokes pleasure or love while the Sublime arises from feelings of awe or terror. By way of contrast, Burke continues: "Sublime objects are vast in their dimensions, beautiful ones comparatively small; beauty should be smooth and polished; the great, rugged and negligent . . . Beauty should not be obscure; the great ought to be dark and gloomy; beauty should be light and delicate; the great ought to be solid and massive. They are indeed ideas of a very different nature, one being founded on pain, the other on pleasure"[5]

With such passages in mind, Coleridge must certainly have found it amusing that a fellow observer of the waterfall would use the two terms interchangeably. But for Lewis the key question is whether the waterfall might be considered objectively sublime or whether that is merely the subjective emotional response of a particular observer:

> Until quite modern times all teachers and even all men believed the universe to be such that certain emotional reactions on our part could be either congruous or incongruous to it—believed, in fact, that objects did not receive, but could *merit*, our approval or disapproval, our reverence or our contempt. The reason why Coleridge agreed with the tourist who called the cataract sublime and disagreed with the one who called it pretty was of course he believed inanimate nature to be such that certain responses could be more "just" or 'ordinate' or 'appropriate' to it than others. And he believed (correctly) that the tourists thought the same. The man who called the cataract sublime was not intending simply to describe his own emotions about it: he was also claiming that the object was one that *merited* those emotions.[6]

Such assertions of Natural Law are more easily defended in the realm of ethics than in aesthetics. As Lewis himself shows in the appendix of *The Abolition of Man*, there seems to be a broad cross-cultural consensus approving of altruism, honesty, and fidelity, while disapproving of murder, adultery, and cowardice. But the evidence of history suggests that aesthetic values are often culturally constructed, shaped by particular contexts, not innate responses to objective Beauty. Lewis himself seemed to acknowledge this fact in several of his other books.

In her classic study *Mountain Gloom and Mountain Glory: The Development of the Aesthetics of the Infinite* (1959), Marjorie Hope Nicholson traces a cultural sea-change regarding people's responses to the natural world, particularly features such as mountains and waterfalls that later observers would call sublime. The opening of Nicholson's book sums up her thesis clearly:

> "To me," said Byron's Childe Harold, "high mountains are a feeling." We comfortably agree, believing that the emotions we feel—or are supposed to feel—in the presence of grand Nature are universal and have been shared by all men at all times. But high mountains were not a "feeling" to Virgil or Horace, to Dante, to Shakespeare, or Milton .... Like men of every age, we see in Nature what we have been taught to look for, we feel what we have been prepared to feel"[7]

Nicholson goes on to document in great detail changing sensibilities in Western culture about finding the sublime in Nature. In literature, there are no grand descriptions of craggy peaks or majestic panoramas among the classical poets, and the mountains of the medieval and early modern era usually appear not as objects to be admired in themselves, but as allegorical imagery (e.g., Dante's Mount Purgatory, Bunyan's Hill of Difficulty).

In 1844, poet William Wordsworth observed that "elaborate gardening, with topiary works, were in high request, even among our remote ancestors. But the relish for the choice and picturesque *scenery* is quite recent of origin." Noting one possible exception [Thomas Burnet], Wordsworth concludes that before the late 18th century, "There is not, I believe, one English traveler whose published writings would disprove the assertion that, where precipitous rocks and mountains are mentioned at all, they are spoken of as objects of dislike and fear, and not of admiration."[8] In the following decade, art critic James Ruskin (1856) noted in *Modern Painters* that he could not find awe-inspiring mountainscapes (or impressive ruins) in classical, medieval, or Renaissance paintings, but then they appeared with sudden profusion in the Romantic era.

Nicholson surveys the major figures in English literature and finds mountains repeatedly described with fear or contempt, not with awe or admiration. In a poem written in 1611, John Donne called mountains "disfigurements" in the round circle of the globe, "warts and pock-marks in the face of the earth."[9] Donne's contemporary Andrew Marvell agreed that mountains spoiled the circularity of the earth, calling them "unjust" and "hook-shouldered," ill-designed "excrescences" that deformed the earth and frightened the heavens. In a similar vein, John Milton wrote in *L'Allegro* (1645), of "mountains, on whose barren breasts/The labouring clouds do often rest."

According to Nicholson, it was not until the 18th century that theologians and poets began to associate the Infinite nature of God with his creation, as the rapidly developing sciences revealed first the vastness of the cosmos, then the many wonders of our terrestrial globe. By the early 19th century, especially in the works of Byron, Shelley, and Wordsworth, mountains, waterfalls, and other grand scenes from nature could be admired in and of themselves, not merely as expressions of God's grandeur. So when Coleridge and other tourists hiked up to see a waterfall in Scotland, their very impulse to do so was still something of a novelty. Nicholson borrows the terms "Mountain Gloom" and "Mountain Glory" from John Ruskin to describe the radical change in attitude toward nature that divides classical, medieval, and early modern poets from those in the late 18th century and afterwards.

However much one may want to quibble with Nicholson's explanation of this appearance of the Sublime in nature, the mere wealth of data she provides certainly casts doubt on Lewis's bald assertion in *The Abolition of Man* that until modern times all thinkers would agree with Coleridge that the waterfall he so admired *merited* the response that he felt within. Even Byron's "To me high mountains are a feeling" suggests that the sublimity exists in the relationship between the object and its observer; it is not an objective trait of a waterfall, such as its height or volume of water.

In *Reflections on the Psalms* (1958), Lewis acknowledged that people's response to nature changes with their changing cultural conditions. Describing the Jews who composed the psalms, Lewis notes:

> Everyone was close to the land, everyone vividly aware of our dependence on soils and weather. So, till a late age, was every Greek and Roman. Thus part of what we should now perhaps call "appreciation of Nature" could not then exist—all that part which is really a delight "in the country" as a contrast to the town. Where towns are few and very small and where nearly everyone is on the land, one is not aware of any special thing called "the country." Hence a certain sort of "nature poetry" never existed in the ancient world till really vast cities like Alexandria arose; and after the fall of ancient civilization, it never existed again until the eighteenth century. At other periods what we call "the country" is simply the world, what water is to a fish.[10]

Lewis's observation that "the appreciation of Nature" can only arise when people live apart from nature—in big cities—is exactly in accord with Marjorie Hope Nicholson's *Mountain Gloom and Mountain Glory*, published one year after *Reflections on the Psalms.* But his own cultural analysis seems to undermine his earlier idea, expressed in *The Abolition of Man,* that until recent times people's responses to natural objects were considered to be merely a natural acknowledgment of their innate features, not a conditioned response based upon their own cultural milieu.

In his other writings, Lewis himself questioned the idea of universal aesthetic responses. In his essay "Hedonics" (1945), Lewis described a feeling of extreme pleasure and well-being while riding on the London Tube and emerging from underground into the suburbs. Lewis seems at a loss to describe his own sense of happiness. The other people on the train were not particularly admirable or attractive; their drab and commonplace neighborhoods were certainly not of the sort that would *merit* aesthetic appreciation. Yet some dim awareness inside him of all the domestic scenes taking place—turning on of lights, hanging up of hats, the familiar smells in the hallway—created in Lewis a sensation of cozy exuberance. Lewis ends the essay noting that "the *weather* of consciousness" is only loosely related to one's surroundings at any particular moment.[11] This insight would seem to apply as much to the "sublime" as to the suburbs. While any rational observer will agree as to the objective height or coloring of a waterfall, different observers might have widely diverging aesthetic responses to the scene—depending upon the time and place in which they live or perhaps even the weather or the "inner weather" of one's mood.

> In *An Experiment in Criticism* (1965), Lewis underscored the vagaries of another kind of aesthetic response, one's reaction to the products of human creativity. According to his theory suggested in *The Abolition of Man*, one might expect some "appropriate" or "ordinate" response shared by all to works of art. But he admits that, upon hearing a Zulu war chant intended to inspire ferocity and fearlessness, he thought it sounded as wistful and gentle as a lullaby.[12] Lewis also notes that aesthetic values may vary widely, even wildly, from one generation to another. Speaking of literary reputations, Lewis remarked, "'Taste' in this sense is mainly a chronological phenomenon. Tell me the date of your birth and I can make a shrewd guess whether you prefer Hopkins or Housman, Hardy or Lawrence . . . . All you can really say about my taste is that is it old fashioned; yours will soon be the same."[13]

Lewis's sensibilities were heavily shaped by Platonism and Romanticism, so he may have too quickly attached the *Idea* of Beauty to the waterfall, assuming his own delight in nature was a universal human trait, not the product of his own Wordsworthian temperament and his love of the outdoors.

Ultimately, Lewis's own response to nature was as much mystical as aesthetic, more like the "garment of God" than the embodiment of platonic Beauty. In *Mere Christianity* Lewis gives an account of everything in the cosmos as a mirror of God's nature. Space, in its very immensity, is a symbol of God's greatness, a "translation of it into non-spiritual terms."[14] The physical energy in matter reminds us of the spiritual power of God. Growing plant life is a sign of the living God, as animal life is a sign of his ceaseless activity and creative power. And humans, in their ability to think and will and love and create, are the most complete and fully realized image of God in this earthly realm. Lewis's aesthetic theories seem most persuasive when he views varied experiences of Beauty less as embodiments of a neo-platonic principle than as glimpses of a Person.

ENDNOTES

1 Alec King and Martin Ketley. *The Control of Language* (London: Longmans, Green and Co, 1940), 17.
2 King and Ketley, 18.
3 C.S. Lewis, *The Abolition of Man, or Reflections on Education with Special Reference to the Teaching of English in the Upper Forms of Schools* (New York: Macmillan, 1947), 15.
4 Dorothy Wordsworth. *Recollections of a Tour in Scotland, A.D. 1803*. Ed by J.C. Shairp (1874), 37.
5 Edmund Burke. *Philosophical Inquiry into the Origin of Our Ideas of the Sublime and Beautiful.* Qtd. in Adams. *Critical Theory Since Plato* (New York: Harcourt Brace Jovanovich, 1971), 311.
6 *Abolition of Man*, 25.
7 Nicholson, 1.
8 Qtd. in Nicholson, 18.
9 Nicholson, 28.
10 C.S. Lewis. *Reflections on the Psalms* (New York: Harcourt Brace Jovanovich, 1958), 76-77.
11 C.S. Lewis. *Present Concerns*. Ed by Walter Hooper (San Diego: Harcourt Brace Jovanovich, 1987), 53.
12 C.S. Lewis. *An Experiment in Criticism* (Cambridge: Cambridge University Press, 1961), 22.
13 *Experiment*, 106.
14 C.S. Lewis *Mere Christianity* (New York: Macmillan, 1952), 139

WORKS CITED

Adams, Hazard. *Critical Theory Since Plato* (New York: Harcourt Brace Jovanovich, 1971).

Burke, Edmund. *Philosophical Inquiry into the Origin of Our Ideas of the Sublime and Beautiful.* Ed. by J. T. Boulton (1958).

King, Alec and Martin Ketley. *The Control of Language*. London: Longmans, Green and Co., 1940.

Lewis, C.S. *The Abolition of Man, or Reflections on Education with Special Reference to the Teaching of English in the Upper Forms of Schools*. New York: Macmillan, 1947.

_________. *An Experiment in Criticism*. Cambridge: Cambridge University Press, 1961.

_________. *Mere Christianity*. New York: Macmillan, 1952.

_________. *Present Concerns*. Ed by Walter Hooper. San Diego: Harcourt Brace Jovanovich, 1987.

_________. *Reflections on the Psalms*. New York: Harcourt Brace Jovanovich, 1958.

Wordsworth, Dorothy. *Recollections of a Tour in Scotland, A.D. 1803*. Ed by J.C. Shairp, 1874.

At the Table With Our Guard Down: Submission, Courtesia, and Symbol in the Theories of C.S. Lewis, George Steiner, and Hans Georg Gadamer

BRUCE HERMAN

C.S. Lewis is a popular figure in Christian circles and he has been for better than a half-century. Yet few have read his literary theory, and fewer still realize that he was part of a larger cultural conversation that reaches beyond Christian apologetics and into questions surrounding the very fabric of a shared cultural vision—of civilization itself. I attempt in what follows to offer evidence that Lewis's thought harmonizes well with two other, perhaps less well-known but no less important culture critics—the English linguist and critic George Steiner and the German philosopher, Hans Georg Gadamer. Both Steiner and Gadamer are read among academics and specialists, but their thought has far reaching implications for all of us—and I believe that Lewis's literary reflections are in substantial agreement with these other two thinkers whose religious commitments are far from clear. First, a look at C.S. Lewis's theory and then an attempt to show where he is in deep agreement with Steiner and Gadamer.

In *Experiment in Criticism*, C.S. Lewis makes an argument employing "the use of pictures"—visual art—as a paradigm for understanding how different readers approach the reading of literature. In this extended argument Lewis aims to persuade the reader to "submit" to a story—open ourselves up to a poem's emotive power and risk being changed by it. This flies in the face of pragmatism, utilitarianism, and reductionism—three of the most influential modes of our times. But something also occurs in Lewis's initial discussion of his literary theory: he mounts a persuasive defense of the Romantic dictum of art for art's sake—not as a conscious stratagem, but as a collateral outcome. In the course of his opening chapters, Lewis makes it clear to his reader that he is on the side of the angels—which is to say, the side of those who approach art without ulterior motive or guarded self protection. The good reader, in his argument, is the one who doesn't read or look at art in order to satisfy a prejudice or pre-existing appetite for, say, racy plot lines, page-turning murder mysteries, or happy sunsets that remind one fondly of places one has been. On the contrary, the good reader comes to the story, as the good viewer to a painting, ready to savor its brushstrokes as much as the image depicted; appreciating the color and texture and composition as much as the portrait or still-life; character development as much as plot. The good reader comes to the story willing to suspend disbelief and to encounter imaginary persons with their joys and sorrows, their triumphs and failures, their pain and pleasure. In a word, literature and art are not for the philistine enjoyment of superficial or sentimental trivialities. Art is for those who are willing to suspend disbelief and *submit*, to pass through the magic portal of the book or painting to another world—complete with its own persons, places, and internal logic.

In George Steiner's *Real Presences*[1] the British critic advances a theory of literature and the arts that comports well with Lewis's call for submission to the work: more than a third of Steiner's book is devoted to elaborating his concept of *courtesia*—a certain intellectual hospitality that welcomes the text, the painting or poem, novel or symphony into one's intimate place of being much as one welcomes a guest to one's home, thereby risking the same change and emotional transcendence that Lewis is at pains to defend in *Experiment*. Steiner's theory of "real presences" is conceived as an antidote to the dead-end of deconstruction wherein the author and reader are both adrift in "free-play of signifiers" (which amounts to a free-fall in terms of meaning). The presence that Steiner is referring to is not only that of authorial intent, but also voices of the "dead poets" asserting themselves via the tradition and the language itself. He is arguing for nothing less than *real* encounter with the imaginary persons and situations mediated by the tradition. In effect, the characters in Dante's *Divina Comedia* are *real* in the sense of having been wrought and coming to life through the pen of the master and by entering our memories and imaginations. To fail to welcome these literary characters into one's consciousness is to miss the point of literature—and to operate on the text aggressively by asserting one's own prerogatives, over against the call to submission, is likewise a failure on the reader or viewer's part. Such a posture is akin to the "bad" reader in Lewis's theory—i.e., the reader who, like a boorish host, has no real interest in his guest (the story) as such—but sees it merely as a means of recalling his own memory or prejudice or solipsistic agenda. Steiner's call for humility and receptivity has much in common at the fundamental level with the aesthetic theory of German philosopher Hans Georg Gadamer. His essay *The Relevance of the Beautiful* is a masterful summary of the philosopher's essential theory of art—which is broken down into three major investigative sub-essays: Play, Symbol, and Festival. For our purposes it is Gadamer's meditation on "symbol" that has immediate relevance. The philosopher recounts the origins of the word "symbol" as a *tessera hospitalis*—that is, a tile of welcome that was ritually broken when a guest entered one's home. Half of the broken tile (symbol) was handed to one's guest with words like, "Henceforth you, and anyone to whom you give this piece of tile, is welcome in my dwelling." And the test of a trustworthy guest would become the fitting together of the broken pieces—hence the original meaning of the word-concept "symbol" was an act of hospitality, of welcome.

For meaning to occur—for the symbol to make sense, at least two parties are needed. In this case a reader and an author, an artist and a responsive viewer. The meaning is discovered in the encounter of "real presence"—that is, a work of art that is authentic and costly and like good hospitality, an act of welcoming love. The symbol is completed with the two halves joined, and meaning is enjoyed as a form of communion.

It doesn't take much to see the deep simpatico between Steiner's *courtesia*, Gadamer's *symbol*, and Lewis's *experiment* in receptivity to the text or painting or musical piece. And what all three share is the call to openness, to submission and welcome and receptivity. Without this initial step on the part of the reader or viewer, a work of art remains dormant on the wall; the book remains closed, shelved, un-read.

SUBMISSION AND TRANSGRESSIVE ART

What then do we make of this dynamic trio and their requirement of intellectual welcome, of unguarded submission to the work of art when we live in a world of bad players—transgressive artists whose primary aim appears to be the ridicule and attack on all bourgeois values—anything traditional or conservative or smacking of sincere religion? It is a well-known reality that the contemporary art world has been on attack mode with regard to traditional values for more than a century. There is even a category in contemporary art theory referred to as the "transgressive"—which is understood as a primary thrust of much of contemporary painting, sculpture, installation art, and new media productions. This aim on the part of the artist is overtly hostile toward much that conservative Christians hold dear. In such a cultural environment how is one to practice Lewis's call to submit to the art or text? How is one to open oneself to the *courtesia* enjoined by Steiner?

Of course Steiner and Lewis and Gadamer were all aware of modern art—and in fact Gadamer's essay cited above is in large part inspired by the problem of the modern artist as a maker of things that do not fit easily with the expectations of the general populace—and where the artists find themselves frankly out of a job (in the sense of having no real audience for their works other than fellow transgressive artists). But where did this breakdown begin? Where and how did the tacit understanding and general hospitality of the arts begin to be withdrawn from both parties? One can trace the beginnings of transgressive art and literature to the late 19th century and the writing of Charles Baudelaire and Arthur Rimbaud, the scandals surrounding the paintings of Gustave Courbet and many that followed. The term *succès de scandale* became a commonplace, accompanying the exhibitions, concerts, operas, and happenings of from the Surrealists and Dadaists to Stravinsky's *Le Sacre du Printemps*—and this public outcry was invariably followed by financial success and social acclaim. What starts in the art world as an outrage becomes all the rage.

Yet where do we learn the benefit of genuine immersion, true submission to the text, the painting or poem or symphony when all that is really asked of us is that we react in disgust or the rubbernecking curiosity that raging scandals elicit? As long ago as the mid-19th century Leo Tolstoy was lamenting the domination of "interesting" as a prime value in the arts—i.e., the mere novelty or titillating thing prized only for its newness to a jaded audience filled with *ennui*. All this said, I do think that Lewis, in the mid-20th century continued to hope that artists and poets and composers would craft thoughtful, rigorous texts that would demand of us all that we possess by way of intelligence and aesthetic sensibility. And Gadamer's theory assumes a good-faith relationship between artists and their public, their community.

And this last word—community, as shopworn as it has become of late, goes right to the heart of the matter. The root of this word is the same as that of communion, communication, etc.—the root is "common"—that is, shared ground, common ground. For a work of literature to demand our submission, it must first pass the test of community—that is, it must be crafted within the context of faithfulness to common or shared standards, ideas, values, aims, stories, hopes. If the avant-gardist art of the last century had a community, it became a shrunken one indeed—and necessarily so, given the almost sacred task of *shocking* the public that most modern artists were saddled with.

The requirement to shock or transgress is at loggerheads with the requirement that one shall produce a poem or painting or sonata that satisfies a communally shared set of values—be those values totally abstract (as in a piece of music), or be they representational or implicitly narrative (as in a landscape or portrait painting or short story). If the artist must first create a shocking and novel object or event, she cannot hope to share common ground with anyone except fellow shock-artists. This is clearly an untenable situation. Even if an artist or poet feels their calling is to stretch the bounds of their art form, they must begin with shared ground—not with alienation and anomy, however honest such modes might seem at a given moment in cultural history. The hospitality and *courtesia* must work in both directions, and the artist must extend the olive branch in order to win sufficient trust to stretch the boundaries of her audience.

The viewer of a given painting and the one who painted it share the common requirement of opening themselves to one another—the tacit understanding that respect and welcome be extended to the stranger, the visitor to one's place of intimate being, feeling, and contemplation. Without this elemental trust there can be no shared value and thence, no meaning. Meaning is predicated upon communal values right at the level of language itself. If one speaks an idiosyncratic tongue, no one can understand, much less enjoy or celebrate the utterance.

And this perhaps is the crux of our topic: that trust must first be established before it can be stretched or expanded—extended to include the authentically new form of music, literature, or art. If there is an unrepaired rupture between artist and audience, no further movement toward the mystery of communication is possible before that trust is restored. My hunch about our times is that we are in what Steiner calls a "holy Saturday" of waiting for resurrection of meaning, of the possibility once more of a shared vision of worth and purpose in the arts.

After more than a century of experimentation and stretching of all conceivable boundaries, we have something like viewer and reader and listener fatigue. Artists have stretched the credulity of their audiences to the breaking point, and many readers and viewers have now developed a habitual posture of skepticism and suspicion, just as the deconstructionists indicate. All speech, all art, all social acts are suspected to be power plays and naked or veiled attempts to colonize the public square. The avant-garde has lived up to its literal meaning: the advance guard of militant shock troops. The audience, in this analogy, is the enemy army—and has been treated as an opponent, not as a friend.

• • •

In conclusion I would offer three responses to our current impasse between contemporary art and artist and the bewildered general populace. First, a recapitulation of the main point above: artistic meaning is only possible where intellectual hospitality works both ways—with artist and audience extending elemental trust and the safety of unguarded receptivity to the work of art. Second, in order for a robust community of patronage and large cultural audiences for contemporary art to develop, there must be an extended period of carefully managed rapprochement—with the galleries, museums, art historians, and critics consciously addressing the gulf that exists between a public bewildered by shock tactics and artists who seek to push the envelope. This could be accomplished by analyzing the historical forces at play over the past hundred fifty years—Marxism, Freudianism, and other forms of philosophical disenfranchisement of shared meaning—i.e., the reductionist habit of mind needs dismantling.

Finally, I would look for a fresh investigation of the relationship between image, story, music, and drama and the deeply natural religious impulse in individuals and society. This could take the form initially of a careful critique of the prejudice that religion and enlightened intellectual and artistic taste are mutually exclusive. Religious faith was historically the north star of the arts, and it nearly always has been—even when it is placed as background for a given storyline or poem or painting (as in *Brothers Karamazov* and many other great works of art). Without a deeply shared vision of what matters, the arts founder and default to the highest dose of shock. Simply put, when there is no shared artistic vision, the people and their culture perish. And this is true not only for those committed to a biblical theology. It is true for any human being—as a century or more of rootless, vision-less cultural experimentation has revealed. Experimentation is crucial as an element in the advance of art, but it is never, by itself, enough. And where it is enshrined as the only legitimate value in art, there is little room for the shared meaning and mutual submission required in the communion of art.

Lewis, Gadamer, and Steiner are right—without that elemental submission of trust extended to the text, the painting, the musical score, the audience cannot receive what is being offered by artist, poet, or composer. Yet this principle of unguarded openness to visual, literary, or music texts must be underwritten by faith in a larger order, a big-picture understanding of spiritual and cultural values that are normative for all human beings. Without this vision of worth, the reader or viewer or listener cannot become a participant in the work of art—it just isn't safe—and without participants, there is no festival, no celebration of the arts.

The arts depend on festival. The communal celebration of color, sound, beautiful language, and shared stories is essential. Without participants, there is no flourishing or staying power in the arts—they simply go fallow, becoming fruitless. But when a shared vision develops, an entire civilization flowers and leaves a lasting legacy of beauty and hope. That hope is a natural by-product of trust and the ability of a society to let down its guard—to laugh and cry and celebrate what it means to be human—as in a wonderful dinner party. This is the common ground, the common table that must be reclaimed in and through revitalized arts, practicing authentic hospitality and courtesy between artist and audience who can finally let down their guard.

ENDNOTES

1 Steiner, George; *Real Presences*, (Chicago: University of Chicago Press, 1989).

The Moral Aesthetic of *Perelandra*

SCOTT B. KEY

Our culture is captivated by style. Companies in all areas of commerce are realizing that style is becoming even more important than content. Ordinary kitchen tools are being re-designed to make them more pleasing to the eye. Sometimes the changes include real improvements in performance but more often the changes are merely cosmetic, rendering the tool even less functional and more prone to breakage and obsolescence. This same general comment can be made concerning other major areas of our daily cultural encounters. In electronics, Apple products are good; however, what draws customers is their sleek style and ease of use and not the performance statistics generated by comparison tests. Other areas of consumer electronics have tried to match Apple's stylistic competence. The wide-spread use of computer generated special effects by the movie industry also reflects the growing devotion to style. The special effects, the look, and the "atmosphere" of the movie are increasingly the most important aspects of the experience. Character development, story, and reflection on the human experience are, in many cases, unimportant qualities to which little attention is given. It is not difficult to see this yearning for "style" in the markets of apparel, sports equipment, food presentation, interior decoration, product displays in many retail establishments, and even in our places of education and worship. Obviously, this concern for style is the staple of advertising which has always understood that the emotional response of consumers, and not solid facts about the merits of the product, motivates sales.

These wide-spread cultural expressions, all concerned in one way or another with style as the focal point of design, point to a deeper and more significant cultural shift. During the period that we now broadly term the Modern Age (approximately 1600 to mid-20th Century), the age whose central focus was the Enlightenment Project, the compelling question that stimulated development in every area of Western life was the epistemological question: How do I know what I know? It appears, to this observer (regardless if one argues that present culture is at the end of the Modern or the beginning of the Post-Modern or if the Post-Modern has already passed into something else), that the driving questions of culture are currently axiological in nature: What is good and what is beauty?

Our compulsions related to style are driven by a deep concern for the nature of value. Style is a cipher for our culture-wide longing for beauty—a deeper beauty that is marked by goodness. It is the thesis of this essay that the re-discovery of real beauty demands the retrieval of a comprehensive aesthetic-moral vision that re-sacralizes the cosmos as the living context in which the personal Creator God discloses His Glory as a ransom for alienated humanity. This desire is a fulfillment of the longing for beauty, goodness and truth that lies at the center of each person. The various ways in which these longings are distorted are the root of our profound "homelessness" and "dis-ease." The Christian vision of the cosmos bears witness that it is created through Him, for Him, by Him, and in Him (Col. 1:15–20). C.S. Lewis argues (in a variety of ways) that only when our understandings of beauty are informed by this revelatory insight can the subjective, private, formal, and emotive conception of beauty defined by culturally determined aesthetic geniuses be overcome and a robust and meaningful reconnection of beauty and goodness be possible. The elements of this thesis will be developed more fully in the discussion to follow.

The Lewisian focus of this essay will be *Perelandra*. The themes of this engaging novel are resounded in many places in the corpus of Lewis's work but I will not seek to trace all of them.[1] To gain a more complete insight into the remarkable nature of the *Space Trilogy* as a whole, and *Perelandra* in particular, it is necessary to briefly examine first the notions about beauty commonly held during the mid-20th Century. A second step in the argument involves the exploration of the "Great Tradition" as Lewis interprets it and uses it to provide a larger context for his own consideration of the relationship between beauty, moral goodness, and knowledge.[2] Only an outline can be given on these matters that will point and highlight the context in which *Perelandra* serves as the focal expression. The third section will seek to demonstrate the ways in which Lewis draws together the moral imagination with the aesthetic envisioning of the moral. It is this link (that is, between the moral and the beautiful) that modernity has sought to sever. The reestablishment of this relationship is essential to the revitalization of worship as the celebration of the glory of God. Ransom's experience on Perelandra reaches its climax in worship. This enables him to properly interpret the meaning of his passionate struggle against Weston and, thereby, deepen his understanding of the link between the moral and the beautiful. In the last section of this essay an effort will be made to evaluate the implications of the vision of Lewis for a culture longing for beauty (even if it is only transient style) and a church whose calling is to give witness in all things to the One whose beauty makes all things real.

THE COMMON PROBLEM OF BEAUTY

The Post-Kantian discussion of aesthetics is a complicated one. The thesis I am pursuing in this essay requires only that a general description of the mid-20th Century understanding of aesthetics be sketched.[3] Three elements of the more complex Kantian analysis became central to the 20th Century discussion, which then added a few twists of its own. First, a generally accepted "truism" of the mid-20th Century could be stated this way: "That (X) is beautiful" is a statement expressing the subjective and emotional reaction of the speaker and not the clearly recognizable beauty of the object lying before the speaker.[4] "Beauty is in the eye of the beholder" served as the motto of this understanding.

Secondly, in a more subtle way, there was an assertion that the object about which the speaker is exclaiming can be known only in a formal sense, that is, as being composed of abstract concepts such as lines, points, arcs, and, most obscurely, as color. These formal realities are more reflective of the structure of the mind of the speaker than of the entity or object.

Lastly, only the "aesthetic genius" can accurately provide a description of the aesthetic qualities of the object or render them in some artistic form that communicates the sublime. The "genius" possesses qualities of the imagination to sense the ineffable features of the "thing-in-itself" (the object in question). This "beautiful" object initiates the sense experience, but "what it is" cannot be directly grasped by reason; rather, reason constructs its significance by means of the *a priori* structures of the mind. The imaginative genius is able to sense the ineffable qualities of the object and give expression to them, in such a way, that the general population can acquire a proper sentiment and a more cultivated taste for that which is beautiful. Thus, the statement, "That is beautiful," in the final analysis, is an expression of the emotive response of the speaker to abstract forms located in the speaker's mind and only intimated by imagination as related to the object in question and the judgment of personal taste expressed by the speaker.

Early 20th Century thinkers tended to focus upon two interpretations of this general neo-Kantian account of beauty. First, if the identification of an object as beautiful is ultimately a matter of taste, even the taste of the critic, then it is ultimately a reflection of the speaker's emotional life and nothing more. Secondly, if it is merely emotive, then it is completely relative. Judgments about beauty are completely individual, emotive, relative, reflective of personal taste, and, hence, devoid of any universal value or significance. In such an interpretive world beauty ceases to have any value and other concerns such as functionality, artistic protest, experimentation, abstraction, and individual expression become paramount. It goes largely unnoticed by the critic or the general public that the list of concerns just enumerated are themselves "value-laden" realities that within the generally accepted paradigm would be understood as ultimately valueless, emotive expressions.

This section provides a general context against which the assertions of Lewis can be measured and the contrast provided by the "Great Tradition" can be readily understood. Lewis enters this discussion, with his imagination baptized, his convictions centered in historic Christianity, and his reason very critical of the course of modernity and the implications, clearly evident, of a culture dominated by men and women without concern about reality, values, and the virtue-based convictions that temper both reason and emotion.[5]

THE GREAT "SACRAMENTAL" TRADITION

Lewis provides a clear understanding of his use of "sacramental" in his profoundly moving sermon first given on the Feast of Pentecost, May 28, 1944, at Mansfield College, Oxford. He later expanded the sermon in 1961 and the additional sections transform the sermon into one of great depth and beauty.[6] The title, "Transposition," is a reference to its central metaphor. In a variety of ways it is natural for humans to move from one "higher" dimension to another "lower" dimension and back again. For example, one can move from the relative simplicity of sensation to the far more complex arena of emotion.[7] There is not a one-to one correspondence between the two. Sometime, most often, the same sensation can be understood, in different contexts, as indicating very different emotions. Or a composition for orchestra can be re-written for solo piano.[8] The complexity and richness of the original composition cannot be fully rendered in the second. As a result, we can understand fully the more simplified version only when we know the more complex. In the visual arts, a two-dimensional painting seeks to render a three-dimensional world.[9] We accept the painting only because the illusion created by the proper rendering of perspective which gives value to the two-dimensional is understood in light of our knowledge that the world is three-dimensional. Lewis argues that symbolism is not "adequate in all cases to cover the relation between the higher medium and its transposition in the lower."[10] He writes, "If I had to name the relation I should call it not symbolical but sacramental."[11]

Only by approaching the transposition from above can one fully understand the relationship of the emotion to the sensation, the orchestra to the solo piano, the three-dimensional world to the two-dimensional rendering in a painting, and the spiritual dimension of love to animal lust.[12]

The sacramental is born in the insight that the lower can only be truly known by the higher, and the higher encompasses and re-interprets the lower in such a way that the lower is given meaning and value within that which is greater. When we begin to understand the world this way, then it becomes alive with meaning, value, and significance that was once denied us. Lewis writes:

> It is the present life which is the diminution, the symbol, the etiolated, the (as it were) "vegetarian" substitute. If flesh and blood cannot inherit the Kingdom, that is not because they are too solid, too gross, too distinct, too "illustrious with being." They are too flimsy, too transitory, too phantasmal.[13]

This understanding of the sacramental informs all of Lewis's work including *Perelandra* and it reflects the great tradition of Christian thinking. It is this vision that shapes the Christian assertion that aesthetics is related to the moral life. The contours of this relationship reflect important themes like the colors of a beautiful tapestry.

The "tapestry"[14] of the "Great Sacramental Tradition" is an intricate weave with many different hues, subtle themes, riveting colors, and mysterious shadows. It is too easy to view it as a study in contrasts and so pit one pattern against another. To highlight an emphasis can be a suitable pedagogy but as a picture of the whole tapestry it proves to be a distortion. What is shared within the weave of the tapestry is greater than the distinctions that one can establish.

In the fullness of the tapestry, human knowledge is real but not absolute or total. Reality is truly "real" in an ontological sense but not fully experienced by the human. Yet, the human, made in the image of the Creator, is capable of discovering much about the real cosmos. Everything so discovered is embedded in a larger reality to which word and deed, matter and spirit, will and reason, and imagination and valuation are pointers and ciphers. The Christian understanding asserts that the incarnational model lies at the center of all reality such that the depths of human experience and understanding are raised into a larger reality that encompasses and embraces the partial and unfinished.[15] Lewis puts it this way in "The Weight of Glory" and refers to our longing for beauty that transcends our experiences and our memory:

> These things—the beauty, the memory of our own past—are good images of what we really desire; but if they are mistaken for the thing itself, they turn into dumb idols, breaking the hearts of their worshippers. For they are not the thing itself; they are only the scent of a flower we have not found, the echo of a tune we have not heard, news from a country we have never yet visited.... We do not want merely to *see* beauty, though, God knows, even that is beauty enough. We want something else which can hardly be put into words—to be united with the beauty we see, to pass into it, to receive it into ourselves, to bathe in it, to become part of it.[16]

The Great Sacramental Tradition is based upon three important understandings rooted in the biblical revelation: the incarnational model; the hierarchy of value; and the eschatological *telos* of the created order. It is important to note that at its center lie two significant assumptions: the dynamic, relational structure of reality and the created and real nature of matter. A beautiful flower is a real "thing" created and material yet in vital relationship with all the cosmos and with the Creator God. Its beauty is discoverable and yet it does not exhaust the meaning of beauty nor does it serve as the *telos* of beauty. This will be more clear as we examine the flower in light of the three understandings mentioned above.

The biblical God is the creator of all there is. God creates, not out of need, but out of love and joy. The Triune nature of God reveals that relationality lies at the center of all reality. God creates and each created "thing" bears His "stamp." God creates by means of the Word/Deed who becomes flesh and blood for us (John 1:1-14). Even the simplest realities, like bread and wine, can reveal the presence and glory of the Creator God. The incarnational model helps center Christian thought in time and space, in word and deed, and in relationship and community. Neither a vague transcendentalism nor a cold materialism can contain the power and vitality of the "Word become flesh." This is not a matter of development, Lewis writes, as if the natural grew and changed into the spiritual but rather the "... Spiritual Reality, which existed before there were any creatures who ate, gives this natural act a new meaning, and more than a new meaning: makes it in a certain context to be a different thing. In a word, I think the real landscapes enter into pictures, not that pictures will one day sprout out into real trees and grass."[17] The flower, whose beauty we discover, reflects the very beauty of God as Augustine writes, "... too late have I loved you, O beauty so ancient and so new, too late have I loved you!"[18] In this understanding the real world of material "stuff," the ordinary actions of people in community, the simple tasks of living, the basic necessities of life are all made alive with the presence and power of God.

The second understanding is that the Creator God is the source of all reality and the highest value. The reality of the cosmos depends upon the creative action of God. Rather than detailing arguments for the existence of God or the difference between necessary and contingent entities, the Bible assumes that God, and only God, is God. All glory belongs only to Him. If this is true then God is the highest of all values. Thus, in creation a hierarchy of being is created as God creates, beginning from the most fundamental of realities (light energy) to the highest of the created realities (humankind). And, a hierarchy of value is created that extends from the highest creature (humans) to the lowest value (matter). The flower has value in relation to that which has greater value.

The third feature of this tapestry is the understanding that all things are moving toward a God ordained end. There is purpose and meaning to individual lives, to history, to social reality, and to the cosmos itself. Purpose provides the context for meaning and value. Relationality[19] asserts that even what appears to be the least can be the greatest in the economy of God's purpose. The discovered beauty of the flower transcends the possible utility of its construction and, if understood from within the Great Tradition, serves as an individual expression of the fecundity of the love and goodness of God.

MORAL IMAGINATION AND BEAUTY

For modernity, beauty has largely been understood as a matter of personal taste that is ultimately subjective and relative. The current revival of interest in "style" and in questions of value serve as a reminder that relegating beauty to the private sphere does not quell the longing in the human for the good and the beautiful. A recovery of the "Great Tradition" of Christian thinking about beauty is a necessary step in the engagement with culture. It is here that Lewis can provide a model of a literary artist who is both academically and theologically astute and culturally aware.

The woven "atmosphere" of *Perelandra* provides a subtle setting for demonstrating the necessary connection between goodness and beauty. Through an examination of the language that Lewis employs we can begin to understand the way in which the moral imagination informs and shapes our understanding of beauty. Although the novel does not provide a formal exposition concerning the nature of value, there is an implicit argument embedded within its fabric that serves to demonstrate the relationship between moral understanding and the imaginative appreciation of the beautiful.

Ransom, as he tells of his adventure to Lewis and Humphrey, makes it very clear that from his first moments on Perelandra he was struck by its vivid beauty. The "golden or coppery" color gave way to an "indescribable confusion of color."[20] Immersed in warm water undulating with curving swells and rushing descents, Ransom got a mouth full of water that gave him "quite astonishing pleasure."[21] In fact, during those first moments on Perelandra he experienced "excessive pleasure" in that "warm, maternal, delicately gorgeous world."[22] It was not a "non-sensuous" but a "trans-sensuous"[23] experience where he was lifted into a higher reality. Wonder upon wonder engaged his attention. After he made it onto one of the floating islands he was overwhelmed by the smells and the sounds and the tastes he encountered such that it was "the discovery of a totally new *genus* of pleasures, something unheard of among men, out of all reckoning, beyond all covenant."[24] It was a world unsullied by sin and guilt.

The encounter with the "green Lady" changes everything. She shatters all the "normal" categories of human thought. As Ransom put it:

> Opposites met in her and were fused in a fashion for which we have no images. One way of putting it would be to say that neither our sacred nor our profane art could make her portrait. Beautiful, naked, shameless, young—she was obviously a goddess: but then the face, the face so calm that it escaped insipidity by the very concentration of its mildness, the face that was like the sudden coldness and stillness of a church when we enter it from a hot street—that made her a Madonna..... there was in her face an authority, in her caresses a condescension, which by taking seriously the inferiority of her adorers (the animals on Perelandra) made them somehow less inferior—raised them from the status of pets to that of slaves.[25]

This word picture reflects her innocence and purity, her value in relationship to the animals, and her power centered not in coercive force but in her moral presence and role in her world. She embodies goodness and beauty in their proper relationship. It is important to note that her moral character is not a static abstraction but is rather a growing and dynamic personal reality—"alive and therefore breakable"—a "balance maintained by a mind and therefore, at least in theory, able to be lost."[26]

The source of this dynamic understanding lies in the ontological character of the relationships that shape her existence. It is not a matter of taste. It is not a matter of autonomous individuality. Her existence is centered in a set of profound ontological relationships which includes, first, Maleldil the Creator God; second, the King of Perelandra who is currently physically separated from her; third, Ransom; fourth, the animals; and lastly, the rest of Perelandra. At the center lies her relationship with Maleldil. She tells Ransom,

> It is a delight with terror in it! One's own self to be walking from one good to another, walking beside Him as Himself may walk, not even holding hands. How has He made me so separate from Himself? How did it enter His mind to conceive such a thing? The world is so much larger than I thought. I thought we went along paths—but it seems there are no paths. The going itself is the path.[27]

In this primordial and sinless world the experience of pleasure and beauty is automatically associated with and gives knowledge of the good—especially the good purposes of Maleldil. Even the law not to sleep on the "fixed land" is an expression of the goodness of Maleldil and shapes and informs the role of creator and creature. "I am His beast, and all His biddings are joys."[28]

Ransom is not the only outside visitor to this world. Weston, under the inner compulsion of the "bent" Eldil of the "Silent Planet," plunges into Perelandra. He is intellectually driven by a vague notion of "emergent evolution" that results in a monistic idealism that celebrates the evolutionary movement of "Life" toward a transcendental spirituality of "Pure Spirit."[29] This intellectual vision serves as an outer expression of an inner and demonic attempt to corrupt the Green Lady, and with her, all of Perelandra. In a critical moment, Weston howls, "I am the Universe. I, Weston, am your God and your Devil, I call that Force into me completely. . . ."[30] And, as he does so, he ceases to exercise any personal control of himself and accepts control by the rebellious Eldil who eventually leaves Weston to die.[31]

Weston (now the "Un-man) seeks to sway the Green Lady to disobey "the law of the fixed land" through an almost ceaseless conversation. Ransom attempts to intervene but the sheer relentless struggle of the dialogue brings him to the edge of fatigue. After a brief period of rest, Ransom attempts to track the movements of the conversing pair and uncovers the "face" of the ugly and of evil.[32] He discovers the ripped and lifeless bodies of brightly colored frogs. These were the first "dead or spoiled"[33] things he had seen on Perelandra. Following the trail of mutilated frogs, Ransom comes upon Weston meticulously ripping apart a frog and throwing it to the ground.[34]

In contrast to the "face" of the Lady, Weston, though still in human form, had the face of death, the face without human expression, the face with a devilish smile, the face of evil.[35] It was no longer Weston. It was the "Unman."[36] "The extremity of its evil had passed beyond all struggle into some state which bore a horrible similarity to innocence. It was beyond vice as the Lady was beyond virtue."[37]

Ransom collapses in a faint before the face of evil. He recalls later the terror of that moment connecting this experience to the wisdom of "certain old philosophers and poets" whose insight he summarizes:

> As there is one Face above all worlds merely to see which is irrevocable joy, so at the bottom of all worlds that face is waiting whose sight alone is the misery from which none who beholds it can recover. And though there seemed to be, and indeed were, a thousand roads by which a man could walk through the world, there was not a single one which did not lead sooner or later either to the Beatific or the Miserific Vision. He himself had, of course, seen only a mask or faint adumbration of it; even so, he was not quite sure that he would live.[38]

The Unman continues its efforts to corrupt the Lady through an almost unending series of dialogues and challenges. Ransom responds to the call of the "Voice" and initiates the final crisis of the story.[39] A life and death struggle between Ransom and the Unman finally results in the death of the Unman—now abandoned by the evil that had once controlled him. Ransom is raised from what he believes is certain death in a deep cave by sliding into a fast moving stream of water that takes him to the surface. After he regained his strength and created a memorial for Weston, Ransom, with his wounded heel, follows the sound of a Song, "low and ripe and tender, full-bellied, rich and golden-brown: passionate too, but not with the passions of men."[40]

He is led by the Song of Maleldil to the great celebration that marked the true beginning of Perelandra: the coronation of the King and the Queen, the gathering of the Eldila of Malacandra and Perelandra, the worship of Maleldil through the litany of the Great Dance and, in the end, Ransom is placed in the casket for his transport back to earth. Throughout the closing celebration the interweaving of beauty and goodness is emphasized. The "pure, spiritual, intellectual love"[41] of the Eldila, the light resting upon but not "emanating from"[42] the young King and Queen in their purity and embodiment created in the image of Maleldil, the willing obedience of the King and Queen to the Eldila and beyond them to Maleldil as willing participants in the Great Dance, and the Great Dance itself in word and vision all suggest the great tapestry. In this climax the themes of incarnation, the creator God as the source of all being and value, the glorious consummation of the purposes of God are sounded. "*Maleldil* Himself will go to war,"[43] the siege of Thulcandra (the silent planet, earth) will end, the Dark Lord defeated and the evil cleansed. Then and only then will the false start be wiped out and "the world may then begin."[44] "... [I]t will be whispered that the morning is at hand:"[45] the morning of the fulfillment of the Great Dance.[46]

The language employed by Lewis in *Perelandra* brings together within the narrative movement of the text the ideas of moral insight and aesthetic judgment. Ransom is able to appreciate the beauty of *Perelandra* more fully than Weston because his aesthetic sensibilities are sharpened by his development in virtue and moral understanding. In the presence of the beauty and innocence of the Green Lady, Ransom is ever more aware of the need to be honest, to be engaged in the moral struggle, and listen to the Voice. In the same way, his moral development and his faith in the meaningful structure of the universe and the loving nature of the Creator allows him to enjoy the pleasures and beauties of *Perelandra* to a much greater degree than Weston.

Weston is driven and controlled by evil. He willingly gives himself over to the destructive power of the Bent One. He destroys and wantonly kills beautiful animals. His dialogue is a dialogue of lies. He seeks the moral and spiritual demise of the Green Lady. He desires her downfall. He distorts human history and experience. Not once does he acknowledge the beauty that surrounds him. To him the purity and innocence of the Green Lady is evidence of immaturity and ignorance and not of growing maturity and wisdom.

In the end Weston loses all hope. His vision of the Spiritual Force that is the goal of all reality, of which he is the spokesman, dissolves into fear, failure, and futility. Life loses all meaning. Near the end of the spiritual battle with Ransom, Weston, the Unman, tries to justify his understanding of the universe. Words like "real" and "unreal," "true" and "false" have no ontological reality. They refer to the "surface" of things and so: "The only point in anything is that there isn't any point."[47] The net of effect of Weston's position is nihilism. All values are relative and ultimately meaningless. Ransom then confronts Weston with the central existential question: "Are you Weston?"[48] This question cuts to the heart of the matter and he is only able to express his profound fear of losing the small shred of himself that was left. Then, the terror of the darkness came and Ransom calls out to Weston to "say a child's prayer if you can't say a man's."[49] The Unman cannot "bear it" and drags Ransom down into the water. The power of this exchange lies in the way it reveals the spiritual bankruptcy of "deflationary"[50] understandings of value that are the dominant positions in the current debates about truth, goodness, and beauty. Lewis dramatically lays out a different understanding rooted in the sacramental tapestry that grows out of the Christian worldview.

CONCLUSION

Mid-20th Century understandings of beauty continue to dominate the cultural perspective at the beginning of the twenty-first. Beauty, and with it all questions about value, including the meaning of "goodness," are relegated to the realm of the subjective, private, formal, and emotive. Devoid of value, life is now measured in terms of utility, the individual quest for pleasure, and notions of freedom that bear no relationship to a discussion of the end or goal of human community and its flourishing. Lewis challenges these understandings by pointing back to an earlier vision of the shape of reality: the "sacramental" tapestry rooted in the Christian worldview. It is important to re-examine the four general features of mid-20th Century aesthetic which Lewis engages in *Perelandra* and other writings. It is the intention of Lewis to confront and dismantle each of these characteristic positions by developing a more robust understanding rooted in the Great Tradition. In this process Lewis argues to the best explanation.

Rather than trying to directly confront the solipsism of subjectivism, Lewis presents Perelandra as a world alive with beauty, life, motion, and exquisite pleasure that overwhelms Ransom, in such a way that there is no question concerning the value and beauty of the external world. In this way it is clear that Ransom discovers rather than constructs Perelandra. Each discovery serves as a refutation of contemporary subjectivism. The world that he discovers is greater than the world within his mind and the world within his mind finds meaning and fulfillment in the larger reality of the world he discovers.

This is related directly to the public character of value and virtue. The wanton destruction of life perpetrated by the "Unman" is not a private affair reflective of private values with no social or transpersonal effect. The contempt for life and the repudiation of beauty has immediate and unmistakable public consequences. The beauty of Perelandra is littered with the bleeding carcasses of the eviscerated "brightly coloured frogs."[51] Evil is not a private or closed phenomenon. Evil, by its very nature, dehumanizes, destroys, manipulates, distorts, and subverts all domains of human relationship.

The formalizing of beauty to a reflection of the "a priori" structure of the Neo-Kantian mind requires a more subtle critique. It is an expression of modern reductionism in which the presumably smallest building blocks of any phenomenon are treated as providing the determining and supreme value and power over the whole. Thus, for example, cell function determines the viability of the whole organism. The intricate and inter-woven nature of Perelandra serves as a reminder that the "parts" reflect the "whole" and that the greater whole provides order and value to each of the parts. In the climatic celebration of worship Ransom directly experiences the cosmic structure of reality within which the dynamic and pulsating life of Perelandra finds her meaning and true value.

As indicated earlier in this essay, it is a commonplace assumption of our time that values merely reflect the internal, emotional life of the person. Although this position can be seen as a sub-category of subjectivism, it is concerned more with the nature of value than the source of value. The emotivist argues that values contain no cognitive content and do not reflect, in any way, the contours of reality. In the struggle with Weston to protect the innocence of the Green Lady, Ransom responds to Weston's argument that the law forbidding anyone from staying the night on the fixed island is only given to provoke the Green Lady to courageously stand up against Maleldil expressing her own desire over-against His command. Ransom interjects that obeying all the other commands seems "good in your own eyes also."[52] But where is there a command calling you to the "joy of obeying" that comes from doing something for which "His bidding is the *only* reason?"[53] Here Lewis provides an example of the true nature of value whose source is not our desires but the will of the One who calls us to fulfill all our longings in Him. The Green Lady responds in the best possible way, in worship and understanding:

> Oh, how well I see it! We cannot walk out of Maleldil's will: but He has given us a way to walk out of *our* will. And there could be no such way except

> a command like this. Out of our own will. It is like passing out through the world's roof into Deep Heaven. All beyond is Love Himself. I knew there was joy in looking upon the Fixed Island and laying down all thought of ever living there, but I did not till now understand.[54]

The principles rooted in the Great Tradition that undergird the narrative of *Perelandra* can be summarized in the following way:

- God is the source of value and being;
- A higher reality in value and being raises the lower reality and gives to the lower its dignity and meaning;
- Truth, goodness, and beauty are real (not in a purely Platonic sense) and are ultimately rooted in God and this makes them ontologically related;
- The longing for beauty can draw us to the source of beauty and the beatific vision is a transformative reality that points to God's ultimate mission and purpose;
- Goodness and beauty are so related that development in virtue can make beauty more discoverable and knowable;
- The ugly is not outside of the Christian vision nor is the realistic and gritty understanding of human brokenness and sin. But the Christian vision also understands that hope is real, redemption is possible by grace, and that ultimately, the presence of radical evil does not count against the covenantal justice of the Triune God whose love and power is revealed in the resurrection of the crucified One;
- The mission of the contemporary Church must include the intentional development of all of the Arts understood within the broad contours of a sacramental understanding of the cosmos and an acceptance the revelatory reality of God's gracious Spirit at work in his people who do all things, in all areas of life, for the glory of God.

The longing for "style" is a continuing cultural reflection of the desire for beauty. A recovery of the "Great Tradition" can provide resources for the creative engagement with this cultural moment. It is crucial that people of faith embrace the dynamic creativity of the creator God who beckons us to join Him in the Cosmic Dance. As the climax of the litany of the Great Dance intones:

> All things are by Him and for Him. He utters Himself also for His own delight and sees that He is good. He is His own begotten and what proceeds from Him is Himself. Blessed be He!
>
> All that is made seems planless to the darkened mind, because there are more plans than it looked for. In these seas there are islands where the hairs

of the turf are so fine and so closely woven together that unless a man looked long at them he would see neither hairs nor weaving at all, but only the same and the flat. So with the Great Dance. Set your eyes on one movement and it will lead you through all patterns and it will seem to you the master movement. But the seeming will be true. Let no mouth open to gainsay it. There seems no plan because it is all plan: there seems no centre because it is all centre.

Blessed be He!

Yet this seeming also is the end and final cause for which He spreads out Time so long and Heaven so deep; lest if we never met the dark, and the road that leads nowhither, and the question to which no answer is imaginable, we should have in our minds no likeness of the Abyss of the Father, into which if a creature drop down his thoughts for ever he shall hear no echo return to him.

Blessed, blessed, blessed be He![55]

ENDNOTES

1 The themes in the other books of the Space Trilogy, *Out of the Silent Planet* and *That Hideous Strength*, intersect with those of *Perelandra* but also similar themes can be found in such diverse works as: *Mere Christianity*, *Till We Have Faces*, *The Abolition of Man*, *The Problem of Pain*, *Screwtape Letters*, *The Chronicles of Narnia,* and the collection of essays in *The Weight of Glory.*

2 The inclusion of knowledge in this sentence is deliberate. One of the clear implications of mid-20th Century understandings of aesthetics in particular and axiology in general lies in its denial of any noetic content present in value judgments. As this essay will try to make clear, Lewis seeks to illustrate in *Perelandra* that moral insight provides a context within which the content of knowledge claims can be properly assessed.

3 For additional introductory detail see *Philosophy and the Arts: An Introduction to Aesthetics,* 3rd ed., by Gordon Graham, *Philosophies of Art and Beauty: Selected Readings in Aesthetics from Plato to Heidegger,* ed. By Albert Hofstadter and Richard Kuhns, and *The Beauty of the Infinite: The Aesthetics of Christian Truth,* by David Bentley Hart among many other works that explore philosophical aesthetics of the mid-20th Century period.

4 Generally speaking one could point to Hume, Mill, Dewey, and, to some extent, Derrida as representative of this position.

5 See *Surprised by Joy*, *Abolition of Man*, and *That Hideous Strength* for the arguments and the literary examples that illustrate his assumptions. This will be developed with more detail in the remaining sections of the essay.

6 Walter Hooper, "Introduction," to C.S. Lewis, "Transposition," *The Weight of Glory*, ed. by Walter Hooper, (New York: HarperSanFrancisco, 2001), 18-20.

7 C.S. Lewis, "Transposition," *The Weight of Glory*, ed. by Walter Hooper, (New York: HarperSanFrancisco, 2001), 98-99.

8 Lewis, "Transposition," 100-101.

9 Lewis, "Transposition," 101.

10 Lewis, "Transposition," 102.

11 Lewis, "Transposition," 102.

12 Lewis, "Transposition," 103.

13 Lewis, "Transposition," 111.

14 See, Hans Boersma, *Heavenly Participation: The Weaving of a Sacramental Tapestry*, (Grand Rapids: Wm. B. Eerdmans Publishing Co., 2011), 19-26.

15 The reference here to the "Incarnation" and later to the "Triune nature of God" is an important link to the "Mere Christian" understanding of Lewis and to the center of the "Great Sacramental Tradition." A full development of these ideas lies outside the scope of this essay but are deeply reflected in the narrative of *Perelandra* and its relationship to the rest of the Space Trilogy. The central theme of "Transposition" is also reflected in these comments: the "higher" is necessary to understand and interpret the "lower."

16 C.S. Lewis, "The Weight of Glory," *The Weight of Glory*, ed. by Walter Hooper, (New York: HarperSanFranscisco, 2001), 30-31, 42. The Italicized word is in the original text.

17 Lewis, "Transposition," 112.

18 Augustine, *Confessions*, Book X, chapter 27, line 38.

19 The meaning of this word in this context can be indicated in the following way. Because the creator God is eternally Father, Son, and Holy Spirit (Love, Lover, and Loving) in eternal relationship, the creation which bears the stamp of the Creator is also intricately interwoven in such a way that all parts are related to every other part and to the whole. This fact is becoming increasingly acknowledged by all areas of science.

20 C.S. Lewis, *Perelandra*, (New York: Scribner, 2003), 30-31 and see also Michael Ward, *Planet Narnia: The Seven Heavens in the Imagination of C.S. Lewis*, (Oxford: Oxford University Press, 2008), 164-171.

21 Lewis, *Perelandra*, 32.

22 Lewis, *Perelandra*, 33, 32.

23 Lewis, *Perelandra*, 30.

24 Lewis, *Perelandra*, 37.

25 Lewis, *Perelandra*, 56.

26 Lewis, *Perelandra*, 59.

27 Lewis, *Perelandra*, 60. See also John 14:1ff.

28 Lewis, *Perelandra*, 65.

29 Lewis, *Perelandra*, 78-79.

30 Lewis, *Perelandra*, 82.

31 Lewis, *Perelandra*, 155.

32 Lewis, *Perelandra*, 93-94.

33 Lewis, *Perelandra*, 94.

34 Lewis, *Perelandra*, 94-95.

35 Lewis, *Perelandra*, 95.

36 Lewis, *Perelandra*, 105.

37 Lewis, *Perelandra*, 95.

38 Lewis, *Perelandra*, 96.

39 Lewis, *Perelandra*, 119-156.

40 Lewis, *Perelandra*, 159.

41 Lewis, *Perelandra*, 171.

42 Lewis, *Perelandra*, 175.

43 Lewis, *Perelandra*, 182.

44 Lewis, *Perelandra*, 182.

45 Lewis, *Perelandra*, 183.

46 Lewis, *Perelandra*, 183-187.

47 Lewis, *Perelandra*, 144.
48 Lewis, *Perelandra*, 145.
49 Lewis, *Perelandra*, 146.
50 Pascal Engel, *Truth* (Montreal: McGill-Queen's University Press, 2002), 41-63.
51 Lewis, *Perelandra*, 93.
52 Lewis, *Perelandra*, 101.
53 Lewis, *Perelandra*, 101 (italics in the original).
54 Lewis, Perelandra, 101-102 (italics in the original).
55 Lewis, *Perelandra*, 186-187

WORKS CITED

Adams, Doug and Diane Apostolos-Cappadona. *Art as Religious Studies*. New York: Crossroad Publishing Company, 1987.

Adams, Marilyn McCord. Horrendous Evils and the Goodness of God. Ithaca, New York: Cornell University Press, 2000.

Augustine, *Confessions*, translated by John K. Ryan. New York: Image Books, 1960.

Bagger, David, Gary R. Habermas and Jerry L. Walls. C.S. Lewis as Philosopher: Truth, Goodness and Beauty. Downers Grove, IL.: InterVarsity Press, 2008.

Boersma, Hans. *Heavenly Participation: The Weaving of a Sacramental Tapestry*. Grand Rapids: Wm. B. Eerdmans Publishing Co., 2011.

Engel, Pascal. *Truth*: Montreal: McGill-Queen's University Press, 2002.

Gadamer, Hans-Georg. *The Relevance of the Beautiful and Other Essays*, ed. by Robert Bernasconi. Cambridge: Cambridge University Press, 1988.

Gay, Peter. *The Enlightenment:The Rise of Modern Paganism*. New York: W. W. Norton and Company, 1966.

_________. *The Enlightenment:The Science of Freedom*. New York: W. W. Norton and Company, 1969.

Graham, Gordon. *Philosophy and the Arts:An Introduction to Aesthetics*, 3rd Ed. London: Routledge, 2005.

Hart, David Bentley. *The Beauty of the Infinite: The Aesthetics of Christian Truth*. Grand Rapids: Wm. B. Eerdmans Publishing Co., 2004.

Hazelton, Roger. *A Theological Approach to Art*. Nashville: Abingdon Press, 1967.

Hofstadter, Albert and Richard Kuhns, eds. *Philosophies of Art and Beauty: Selected Readings in Aesthetics from Plato to Heidegger*. Chicago: The University of Chicago Press, 1976.

Lewis, C.S. *Abolition of Man: or Reflections on Education with Special Reference to the Teaching of English in the Upper Forms of Schools*. HarperSanFrancisco: HarperCollins, 2001.

_________. *Mere Christianity:A Revised and Enlarged Edition, with a New Introduction, of the Three Books The Case for Christianity, Christian Behaviour, and Beyond Personality*. New York: Macmillan Publishing Co., Inc., 1952.

_________. *Out of the Silent Planet*. New York: Scribner, 2003.

_________. *Perelandra:A Novel*. New York: Scribner, 2003.

_________. *Prince Caspian:The Return to Narnia*. New York: HarperCollins, 1979.

_________. *Surprised by Joy:The Shape of My Early Life*. New York: Harcourt, Brace and World, Inc., 1955.

_________. *The Horse and His Boy*. New York: HarperCollins, 1982.

_________. *The Last Battle*. New York: HarperCollins, 1984.

_________. *The Lion, the Witch and the Wardrobe*. New York: HarperCollins, 1978.

_________. *The Magician's Nephew*. New York: HarperCollins, 1983.

_________. *The Problem of Pain*. New York: HaperCollins, 2001.

_________. *That Hideous Strength: A Modern Fairy-Tale for Grown-Ups.* New York: Scribner, 2003.

_________. *Till We Have Faces: A Myth Retold.* Orlando: Harcourt, Inc., 1984.

_________. *The Screwtape Letters.* West Chicago, Illinois: Lord and King Associates, Inc., 1976.

_________. *The Silver Chair.* New York: HarperCollins, 1981.

_________. *The Voyage of the "Dawn Treader."* HarperCollins, 1980.

_________. "The Weight of Glory," *The Weight of Glory*, ed. by Walter Hooper. New York: HarperSanFrancisco, 2001.

_________. "Transposition," *The Weight of Glory*, ed. by Walter Hooper. New York: Harper San Francisco, 2001.

Markos, Louis. *Restoring Beauty: The Good, The True, and The Beautiful in the Writings of C.S. Lewis.* Colorado Springs, CO.: Biblica Publishing, 2010.

Smith, John E., Harry S. Stout, and Kenneth P. Minkema, eds. *A Jonathan Edwards Reader.* New Haven: Yale University Press, 1995.

Thiessen, Gesa Elsbeth, ed. *Theological Aesthetics: A Reader.* Grand Rapids: Wm. B. Eerdmans Publishing Co., 2005.

Treier, Daniel J., Mark Husbands, and Roger Lundin, Eds. *The Beauty of God: Theology and the Arts.* Downers Grove, IL.: InterVarsity Press, 2007.

Ward, Michael. *Planet Narnia: The Seven Heavens in the Imagination of C.S. Lewis.* Oxford: Oxford University Press, 2008.

The Art of C.S. Lewis's Poetry[1]

DON W. KING

C.S. Lewis's popularity as a writer rests squarely on a prose style that is clear, lucid, and engaging. Lewis's attractive prose is not limited to one or two genres, but instead is apparent in his literary criticism as well as his children's stories, in his devotional works as well as his science fiction, in his apologetics as well as his letters. It is a commonplace, then, to underscore the enormous success his prose brought him. Yet Lewis began his publishing career as a poet with *Spirits in Bondage* (1919), a volume of lyrical poems, and followed this with *Dymer* (1926), a long narrative poem in rhyme royal (both published under the pseudonym, Clive Hamilton, using his own first name and his mother's maiden name). Moreover, throughout his life Lewis continued to write poetry; some poems were included in prose works like *The Pilgrim's Regress*, the Chronicles of Narnia, and the Ransom Space trilogy, and others were published independently in magazines, journals, and newspapers. Many were collected by Walter Hooper and published in 1964 as *Poems*.[2]

Anyone interested in Lewis as a writer should become aware of the important role poetry has in shaping his literary life, particularly his aspirations to achieve acclaim as a poet and the literary influences that shaped him. Owen Barfield remembers Lewis when he first met him as one "whose ruling ambition was to become a great poet. At that time if you thought of Lewis you automatically thought of poetry."[3] Tracing these aspirations and influences as he moved from boyhood to mature adult is fascinating and sheds significant light upon the prose for which he later became best known. His autobiography, *Surprised by Joy*, letters, particularly to Arthur Greeves, diaries, and journal entries provide ample chronological evidence of his early enthusiasm for poetry, the writers most influencing him, and his sustained desire to achieve acclaim as a poet. Furthermore, throughout we see his attempt to establish his own theory of poetry, something he pursued throughout his life via a number of different forums culminating in his published debate with E. M. W. Tillyard, *The Personal Heresy*. What all these sources make clear is how integral poetry was to Lewis's life. He did not sip or taste poetry in a casual, off-handed manner; rather, it was for him a stream intricately weaving through his life becoming a literary well—a nourishing reservoir almost without bottom—one from which he drank deeply and passionately.[4]

Accordingly, the focus of this essay is on Lewis as poet and artist. In a lengthy correspondence with Ruth Pitter, an accomplished poet, Lewis frequently reveals his deep desire to write beautiful and powerful poems. In response to her critiques of several of his poems, he writes: "In most of these poems [that he sent her] I am enamoured of metrical subtleties—not as a game: the truth is I often lust after a metre as a man might lust after a woman" (August 10, 1946).[5] In addition, he writes New Zealander Rhona Bodle commenting on the way poetry makes language concrete:[6]

> Indeed, in a sense, one can hardly put anything into words: only the simplest colours have names, and hardly any of the smells. The simple physical pains and (still more) the pleasures can't be expressed in language. I labour the point lest the devil shd. hereafter try to make you believe that what was wordless was therefore vague and nebulous. But in reality it is just the clearest, the most concrete, and most indubitable realities which escape language: not because *they* are vague but because language is . . . Poetry I take to be the continual effort to bring language back to the actual.[7] (June 24, 1949)

In writing to Martyn Skinner about his *Two Colloquies*, Lewis says:

> I didn't want to write until I had given them a sympathetic reading and somehow I never was in quite the mood for them till tonight. (Reading collection papers, like marking School Cert., I have always found a great whetter of appetite for poetry. Fact! I don't know why). The right mood for a new poem doesn't come so often now as it used to. There is so little leisure, and when one comes to that leisure untired—well, you know *Ink* is a deadly drug. One wants to write. I cannot shake off the addiction.[8] (October 11, 1950)

In a letter to Dom Bede Griffiths, Lewis expresses his well-known distaste for modern British poetry and a surprisingly positive evaluation of some modern American poets: "I feel as you do about modern English poetry. American is better. Lee, Masters, Frost, and Robinson Jeffers all really have something to *say* and some real art"[9] (April 22, 1954). During a dry period in writing his own poetry, he writes Pitter: "It is a long time since I turned a verse. One aches a little, doesn't one? I should like to be 'with poem' again" (March 19, 1955).[10]

Lewis's penchant to be "enamoured of metrical subtleties," his lusting "after a metre as a man might lust after a woman," his ache to turn a verse and "be 'with poem' again," was lifelong, suggesting how intently he focused upon crafting his poetry, including both his tendency to revise his poems and his fascination with prosody. While he certainly dashed off quick initial drafts of poems, he labored as an artist to make the final draft as polished as possible. Walter Hooper has noted that while Lewis the prose writer worked quickly and wrote few drafts, Lewis the poet was painstaking, often writing several versions of the same poem: "Most of Lewis's prose came from his head almost exactly as it appears on the printed page, with only an occasional word being changed. It was not like this with his poetry. They went through endless revisions.[11] We know, for example, that Lewis sent friends drafts of poems and asked for criticism. On

December 20, 1920, he writes Leo Baker: "I am sending you the revised Wild Hunt [a poem that has not survived] and await your criticism... I have not time today to discuss your theory of poetry; we seem to be agreed on fundamentals, tho' there are still points of difference—real ones, not 'misunderstandings.'"[12] About an autobiographical poem concerning in part his spiritual journey, Lewis writes Barfield: "It really takes a load off my mind to hear that you like the poem ["I Will Write Down"[13]]. Couplets, however dangerous, are needed if one is to try to give to the subjective poem some of the swing and narrative zest of the old epic ... I send ... the opening of the poem. I am not satisfied with any part I have yet written and the design is ludicrously ambitious. But I feel it will be several years anyway before I give up" (May 6, 1932).[14]

Lewis's extensive correspondence already alluded to with Ruth Pitter shows him seeking criticism about drafts of poems. Given Lewis's deep affection for Pitter's poetry, it is not surprising that he seeks her advice about his own poetry. In her he found one who shared similar poetic sensibilities, so he felt comfortable asking her to critique his verse. In fact, he asked her to be straightforward in her criticisms: "Now remember ... you won't wound a sick man by unfavourable comment ... I know (or think) that some of these contain important thoughts and v. great metrical ingenuity. That isn't what I'm worrying about. But are they real poems or do the content and the form remain separable—fitted together only by force?"[15] At one point he asks her to judge between two versions of his poem "Two Kinds of Memory":

> I want some advice. I have written two different versions of a poem and all my friends disagree, some violently championing A and some B, and some neither. Will you give a vote? Firstly, is either any good? Secondly, if so, which is the good one? Don't be in the least afraid of answering NO to the first question: kindness wd. only be an encouragement to waste more time... I could almost make myself hope for your sake—and lest you spend more time and attention on them than is reasonable for me to exact—that both are bad![16]

Accordingly, on the basis of his friend's criticisms as well as his own desire to craft the best poetry possible, Lewis frequently re-worked poems. While any number of poems could be cited to show Lewis working as an artist on his poetry, we will consider one here as representative. In *Poems* Hooper publishes the poignant sonnet "As the Ruin Falls," an agonizing recollection about a beloved one's suffering. Three holograph versions of the poem survive, but all are undated.[17] However, based on the internal evidence of the three versions, I surmise the following order of the drafts:

Draft A

This is all flashy rhetoric about loving you;
I never had a selfless thought since I was born.
I am mercenary and self-seeking through and through,
I want God, Man, and you, only to serve my turn.

Pleasure, ease, reassurance are the goals I seek,
I cannot crawl one inch outside my proper skin.
I talk of "love" (a scholar's parrot might talk Greek)
But, self-imprisoned, end always where I begin.

But this at least: you have shown me, dearest, what I lack,
Revealed the gulf, and me on the wrong side of it,
Shown me the impossibility of turning back,
And pointed me the one way from[?] the noisome pit.

For this I bless you for my broken heart. The pains
You cause me are more precious than all other gains.

Draft B

All this is flashy rhetoric, about loving you.
I never had a selfless thought since I was born.
I am mercenary and self-seeking through and through:
I want friends, you, and God only to serve my turn.

Pleasure, peace, re-assurance are the goals I seek;
I cannot crawl one inch outside my proper skin.
I talk of love—a scholar's parrot may talk Greek—
But, self-imprisoned, always end where I begin.

Only that now you have shown me (oh how late) my lack:
I see the chasm; and everything you are was making
Each moment a long bridge by which I might get back
From exile and grow man. And now the bridge is breaking.

Yet so, I bless you for my hammered heart: the pains
You give me are more precious than all other gains.

Draft C

All this is flashy rhetoric about loving you.
I never had a selfless thought since I was born.
I am mercenary and self-seeking through and through:
I want God, you, all friends, merely to serve my turn.

Peace, re-reassurance, pleasure, are the goals I seek,
I cannot crawl one inch outside my proper skin:
I talk of love—a scholar's parrot may talk Greek—
But, self-imprisoned, always end where I begin.

Only that now you have taught me (but how late) my lack.
I see the chasm. And everything you are was making
My heart into a bridge by which I might get back
From exile, and grow man. And now the bridge is breaking.

For this I bless you as the ruin falls. The pains
You give me are more precious than all other gains.[18]

Each draft is written in alexandrines and uses the rhyme scheme of an English sonnet. In the first quatrain, there are few differences between the drafts. "B" and "C" change the opening from "This is all flashy rhetoric" to "All this is flashy rhetoric," and in line four "only" becomes "merely" in "C." In the second quatrain, the "ease" of line five becomes "peace" in "B" and "C"; the alliteration of "pleasure, peace, reassurance" in "B" is weakened in "peace, re-assurance, pleasure" in "C." The only other significant difference is that "(a scholar's parrot might talk Greek)" becomes "—a scholar's parrot may talk Greek—" in "B" and "C."

However the minor tweaking Lewis does in the drafts of the first two quatrains contrasts to major changes in the third quatrain and final couplet. The third quatrain in A is weak. In line nine "but this at least" is jarring, and "dearest" edges the poem to the brink of sentimentality. "Revealed the gulf" in line ten could work, but "me on the wrong side of it" is forced. Line eleven suggests the beloved has shown the speaker "the impossibility of turning back" from his love for her, and this works well with the sentiment expressed in line twelve: that their relationship has saved him from hell on earth ("pointed me the one way from[?] the noisome pit"). Also, the *it:pit* rhyme is odd. The third quatrains of "B" and "C" are considerable improvements. Both drafts remake lines nine and ten-A into the more poetically powerful "Only that now you have taught me (but how late) my lack. / I see the chasm." The next clear sign the poem evolves from weak to stronger occurs when lines ten-B and eleven of "B," "and everything you are was making / Each moment a long bridge by which I might get back" becomes "and everything you are was making / My heart into a bridge by which I might get back" of "C." The shift from the impersonal "each moment a long bridge" to "my heart into a bridge" suddenly transforms the poem from an objective, clinical analysis to a subjective, personal confession. The power of both "B" and "C" is highlighted by the shared conclusion: "And now the bridge is breaking." Lewis deftly describes the pain of heartbreak yet avoids being maudlin.

The final couplet in the three drafts undergoes the most change, particularly line thirteen. In "A," Lewis again verges on the sentimental when he writes "For this I bless you for my broken heart." "B" is a qualitative improvement as we read "Yet so, I bless you for my hammered heart." Indeed the notion his heart has been hammered by a smith shaping molten iron ameliorates the hackneyed use of "bless." However, Lewis nears perfection in "C" when the line evolves to its most powerful expression: "For this I bless you as the ruin falls." Now it all comes out; as he watches her suffering—her physical ruin—he faces squarely his own ruin—his broken life as he anticipates losing her. Yet in the midst of this knowledge, the poem's final line shares the secret of one of life's greatest ironies—the pain of losing one's beloved reinforces the inestimable worth of human love: "The pains / You give me are more precious than all other gains." This review of the three drafts of this poem makes it clear that Lewis is an artist at work—shaping, honing, and molding words into the best combination of sounds and meanings he can. This same dedication to crafting the best poetry possible informs all of Lewis's serious efforts at verse.

Also indicative of Lewis's conscious efforts at the art of poetry is his keen practice of prosody, especially meter, rhyme (exact and slant as well internal and final), and stanza form.[19] As early as March 7, 1916, he writes Greeves and critiques the prosody of several of George MacDonald's poems appearing in *Phantastes*: "There are . . . poems in the tale . . . which with one or two exceptions are shockingly bad, so don't TRY to appreciate them: it is just a sign, isn't it, of how some geniuses can't work in metrical forms."[20] Three months later he tells Greeves "my verse, both in quality and quantity for the last three weeks is deplorable!"[21] On October 12, 1916, Lewis's praise to Greeves of Shelley's *Prometheus Unbound* is tempered by his criticism of the prosody: "Shelley had a great genius, but his carelessness about rhymes, metre, choice of words etc., just prevents him being as good as he might be. To me, when you're in the middle of a fine passage and come to a 'cockney' rhyme like 'ru*in*' & pursu*ing*, it spoils the whole thing."[22]

While Lewis's youthful criticism of Shelley may be querulous, it nonetheless demonstrates how important prosody was to him. Lewis's interest in the making of verse, especially prosody, was lifelong and is also reflected in many of his scholarly writings. In "The Alliterative Metre" Lewis took it upon himself to expound "the principles of this metre to a larger public than those Anglo-Saxon and Old Norse specialists who know it already.[23] Throughout this essay he tries to make the technical aspects of alliterative meter understandable, and he gives a detailed explanation of how the half-line meter works. In addition, he explains lifts and dips, providing multiple examples of how lifts and dips may be arranged in the half-line. In something of a tour de force he ends the essay with his own model alliterative poem, "The Planets." Throughout this essay we follow the serious passion of a poet intent upon demonstrating how important a knowledge of prosody is for those who want to understand alliterative verse. In another example, in "The Fifteenth-Century Heroic Line" he offers a thoughtful discussion of prosody:

> I shall give the arbitrary name 'Fifteenth-Century Heroic' to the line we find in *The Temple of Glas*, *The Pastime of Pleasure*, [Alexander] Barclay's *Ecologues*, [Sir Thomas] Wyatt's *Complaint upon Love to Reason*, and, in general, all those poems which appear at first sight to attempt the decasyllabic line without success. The question I propose is whether the Fifteenth-Century Heroic is, in fact, an attempt at our decasyllabic; and, if it is not, what else it may be.[24]

Lewis offers at one point to demonstrate what he means by an "experiment" in which he offers two contrasting four-line stanzas; while the content of each is roughly the same, the differing meters of each illustrate the point he wishes to make.

In his massive *English Literature in the Sixteenth Century* (1944), Lewis moves easily between literary history, evaluation of various poets (some of which he dismisses rather abruptly), and commentary on prosody. For example, about the poulter's measure (alternating lines of hexameter and heptameter), he writes:

> The vices of that metre are two. The medial break in the alexandrine, though it may do well enough in French, quickly becomes intolerable in a language with such a tyrannous stress-accent as ours: the line struts. The fourteener has a much pleasanter movement, but a totally different one; the line dances a jig. Hence in a couplet made of two such yoke-fellows we seem to be labouring up a steep hill in bottom gear for the first line, and then running down the other side of the hill, out of control, for the second.[25]

In "Metre" published near the end of his life, Lewis the artist again focuses upon prosody. The essay attempts to consider the somewhat thorny question of how to scan lines of poetry. After admitting scansion depends upon phonetic facts and individual differences of pronunciation, he posits: "I am going to suggest that metrical questions are profitable only if we regard them, not as questions about fact, but as purely practical. That is, when we ask 'What is the metre of this poem?', we are not, or should not be, asking which analysis of the paradigm is 'true' but which is most useful."[26]

Lewis's earliest poems illustrate this lifelong fascination with prosody. For example, he enjoyed experimenting with meter from the heroic couplets of "Descend to Earth, Descend, Celestial Nine" to the eight-stressed catalectic trochees of "'Carpe Diem' after Horace" to the rhyme royal of "In Winter When the Frosty Nights Are Long" to the blank verse of *Loki Bound*.[27] Other examples of Lewis's earliest verse, the ten poems that survive from "Metrical Meditations of a Cod"[28] and the lyrics of *Spirits in Bondage* (hereafter *SB*), offer additional insights into Lewis's youthful concerns with prosody. Of these fifty-one poems, thirty-five are tetrameter or pentameter, most often iambs, with trochees less frequent. The other fifteen poems include trimeter, hexameter, heptameter, and several cases of mixed meter.

Several of Lewis's iambic tetrameter and pentameter poems employ rhyming couplets. For instance, the tetrameter couplets of "Satan Speaks" (I) and the heroic couplets of "Satan Speaks" (XIII) indicate the two poems share more than a common title.[29] Both open similarly, including the use of a medial caesura. The "I am Nature, the Mighty Mother / I am the law: ye have none other" of the former sets the stage for "I am the Lord your God: even he that made / Material things, and all these signs arrayed" of the latter. In "The Hills of Down" Lewis disguises his heroic couplets by printing the poem as though lines of iambic dimeter alternate with iambic trimeter:

> I will abide
>   And make my dwelling here
> Whatso betide,
>   Since there is more to fear
> Out yonder. Though
>   This world is drear and wan,
> I dare not go
>   To dreaming Avalon.[30]

What we actually have are heroic couplets with internal rhyme. Lewis weaves the fabric of this poem even tighter when we note the assonance of *abide*, *my*, and *betide* in the first three lines as well as the final *-er* sound of *here*, *there*, *fear*, *yonder*, and *drear* in lines two through six. This assonance and sound repetition occurs throughout the other sections of the poem.

Lewis used tercets less often but to powerful effect as in "Spooks": "Last night I dreamed that I was come again / Unto the house where my beloved dwells / After years of wandering and pain."[31] While the rhyme scheme here is *aba* and not the typical *aaa* of the true tercet, Lewis may have been experimenting with a kind of terza rima since the rest of the poem rhymes *acc*, *dde*, *ffe*, *acca*. However, "De Profundis" utilizes the true tercet rhyme with several sounds repeated in the twelve stanzas: *abcdefgdhige*. In addition, one stanza uses the unusual perfect rhyme: "Yet I will not bow down to thee nor love thee, / For looking in my own heart I can prove thee, / And know this frail, bruised being is above thee."[32] Another example of the true tercet is found in

"Hymn (for Boys' Voices) where Lewis uses trochaic catalectic tetrameter: "Every man a God would be / Laughing though eternity / If as God's his eye could see."[33] We also see tercets in the longest poem of *SB*, "Song of the Pilgrim."

Oddly, although Lewis admired Tennyson's poetry, in these early poems we never see him attempt the *In Memoriam* stanza: iambic tetrameter with the *abba* rhyme scheme. At the same time, most of Lewis's pentameter poems in *SB* use the *abba* rhyme scheme, such as "Of Ships," "French Nocturne," "Victory," "Apology," and "Milton Read Again." Also among his early poems Lewis wrote two Italian sonnets, "Sonnet—To Philip Sydney" and "Sonnet" ("The stars come out; the fragrant shadows fall") both employing the *abbaabba cdcdee* rhyme scheme.[34] In the sonnet to Sydney Lewis appears to be working strictly to form, so much so that the poem is only two sentences: the octave is the first sentence and the sestet is the second. In the sonnet "The stars come out," he more freely uses the caesura producing a poem with five sentences and medial caesuras in lines one, eight, and eleven. A final connection between the two sonnets is his use of the feminine rhyme *hour:bower* in both. While Lewis wrote other sonnets later, it was not a form he particularly favored, so these two early specimens suggest poetic "finger exercises" where he imitated and experimented with the form.

We also see Lewis experimenting with a medieval poetic form—the ballade—in his "Ballade of a Winter's Morning" and "Ballade Mystique."[35] The ballade, which Lewis may have encountered in imperfect form in Chaucer and almost certainly knew from Algernon Charles Swinburne's "Ballad of Dreamland," William Ernest Henley's "Ballade of Dead Actors," and Andrew Lang's "Ballades of Blue China," is highly structured. Most commonly the ballade consists of three stanzas and a final envoy. Each stanza is eight to ten lines and the envoy contains half as many lines as the stanza. The rhyme sound must be identical in the corresponding lines in each stanzas although the rhyming words may vary from stanza to stanza; the most common rhyme scheme for the stanza is *ababbcbc* and for the envoy *bcbc*. However, the one element that marks the ballade is the refrain, which forms the last line of each stanza and the envoy. The envoy "is not only a dedication, but should be the peroration of the subject, and richer in its wording and more stately in its imagery than the preceding verses, to convey the climax of the whole matter, and avoid the suspicion that it is a mere postscript."[36]

Both "Ballade of a Winter's Morning" and "Ballade Mystique" are iambic tetrameter stanzas of eight lines with the *ababbcbc* rhyme scheme and both four line envoys use the *bcbc* rhyme scheme. The refrain in "Ballade of a Winter's Morning" undergoes progressive mutations from "A merry morning we shall spend" to "And make us merry friend by friend" to "To make us merry friend by friend" to "Of him who sang Patroklos' friend" to "Than mine or mine, oh friend, my friend" to the final line of the envoy "We'll tread them bravely, friend by friend." In a poem almost certainly celebrating Lewis's friendship with Greeves, the evolving refrain celebrating friendship is most appropriate. In "Ballade Mystique" Lewis experiments with the refrain as it moves from a question to a declarative to a final combined declarative and question: "What do they know? What do they know?" (repeated in the second stanza) to "They do not know, they do not know" to the envoy's "They do not know: how should they know?" This poem, ostensibly also about friendship, uses the refrain to contrast the distance between the speaker and his friends.

Similarly, the envoy of the former is upbeat ("So while the wind-foot seasons wear / Be glad, and when towards the end / Adown the dusky ways we fare, / We'll tread them bravely, friend by friend!") while that of the latter is dark ("The friends I have without a peer / Beyond the western ocean's glow, / Whither the faerie galleys steer, / They do not know: how should they know?"). Yet both poems link friendship with love for literature. "Ballade of a Winter's Morning," obviously set in winter when all is cold and dead outside, fairly exalts in the anticipation of rich sessions inside where the friends will "take fit books" and "old tomes full oft re-read with care," those perhaps of Spenser, Horace, Malory, and Virgil, as a remedy for the outer cold. Ironically, however, in "Ballade Mystique" the speaker, whose friends think he needs to leave his house in order to enjoy Spring and "the wakening of the year," does not feel the need for their fellowship. He is not, as they believe, "piteously alone / Without the speech of comrades dear." Instead, literature is his comfort:

> That I have seen the Dagda's throne
> In sunny lands without a tear
> And found a forest all my own
> To ward with magic shield and spear,
> Where, through the stately towers I rear
> For my desire, around me go
> Immortal shapes of beauty clear.

As a result, both ballades, highly structure literary forms, center upon the value of literature. While "Ballade Mystique" underscores the speaker's isolation and alienation from his friends, "Ballade of a Winter's Morning" highlights the fellowship and camaraderie the speaker enjoys with one friend.

Although Lewis favored iambic tetrameter and pentameter, he enjoyed writing poems in other meters. "Exercise," for example, utilizes iambic trimeter: "Where are the magic swords / That elves of long ago / Smithied beneath the snow / For heroes' rich rewards?"[37] The trimeter six line stanzas of "Hesperus" employ a unique *ababcb* rhyme scheme.[38] Three poems, "To Sleep," "Our Daily Bread," and "How He Saw Angus the God,"[39] use a kind of English form of the Sapphic stanza with rhyme: four line stanzas of alternate rhyme, with the first three lines in pentameter and the fourth line a trimeter. Lewis plays with an even shorter form in the couplet lines of "The Autumn Morning" where we find quatrains with the first three lines in trimeter and the fourth line in dimeter: "See! The pale autumn dawn / Is faint, upon the lawn / That lies in powdered white / Of hoar-frost dight."[40]

Lewis's only example of hexameter in these early poems is the appropriately entitled "Alexandrines."[41] In addition to experimenting with iambic hexameter in this poem, Lewis also plays with the sonnet form by modifying both the rhyme scheme and the length of the poem. His *ababbccddeeff* is a loose adaptation of the typical English sonnet rhyme scheme and his thirteen line format is one short of the sonnet. The alexandrine is typically characterized by a regular and strongly marked medial caesura, and Lewis's poem includes medial caesuras in lines three, seven, nine, ten, eleven, and twelve. The effectiveness of the medial caesura is best seen in the last four lines: "For in that house I know a little, silent room / Where Someone's always waiting, waiting in the gloom / To draw me with an evil eye, and hold me fast— / Yet thither doom will drive me and He will win at last."

More frequent in these early poems is Lewis's exploration of the heptameter (or septenary). Like the hexameter, the heptameter is marked by a regular and strong medial caesura evident in "Ode for New Year's Day":

Woe unto you, ye sons of pain that are this day in earth,
Now cry for all your torment: now curse your hour of birth
And the fathers who begat you to a portion nothing worth.
And Thou, my own beloved, for as brave as ere thou art,
Bow down thine head, Despoina, clasp thy pale arms over it.[42]

"World's Desire" is written primarily in septenarian couplets, with occasional octameters as well: "And the cold ravine / Echoes to the crushing roar and thunder of a mighty river / Raging down a cataract. Very tower and forest quiver / And the grey wolves are afraid and the call of birds is drowned, / And the thought and speech of man in the boiling water's sound."[43] Lewis uses heptameter tercets throughout "The Roads": "I stand on the windy uplands among the hills of Down / With all the world spread out beneath, meadow and sea and town, / And ploughlands on the far-off hills that glow with friendly brown."[44] In "Prologue" he employs an irregular heptameter:

As of old Phoenician men, to the Tin Isles sailing
Straight against the sunset and the edges of the earth,
Chaunted loud above the storm and the strange sea's wailing,
Legends of their people and the land that gave them birth—
Sang aloud to Baal-Peor, sang unto the horned maiden,
Sang how they should come again with the Brethon treasure laden.[45]

To this oddity Lewis adds lines of octameter as in "Toiling at the stroke and feather through the wet and weary weather."

One of the most interesting heptameter specimens is "The Satyr" where Lewis, as he does with the heroic couplets in "The Hills of Down," disguises the meter by printing the poem so it appears we are reading tetrameter quatrains rhyming *aaba*: "When the flowery hands of spring / Forth their woodland riches fling, / Through the meadows, through the valleys / Goes the satyr carolling."[46] In fact, the meter is heptameter couplets with internal rhyme occurring in the first line of each couplet as in *spring:fling*. Furthermore, Lewis emphasizes particular sounds in each couplet as in *f*lowery, *f*orth, *f*ling, and va*ll*eys and caro*ll*ing. He extends the connection of sounds by creating internal rhyme between pairs of couplets. For instance, the couplet following the one cited above is: "From the mountain and the moor, / Forest green and ocean shore / All the faerie kin he rallies / Making music evermore." In addition to the internal rhyme of *moor:shore*, the alliteration of *m*ountain, *m*oor, *m*aking, and *m*usic, and the emphasis on the sound *-or* as in m*oor*, f*or*est, sh*ore*, and ever*more*, Lewis links the couplets by rhyming *valleys* in the second line of the first heptameter couplet with *rallies* in the second line of the second heptameter couplet. This use of internal rhyme to connect the septenarian couplets continues in the rest of the poem as in *cloven:woven* in lines six and eight and *asunder:wonder* in lines ten and twelve. As this review of Lewis's earliest poetry illustrates, he enjoyed experimenting with meter, rhyme, and lyric forms and this interest extended throughout his poetic career.

Nevill Coghill in "The Approach to English" commented upon Lewis's poetry, recalling that as young men in the 1920s both he and Lewis "hoped to be poets.... It was not until six or seven years later that Lewis said sadly to me 'When I at last realized that I was not, after all, going to be a great man ...' I think he meant 'a great poet.'" He also recalled Lewis's "gusto" for poetry."[47] Coghill's comments are a helpful gloss to Lewis's poetic aspirations, influences, craftsmanship, and prosody, illustrating the degree to which writing poetry and being a poet were fundamental to the way Lewis saw himself. As a poet, Lewis saw himself as an artist in the great tradition of the poets he so admired—Virgil, Dante, Milton, Wordsworth, Yeats, and many others. While he never achieved the kind of acclaim he desired as a poet, his sustained efforts at writing poetry demonstrate a dedicated, passionate, and committed artist at work.

ENDNOTES

1 This essay is adapted from material appearing in Chapter 1, "C.S. Lewis, Poet" of Don W. King, *C.S. Lewis, Poet: The Legacy of His Poetic Impulse* (Kent, Ohio: The Kent State University Press, 2001), 12–26. Copyright © 2001 by The Kent State University Press. Reprinted with permission.

2 Hooper also published *Narrative Poems* (New York: Harcourt Brace Jovanovich, 1969), a volume that reprints *Dymer* as well as three other narrative poems, and *Collected Poems* (London: Fount, 1994), a volume that reprints *Spirit in Bondage*, *Poems*, and a handful of other previously uncollected poems. As this book goes to press, the first comprehensive critical edition of Lewis's poetry, my *The Collected Poems of C.S. Lewis: A Critical Edition* (Kent, OH: Kent State University Press, 2013) is nearing publication; this volume will bring together for the first time all of Lewis's poems arranged in chronological order.

3 Owen Barfield, address at Wheaton College, October 16, 1974.

4 For more on this, see my *C.S. Lewis, Poet*, 1-12.

5 *The Collected Letters of C.S. Lewis, Volume 2: Books, Broadcasts and the War, 1931-1949*. Ed. Walter Hooper (London: Harper Collins, 2004, 735 (hereafter *CL*, 2).

6 Jerry Daniel in his "The Taste of the Pineapple: A Basis for Literary Criticism" emphasizes how wonderfully effective Lewis is in describing the "essence of things." Calling this focus as an "emphasis on the quiddity of things" (10), Daniel offers thoughtful commentary and numerous examples from Lewis's work to sustain his argument. As a reader, Lewis, according to Daniel, "immersed himself in the quality of a story or a poem he was reading," and "whether prose or verse, all works were 'poetry' to him in the sense that the 'feel' or 'taste' was primary" (10,11). Indeed, Daniel uses the image of the "taste" of a poem throughout as a way of describing Lewis's acquisition of poetry. In addition, Daniel applies this same rubric to Lewis as literary critic and imaginative writer. He finds Lewis's love of stock responses in poetry a connection to his desire for the essence of things:

> Lewis felt . . . that literature *ought* to produce stock responses: if a story presents a scene of cruelty, we ought to respond with horror; if a poem describes a mother's love for her child we ought to respond with warm satisfaction. Since he, as an artist, was attempting to impart a vision, he was attempting to elicit a response to that vision; and, believing in absolute values, he preferred to elicit a stock response . . . [Lewis forces] us to attend to the great reality of the poetry, the vision, inherent in so many works written by so many different persons in different ages of our history. (25; Daniel emphasis)

Daniel's essay is must reading for anyone interested in Lewis's poetic language.

7 *CL*, 2, 947; Lewis emphasis.

8 *The Collected Letters of C.S. Lewis, Volume 3: Narnia, Cambridge, and Joy, 1950-1963*. Ed. Walter Hooper (London: Harper Collins, 2006), 56-57 (hereafter, *CL*, 3); Lewis emphasis.

9 *CL*, 3, 461-62; Lewis emphasis.

10 *CL*, 3, 585.

11 "Introduction" to *Collected Poems* (hereafter *CP*), xv-xvi.

12 *The Collected Letters of C.S. Lewis, Volume 1: Family Letters 1905-1931*. Ed. Walter Hooper (London: Harper Collins, 2000), 513-14 (hereafter *CL*, 1).

13 For the text of this poem, see *C.S. Lewis, Poet*, 289-90.

14 *CL*, 2, 77.

15 *CL*, 2, 724; July 24, 1946. The poems he sent Pitter were drafts of "The Birth of Language," originally published in *Punch* CCX (January 9, 1946): 32 and later reprinted in *Poems*, 10-11 (hereafter *P*); "To C.W.," published as "To G. M." in *The Spectator* CLXIX (October 9, 1942): 335, and later revised and retitled "To a Friend" in *P*, 104; and "On Being Human," originally published in *Punch* CCX (May 8, 1946): 402, and later revised and reprinted in *P*, 34.

16 *CL*, 2, 758, 761; February 2, 1947. Interestingly, in her journal recollection of this letter, Pitter writes: "Both versions are very fine, of course: the skill in form alone is enough to drive a small poet to despair: and then the melody, so strong and so unforced, and the solemn images and the contrasting moods. Strange how memory is here *polarised*, as though he could not have encompassed the paradisal without retaining a hellish pain in recollection, an ever-fresh wound" (MS. Eng. lett. c. 220/3, fol. 38; Bodleian Library). Version B with slight changes was published in *Time and Tide* XXVIII (August 7, 1947): 859, and later revised and reprinted in *P*, 100. In another instance, Pitter recalls being flattered Lewis would think her view on his poems important: "'Donkey's Delight,' 'Young King Cole,' 'Vitraea Circe,' [are] magnificent poems to my mind, the technique staggering, vocabulary so wide, learned, & choice, discrimination (moral or spiritual) so lofty. As well might a lion request a mouse to criticise

his roaring: and yet I can imagine a lion doing so" (MS. Eng. lett. c. 220/3, fol. 52; Bodleian Library; July 6, 1947).

17 The holographs are available in Hooper's 1997 deposit to the Bodleian.

18 This is the version Hooper published in *P*, 109.

19 Charles Huttar's, "A Lifelong Love Affair with Language: C.S. Lewis's Poetry," in *Word and Story in C.S. Lewis* (Columbia, MO: University of Missouri Press, 1991) is one of best studies available on Lewis's prosody. Huttar focuses upon both Lewis's love of language and his technical expertise as poet. While relegating Lewis to the role of minor poet, Huttar finds Lewis's "attitudes toward language, including a respect for its illusive and elusive nature and at the same time an overflowing enjoyment of it" (87). Among the chief characteristics of Lewis's poetry is his "sheer love of the sounds of words . . . [often revealed] in his virtuoso deployment in poem after poem of intricate patterns of exact or slant rhyme, both final and internal" (87). Another notable characteristic of his poetry "is semantic change, specifically the alteration of meaning which may disrupt communication between members of a speech community" (92). Huttar then cites poems revealing Lewis's use of semantics as a tool for critiquing contemporary culture. Huttar comments upon concerns the way "Lewis examines language as a fundamental human attribute, one that reveals both our greatness and our limitations" (103). Huttar reviews several poems that celebrate the birth of language, human reason and dominion, and freedom of the will. In addition, he cites letters showing Lewis's admission of the inadequacy of language to communicate effectively anything. Huttar believes Lewis's poems on God best demonstrate the shortcoming of language, and he offers from "Footnote to All Prayers" the following as an example: "To 'attempt the ineffable Name' . . . is to risk worshipping an 'idol' shaped by one's 'own unquiet thought;' the language of prayer references only 'frail images' in the speaker's mind, 'which cannot be the thing Thou art' . . . 'Take not, oh Lord, our literal sense. Lord, in Thy great, / Unbroken speech our limping metaphor translate'" (106). Huttar's work in this essay is thorough and keen; his critical focus upon Lewis's use of language in his poetry is essential reading.

20 *CL*, I, 170; Lewis emphasis.

21 *CL*, I, 190; June 6, 1916.

22 *CL*, I, 232; Lewis emphasis.

23 *Selected Literary Essays*. Ed. Walter Hooper (Cambridge: Cambridge University Press, 1969), 15. Originally published as "A Metrical Suggestion," *Lysistrata* 2 (May 1935): 13-24.

24 *Selected Literary Essays*, 46. Originally published in *Essays and Studies by members of the English Association* 26 (1939): 28-41.

25 *English Literature in the Sixteenth Century* (Oxford: Oxford University Press, 1944), 232-33. The young Lewis experimented with the poulter's measure in the "Prologue" to his *Spirits in Bondage* (hereafter *SB*).

26 *Selected Literary Essays*, 281. Originally published in *A Review of English Literature* I (January 1960): 45-50.

27 For the texts of these poems, see *C.S. Lewis, Poet*, 245-65 and 283-84.

28 See *CP*. The poems are "The Hills of Down," "Against Potpourri," "A Prelude," "Ballade of a Winter's Morning," "Laus Mortis," "Sonnet—To Philip Sydney," "Of Ships," "Couplets," "Circe—A Fragment," and "Exercise." All date from 1915-1917.

29 *SB*, 3 and 22.

30 *CP*, 229.

31 *SB*, 11.

32 20.

33 58.

34 *CP*, 237; *SB*, 33.

35 *CP*, 234-35; *SB*, 53-54.

36 Gleeson White from his *Ballades and Rondeaus* (1893) cited in Raymond MacDonald Alden, ed. *English Verse: Specimens Illustrating its Principles and History* (New York: AMS, 1970), 360.

37 *CP*, 242.

38 *SB*, 65-66.

39 18, 60, 61-62.

40 34-35.

41 41.

42 13.

43 72.

44 63.

45 xli.

46 5.

47 "The Approach to English." In *Light on C.S. Lewis*. Ed. Jocelyn Gibb (New York: Harcourt Brace Jovanovich, 1965), 53 and 62.

Mirrors, Shadows, and the Muses: C.S. Lewis and the Value of Arts and Letters

ROD MILLER

> He must ask himself how it is right, or even psychologically possible, for creatures who are every moment advancing either to heaven or hell, to spend any fraction of the little time allowed them in this world on such comparative trivialities as literature or art, mathematics or biology. If human culture can stand up to that, it can stand up to anything.
>
> *Learning in War-Time*

For those who are, as Lewis was, both Christian and involved in the creation of arts and letters, there are certain questions that require both the asking and an answer. Should Christians be involved in the writing of books, the painting of paintings, the design of buildings? Ought they spend their time reading novels, seeking to understand paintings or buildings? In short, what is the value of the arts for Christians who seek to live devout lives? Is art important, why, and to what degree? Given his stature in the world of literature and in Christian apologetics, one might hope to find some clear answer to these questions from C.S. Lewis. While Lewis does offer direction, commenting specifically in several books and articles on cultural products, it is of a particular sort. As will be demonstrated, it is often in his writings not concerned with arts, that one may find a stronger grounding for the value of cultural products.

To begin is a brief survey of what is meant by the term 'culture', for it is in understanding its altered meaning that one can first grasp the issue, and the subsequent problems. Prior to the 18th Century, the meaning of 'culture' may have been closer to: what a cultural group holds to be true. That is to say, those products, arts, and letters that a group of people created were clearly related to what they thought was true and good about reality. For example, one may assume that Christians in 11th Century France were not thinking about building cultural products; rather, they built Chartres cathedral because its structure and organization was a manifestation of their world view, one held by most of their neighbours in Chartres. During the 18th, and particularly the 19th Century, the notion of culture grew in 'those higher and loftier intellectual things.'

There were lower, more mundane products of a social group, but to be 'Cultured' one needed to understand and intimately perceive the items of a higher, loftier, more spiritual, aesthetic realm. One might think here of Kant or, to take Lewis's own example, Matthew Arnold with his statement about culture being "contact with the best which has been thought and said in the world." But Arnold's was a rear-guard position in any event; Rousseau had earlier laid the groundwork for removing culture from its pedestal. The irony of Romanticism is that while it invigorated the arts by conjuring and demanding a profound emotional response it ultimately trivialized them by associating them with merely one's own subjective responses. That is to say, art was aestheticized, reduced to our own sensation and emotional reactions.

We ended up wondering who was to say what was higher and what was lower? Lewis himself wrestled with this in *An Experiment in Criticism* and, of course, 'High and Low Brows.' The upshot is a reduction of what *culture* means. From 'the best' it has been reduced to something like: all the products that groups of people create and every way in which they live and carry out their lives. One contemporary anthropologist put it, "I use the term culture to refer collectively to a society and its way of life."[1] Raymond Williams stated succinctly, "Culture is ordinary," and proposed that the positing of a higher and lower culture be seen as merely attempts by one group, the rich in this case, to divide themselves from another group.[2] The problem has been amplified, and today any attempt at thinking of cultural products, arts, and letters, in terms of 'higher' and 'lower' can only reflect a sort of unrealistic sense of superiority and is to be received with skepticism or irony.[3] In a very serious way, this is just bad thinking: everything being equal means that *everything is equal.* Nothing, no cultural product, is higher or 'higher' or better than any other. But is that really plausible, or profitable?[4]

Of course, this way of thinking springs from much deeper philosophical sources. One of the other effects of cultural aestheticization, or perhaps its cause, is the denigration of the classical concept of beauty, that is, beauty as the splendor of goodness. Indeed, by Lewis's time there had been a long standing precedent for the reduction of beauty to mere aesthetic pleasure.[5] For example, as early as the 17th century Descartes stated:

> Your question as to how one can ascertain the reason why something is beautiful . . . But neither the beautiful nor the pleasant signifies anything other than the attitude of our judgment to the object in question. And since human judgments are various, it is impossible to find any definite measure for the beautiful or the pleasant . . . [6]

From there one may consider Addison's comments that beauty is merely our response to a thing and Hume's suggestion that, "Beauty is in no quality in things themselves: it exists merely in the mind which contemplates them; and each mind perceives a different beauty . . . ".[7] By the 20th century we have persons such as Barnett Newman stating that, "The impulse of modern art was this desire to destroy beauty."[8] It was from this cultural milieu that sprang different symptoms of a similar problem. For example, neither those who sought biography to explain a work nor the New Critics who focused solely upon the text much considered beauty. This is the aestheticized, beauty-less environment in which Lewis found himself and to which he responded. In regards to ethics and truth Lewis spoke profoundly; in matters of arts and letters he was often, but not always, less successful.

We may begin with the few small articles Lewis published in *Theology* magazine around 1940.[9] Prior to his conversion Lewis admitted that he used to think of culture, 'intellectual and aesthetic activity,' as good; after his conversion he realized there was a problem.[10] How could he reconcile his new belief that the end of man was 'salvation in Christ and the glorifying of God'[11] with the fact that his career was wrapped up in the study and creation of literature? In these articles one finds the attempt, in part, to refute a contemporary notion that being a good Christian has something to do with being culturally sophisticated, of having good taste. Lewis did not want to give too much credit to culture, the intellectual and aesthetic products, lest they become idols. His conclusion is that it is not immoral for believers to be involved with culture, under certain conditions; Lewis's support for culture, in these articles, reads as rather tepid.

In these particular articles, Lewis examines both Scripture and tradition for guidance. For example, he asks what the New Testament has to say about culture. In light of passages like Philippians 3:8 ("More than that, I count all things to be loss in view of the surpassing value of knowing Christ Jesus my Lord, for whom I have suffered the loss of all things, and count them but rubbish in order that I may gain Christ"), he suggests that culture does not come across well. Furthermore, it was, Lewis points out, the unclean (both physically and spiritually) who were drawn to Our Lord and who were made spiritually clean; one's intellectual and aesthetic prowess are not required.

Second, Lewis has a look at what various classical philosophical and theological authorities have had to say about the matter. Aristotle, he suggests, thinks culture acceptable and good; Plato 'will tolerate no culture that does not directly or indirectly conduce to . . . the intellectual vision of the good.'[12] The Church Fathers fall mostly into the group which thinks that culture is not so very important.[13] In an example, Lewis cites Gregory with the idea that we may grasp culture as a sort of weapon with which to convert heathens. Of course, as Lewis points out, this 'weapon' notion is a far cry from the lofty aspirations of culture in his Modern period; it should be laid aside as soon as it has fulfilled its purpose.

Finally, Lewis examines in some detail Cardinal Newman's arguments from his University Education lectures. Newman argued passionately for the importance of culture but only for earthly ends, to make not the Christian but the 'gentleman.' "It does not raise it [the mind] above nature, nor has any tendency to make us pleasing to our Maker."[14] With refreshing bluntness Lewis asks: If it does not make us better in

God's sight, ought we to spend time doing it at all? In this section, Lewis also touches on this interesting suggestion: " . . . it would be possible to hold (perhaps it is pretty generally held) that one of the moral duties of a rational creature was to attain the highest non-moral perfection it could."[15] Lewis suggests this is all still problematic. Indeed, if this was our duty then perfection of the mind would not be, as Newman suggests, "absolutely distinct" from virtue. Furthermore, it is odd that so little is mentioned in the scriptures and history of the Church. So, concludes Lewis, Newman's arguments, while clarifying that culture may give us a non-moral perfection, do not explore the real problem: " . . . that of relating such non-moral values to the duty or interest of creatures who are every minute advancing either or heaven or hell . . . "[16] Having reflected on these sources, Lewis offers the following thoughts, briefly stated here, in regards to the issue:

- Earning one's living by producing cultural products is not in itself an evil.
- Christians working as 'culture-sellers' may provide an antidote to those who 'abuse culture.'[17]

After this, Lewis asks, may we "go a step further and find any intrinsic goodness in culture for its own sake?" His conclusion is:

- Pleasure is a good thing and culture may produce pleasure that is not in conflict with moral law.
- Though the values produced in culture are rarely Christian, they may be, as Lewis puts it, 'sub-Christian.' That is to say, their values, earthly though they may be, might just point towards higher Christian values.

For the believer, Lewis restates that these products produce pleasure. That pleasure may as well take place "in the suburbs of Jerusalem." Lewis continues: "Most men must glorify God by doing to His glory something which is not *per se* an act of glorifying God but becomes so by being offered."[18] In sum, for the Believer, cultural production can bring a mundane pleasure, may bring some few closer to recognizing Christ, and may glorify God if offered to him rightly as sacred labor.

This whole matter appears, on the surface, an odd one for Lewis to have wrestled with. Lewis appears not to answer the issue for which he took Newman to task: the issue of 'non-moral values' and their worth for believers. Or more to the point, if we can offer up our labor as a gift to God, then why not just forget artistic creation altogether for something much simpler if not, indeed, more economical? Using Lewis's points, we may well conclude it equally valuable to operate a winery and produce bottles of wine featuring exciting evangelistic messages on the labels? Surely this could meet his conditions of reaching some with the gospel and producing pleasure. Indeed, the wine would arguably produce a more robust aesthetic response. Or perhaps we may just skip the evangelistic messages and offer our winemaking to God rightly as sacred labor. Lewis's answers here do not provide a satisfactory answer to the question as to why Christian engagement with arts and letters ought to be done at all.

Others have touched upon Lewis's thinking with regard to creativity, often delving into discussions of imagination and often without quite grasping the implicit problems. A portion of Peter Schakel's *Imagination and the Arts in C.S. Lewis* explores Lewis's understanding of the imagination. "Without the imagination, Lewis's life would have been diminished in many ways—dimmer, more constricted, less rich and rewarding."[19] Our imagination is to be engaged for 'enlargement of being' or 'enrichment of life,' and Schakel suggests this is "... because of the potential it holds for the deepening of faith and understanding."[20] What is troubling about this position is the way in which reason is given short shrift. How might we learn whether an imaginative experience has contributed to our faith and understanding? When does one learn just how our being ought to be enlarged or in what regard our life may be enriched? Perhaps the strangest, and most disturbing, element in Lewis's thinking is this romanticized imagination. Even though it was a reaction to the destructive influence of Modern scientism on arts and letters, it does not help us to escape the positivist foundations of that thought. Indeed, it contributes to it.

> To plea for the moral imagination over the trivial imagination of Modernity, or the brutal imagination of the Postmodern will to power, is to accept the positivist dichotomization of science and reason. Left lacking is the idea of Truth (or Being) unfolding by degree in time (or becoming). Lost is the idea of timely progress realized in the pursuit of wisdom. Claims of knowledge are therefore nostalgic or fantasy. As such, pleas for the imagination are vestiges of postmodern Romanticism.[21]

Perhaps Schakel begins to see the problem in Lewis's thinking when he states,

> On the one hand ... Lewis is a critic of the twentieth century who believes in art for art's sake and denigrates the "literary Puritanism." On the other hand, he adheres to the traditions of critics from Horace through at least the eighteenth century who believe art must be useful as well as entertaining.[22]

Indeed, and there are clear reasons for that dichotomy.

In a reply to responses to his first Theology article, there is a clue as to why Lewis takes the positions he does with regard to culture. Attempting to distinguish between the moral and matters of taste (by which he means style), he suggests a problem and admits a dilemma. If a book suggests that lying is a good thing, we may rightly condemn it as genuinely, morally bad, but if a book is filled with 'tawdry writing', this may also be bad, but badness of a different sort.[23] It is this stylistic badness, or lack of taste, that gives Lewis pause. Is this an objective statement about a work of literature or a subjective statement about his own feelings? Lewis writes,

> If I choose the latter, then most criticism becomes purely subjective—which I don't want. If I choose the former then they can ask me, 'What are these qualities in a book which you admit to be in some sense good and bad but which, you keep on warning us, are not 'really' or 'spiritually' good and bad?[24]

The conflict is between wanting to make objective statements about aesthetic issues and yet realizing that one cannot make objective statements about aesthetic issues. Lewis sees the problem clearly. He knew that his moral judgments of a work (i.e., it teaches immorality) must be based on an objective moral law; he wished he could say the same for his critical analysis of a work. In regards to having literary criticism be thought of as subjective he wrote, "I don't want [that]."[25] To put it another way, Lewis was struggling with the nature of aesthetics. He was hardly alone in wanting to place concepts of form, style, usage, and pleasure on some sort of objective basis; he was not alone in his failure to do so. Aesthetics, sensation, and emotional response cannot be pinned down as objective. How could it if it is one's own response?

This whole issue, the attempt to objectify aesthetics, so to speak, really festered in the late 19th Century but was grounded in the earlier considerations of Kant. Much like Kantian ethics, which were to be objectively based upon subjective constructs, Kantian aesthetics posited a sort of aesthetic objectivity. It should not require much reflection to consider how well this idea, with regard to both the arts and morality, has worked in the West. Lewis blurs the distinctions between objective and subjective aesthetics by considering what we may call technique as part of 'taste,' but this gets us no further.[26] Consider this quote from a section where Lewis has suggested culture is justified because it may produce pleasure:

> We should, indeed, be justified in propagating good taste on the ground that cultured pleasure in the arts is more varied, intense, and lasting than vulgar or 'popular' pleasure. But we should not regard it as meritorious. In fact, much as we should differ from Bentham about value in general, we should have to be Benthamites on the issue between pushpin and poetry.[27]

A more intense aesthetic experience would justify the teaching of cultured pleasure as opposed to popular. Is aesthetic experience the only element to poetry? Lewis goes on to suggest that this would not be a 'meritorious' undertaking anyway because, given that it's all about 'taste,' or aesthetics, there's no difference between pushpin, a game of trivia, and poetry. At least Lewis is consistent in his thinking here: if our cultural productions are about pleasure then there really isn't much difference between those things we think of as higher and low culture.[28]

It is at this point that one can begin to make sense of many of Lewis's statements regarding arts and letters. In "Different Tastes in Literature," for example, Lewis stumbles with differentiating between good and bad art. With uncharacteristically sweeping and unsupported assertions, Lewis suggests that "... bad art never succeeds with anyone," and, "... no one *cares* about bad art in the same way as some care about good." What he means by that is, because it is bad, bad art cannot do to a person what he thinks good art ought to: "... it never startles, prostrates, and takes captive." "It is tepid, trivial, marginal, habitual. It does not *trouble* them, nor haunt them."[29] It ought to go without saying that making claims for how others perceive, respond, and care about anything is dubious, to say the least. But more troubling is that it sets up an impossible situation: how can we measure this effect and how do we know if others are having it, or having it sincerely? And if we ourselves do not have it, what does that imply? Ignorance or insensitivity or bad art? It is suggested that Lewis was aware of the problems in thinking of art this way. His comment about 'tawdry' writing above, to mention one example, demonstrates the problem. However, it appears that Lewis did not find his way out of this error by the time of his final comment on arts and letters penned in 1961, *An Experiment in Criticism.*

Within this extraordinarily idiosyncratic work, Lewis offers an argument that becomes a dance around the issue of aesthetics. Since we cannot make objective aesthetic claims, but we do need to make discerning judgments, Lewis proposes we rethink entirely how we consider the value of a work. We ought to take each book on its own terms and, if it is a good book, get the proper sorts of pleasure out of it. Lewis suggests that we value not the text itself but rather how it is read. He urges us to open ourselves up to the text, to be 'receivers' rather than 'users.' Schakel paraphrases Lewis thus:

> To experience a work of art fully, we must lay aside preconceptions, self-absorbed expectations, and personal needs or cravings. We must make room for the work by, and as far as possible, emptying a space for the work to fill: "Get yourself out of the way." Then we must engage with the work by surrendering to it.[30]

In the concluding chapter of *Experiment,* Lewis wrestles with value. He rejects "... the views that literature is to be valued (a) for telling us truths about life, (b) as an aid to culture."[31] Knowing this will lead the reader to question, then, just what values are in literature, he spins off in another direction, explaining that there is no obligation to lay out a formal theory. To judge the value of that would require the Queen of Knowledge. Since we have no agreement there we may fall victim to "fak[ing] the experiences so as to make them support *our* theory" [italics mine].[32] So the answer Lewis proposes here is first, the *Poiema*, the thing made, gives us a sort of pleasure, a very specific pleasure, and suggests, "The experience could not thus affect us—could not give *this* pleasure—unless it were good for us; not good as a means to some end but beyond the *Poiema* ... good for us here and now."[33] The second part of Lewis's proposal is that we read this way because we wish our being to be enlarged.

Correspondingly, Lewis, being so opposed to the 'Vigilant Critics' and their 'using,' claims that anyone using a text for philosophical, theological, or ethical learning is misguided. The art work, the literature, is not a means to an end, it is the end itself. Writes Schakel,

> *An Experiment in Criticism* is Lewis's major defense of the imagination in all the arts. He wrote it as a reply to "Cambridge English," the subjective, evaluative approach to literature promulgated by F. R. Leavis and I. A. Richards at Cambridge University in the first half of the twentieth century. Lewis disagreed strongly with the prescriptive way Leavis and his "Vigilant school of critics" sought to use literature to improve society and with their vigilance against those who promote the wrong literature or ideas. He objected to Leavis partly because Leavis made literature a means rather than an end, and partly because he allowed insufficient scope to the imagination and to appreciation of artistic beauty.[34]

One wonders if many of the authors Lewis cites would have agreed. Did Pope construct prose or poetry so that one could 'enlarge' one's being? Did Dante populate the levels of heaven and hell so later readers could revel in his imagination, the effective way in which he constructed his world, as an end in itself? What of George MacDonald, whom Lewis thought a writer with little literary talent? Lewis considered him the most influential author upon his life and thought.[35]

To sum, in a reaction to the Vigilant critics, Lewis proposes that literature is valuable because we receive a specific pleasure, we desire to be enlarged, and we get these by surrendering ourselves. The obvious question to be asked is: Might there not be an inherent danger in surrendering ourselves? Can not our being be enlarged to nefarious ends? Schakel suggests: Lewis's longing for Joy, fueled by imagination "... which, after his conversion, he came to believe was a desire for unity with the divine (though often intermediate objects are mistaken for the ultimate object)."[36] To say the least, mistaking an intermediate object for the ultimate, a shadow for the real, the mundane for the Divine, is a problem. Lewis, wishing to avoid the pitfalls of the Vigilants, would have us surrender ourselves even when faced with the moral corruption of an author: "One could praise Ovid for keeping his pornography so free from the mawkish and the suffocating, while disapproving pornography as such."[37] Do we really wish to ponder the quality of pornographic writing? It is inconceivable that Lewis would have us corrupt ourselves morally, and yet he vehemently opposes arts and letters that are means to virtue as opposed to ends in themselves. The catch in his thinking can be found at the very end of *Experiment*: When reading great literature, "Here, as in worship, in love, in moral action, and in knowing, I transcend myself; and am never more myself than when I do."[38] But in right worship, love, and moral action there is a right object. It is in the seeking of that right object that we can worship, love, and act rightly. When we discuss what it is we ought to seek, however, we are no longer discussing *Poiema*. Indeed, we may measure quality in arts and letters a more substantial way.

Lewis wrestled with the value of arts and letters, and how to judge them, for at least two excellent reasons. The first, commented upon in many places by Lewis, is the pretension that often results when culture is elevated above its proper place. This situation typically arises, however, because of the second reason: the aestheticization of culture. When culture, and its concomitant products, are aestheticized, reduced to mere subjective emotional reactions and responses, several things occur. The first is that criteria for evaluating, for judging, any cultural product are also aestheticized.[39] If the aesthetic is the goal, the only measure of value, of quality, is aesthetic stimulation. But how ought this to be measured? For example, we find, in *The Personal Heresy*, Lewis making the following strange claim:

> It follows that there is an ambiguity in the expression, 'a great poet.' The skill of concrete utterance, as we have seen, can be used for almost any purpose. Fools use it to utter folly, wise men to utter wisdom, humorous men to make jokes, and vermin to utter poison. It can be used (like the telephone) by great men and little—by any one who can acquire the skill.
>
> By a 'great poet' we therefore mean one of two things. We may mean a great man—a man excelling others in knowledge, wisdom, and virtue—who is also a poet and who uses his poetical skill for the utterance of great things. On the other hand we may mean merely a man who is greatly a poet, who possesses this skill in a high or 'great' degree—as we speak of a great cricketer, a great walker, or even a great bore.[40]

And this is the problem: can one be a great poet, or artist, without goodness? Certainly, we may speak of Mao as a great man and mean what Lewis suggests in the one instance: great in the sense of fame, significance, horror. When we attempt this in regards to an artist we run into a problem. To say an artist is great and mean by it something like, "he made very large art" or "he was technically skilled" is not how anyone speaks. Lewis himself stumbles in the above passage; what exactly is "a man who is greatly a poet"? More to the point, who would wish to discuss this man's poetry? One may mean to pursue another angle and suggest that greatness means, "his work was influential" and thereby have some semblance of coherent meaning. The problem is neither version offers any understanding of quality in regards to art. The point here is that when arts and letters are aestheticized the split of form and content is more easily embraced. This leads to a tragic reduction in meaningful discussion of art and ultimately, life.

Now it is clear as to why, when Lewis tries to make general statements about arts and letters, they do not stand up.[41] In 'High and Low Brows' and 'Learning in War-Time' we are told we ought not to think of arts and letters as something to make us cultured. But what can cultured mean in an aestheticized milieu other than a collection of certain (meaningful or meaningless) knowledge? 'On Church Music' and 'High and

Low Brows' suggest distinctions between what we think of as high and low are a bit muddy because what we consider high today was once popular entertainment.[42] We have no discernment in this? Might not popular and high arts be, at one time or another, decadent? *An Experiment in Criticism* and 'Lilies that Fester' posit that we should seek to 'enlarge' our being. But to what? What can 'enlarge' mean in an aestheticized culture other than personal response? 'Different Tastes in Literature' teaches that we ought to consider the difference between good and bad art in regards to how it affects us? Who can judge the intensity of affects? And so, at least in the sources covered thus far, Lewis falls into the aesthetic trap. The tragic dominance in the West of culture as aesthetic reduces its products, arts, and letters to meaningless statements, taken as worthy if they stimulate, and prone to violent interpretations and assertions of value.[43]

What, then, is the alternative? How might one avoid the problems related to the aestheticization of culture, of arts and letters, and the resultant meaninglessness and violence? It is to consider beauty in the very old sense as being deeply informed, indeed a manifestation of, the Ideal, Truth. That is to say, far from being merely a reflection of our lowly physical, sensual responses, Beauty is a glimpse of the eternal as made manifest; it is, in short, the splendour of wisdom. Art that teaches, demonstrates, or manifests eternal wisdom is the only art deserving of the term and the only creative endeavor that has lasting value for humans. For example, commenting upon classical mythology, Pontynen writes,

> The Ideal is the reason for how things ought to happen. Classical mythology personalizes the Ideal, that is, the notion of why. Those myths attempt to offer insight concerning reality and life. How do they differ and to what degree are they reliable? Certainly they differ in terms of aesthetics vs. beauty. Classical mythology aims at understanding reality and life, but myth can be studied aesthetically, as grounded in obscure superstition, mere tradition, or unverifiable revelation. However, from the point of view of beauty, a myth is valuable only when it embodies a degree of truth, and myths are recognizable as being to some degree truthful only via critical exegesis.[44]

It is in 'Christianity and Literature', written in 1939, that we find Lewis answering in much the same way. Here he displays the clearest, simplest, and best understanding for the value of arts and letters:

> If I have read the New Testament aright, it leaves no room for 'creativeness' even in a modified or metaphorical sense. Our whole destiny seems to lie in the opposite direction, in being as little as possible ourselves, in acquiring a fragrance that is not our own but borrowed, in becoming clean mirrors filled with the image of a face that is not ours... An author should never conceive himself as bringing into existence beauty or wisdom which did not exist before, but simply and solely as trying to embody in terms of his own art some reflection of

> eternal Beauty and Wisdom . . . And always, of every idea and of every method the Christian will ask not 'Is it mine?' but 'Is it good?'[45]

Not only does the idea of the artist as a mirror get to the crux of the matter but it also suggests what might be criteria for criticizing art: the shadow. If the goal in our life and artmaking is the same, and how could it not be, then corruption is when we do not reflect that face that is not ours, when we do not reflect the Truth, but when either the work itself, or we ourselves, act as a shade to that Light, to that face, and merely casts a shadow. We may now well ask, in regards to what we have seen of Lewis later ideas, how valuable is the imagination, to 'enlarge' ourselves, to see with other's eyes, or to create arts and letters that do so for others? A good answer may be: as valuable as the extent to which the work reflects the Light.

In *The Four Loves*, one finds a wonderful illustration, and understanding, that can be applied to arts and letters. Lewis comments on Eros, how when worshipped it can become a demon. Eros must obey God, he must be ruled, or he brings destruction. Surely, we may consider the Muses similarly? Driving our imagination, singing with music that delights our ears, they carry such power we may be deceived into thinking they are able to stand on their own, but they cannot. They cannot be made into good gods, or gods at all, for they become then wraiths, shadows. But the temptation is great. We may apply Lewis's admonition to the Muses: "It is easy to acknowledge, but almost impossible to realize for long, that we are mirrors whose brightness, if we are bright, is wholly derived from the sun that shines upon us. Surely we must have a little—however little—native luminosity?"[46] They can only shine, like we ourselves, when they are highly polished and reflect the Divine.

To conclude, it is worth examining why this whole issue is an issue at all. Arts and letters may very well make a pleasing contribution to our lives but, really, do they matter? Aestheticization of culture leads to exactly the sorts of cultural problems Lewis was fighting against on other fronts. The dividing of form and content, or Logos and Poesis, or fact and value, is symptomatic of the division of science and reason in the West. In art, the result is art for art's sake, in jurisprudence, law for law's sake, and in science, the pursuit of scientific knowledge (presumably) disconnected from value. This leads, as we have seen, to aestheticization in arts, a position to which we have sadly grown accustomed, but one that does not cause us much concern; when applied to legal theory, however, it is terrifying. Lewis recognized the problems in the subjectification of culture in many places. He profoundly addressed the issue in *The Abolition of Man*. But he seemed unable to make the connection between ethical and legal subjectivity and the aestheticization of the arts.

Lewis could have turned to a few important historical examples. John of Damascus (676–749) considered the issue of visual art works vital but in terms of veneration, not worship.

> I do not worship matter. I worship the God of matter, who became matter for my sake, and deigned to inhabit matter, who worked out my salvation through matter. I will not cease from honouring that matter which works my salvation. I venerate it, though not as God. How could God be born out of lifeless things?[47]

John was writing about ikons during the Iconoclastic Controversy in the 8th Century, a moment when the value of visual arts were of pressing importance and much ink (and blood) was spilt over them. Yet his understanding of the connection between the object and its value is useful to all arts and letters. Lewis may have considered another example, the medieval European King, Charlemagne. Charlemagne, and his leading scholar, Alcuin, attempted to transform their culture. Charlemagne understood the need for not merely education but for the arts; he attempted to reform both during his reign. Several centuries later the French Abbot Suger wrote on the new Gothic style: "The dull mind rises to truth through that which is material and, in seeing this light, is resurrected from its former submersion."

Foundationally, of course, there is Augustine: "Physical beauty is not without its value, since it is the work of God; but it is only a reflection of the highest beauty; it is a transitory and relative beauty, whereas the highest beauty is eternal and absolute."[48] Augustine grasps that aesthetics are not enough; to see Beauty we must understand truth. Reads Matthew 13:13, "This is why I speak to them in parables: 'Though seeing, they do not see; though hearing, they do not hear or understand."

> In them is fulfilled the prophecy of Isaiah: "You will be ever hearing but never understanding; you will be ever seeing but never perceiving. For this people's heart had become calloused; they hardly hear with their ears, and they have closed their eyes. Otherwise they might see with their eyes, hear with their ears, understand with their hearts and turn, and I would heal them."[49]

As Christian consumers of cultural products we have the freedom to choose those lower works for mere aesthetic pleasure or those of a higher nature that inspire us rightly, increase our devotion, knowledge, wisdom, and love. Christian duty, however, compels us to mirror in the world as much Truth, Goodness, and Beauty as we know and to do so with as much passion, vigour, and quality as is possible. Our conscience and our reason ought to urge us continuously further to those distant and challenging heights where the splendour of Beauty is naught other than Truth made manifest. Lewis often did so. We ought to expect no less of ourselves.

ENDNOTES

1 This paper was previously published in the C.S. Lewis Chronicle, vol. 6, no. 2, (now the Journal of Inklings Studies), and is reproduced with permission. John H. Bodley, *Cultural Anthropology: Tribes, States, and the Global System* (New York: Mayfield Publishing, 1994) 10.

2 Raymond Williams from his 1958 essay, "Culture is Ordinary." *Resources of Hope* (London: Verso, 1989).

3 The arts, and the discipline of art history, are currently in something of a dilemma in this regard. Are the fine arts higher, better, or just stuff? Interestingly, few art historians would want to equate the work of the much ridiculed Thomas Kinkade with that of, say, Picasso.

4 Jacques Barzun addresses this issue and suggested that a culture that thinks art needs to be taken casually while at the same time held up as something valuable is, to say the least, problematic. See Jacques Barzun, *The Use and Abuse of Art* (Princeton: Princeton University Press, 1974).

5 Another way of stating the problem is clearly put by Aeschliman: "In the absence of that great philosophic tradition with its insistence upon an objective, rationally explicable Good, there is left a great gaping hole in any imaginable intellectual conception of the world, and objective grounds for any and all conduct, including intellectual endeavour, are completely ruled out." It is suggested that when the objective and the Good are removed, what fills its place are the subjective and the aesthetic. Michael D. Aeschliman. *The Restitution of Man: C.S. Lewis and the Case Against Scientism*. (Grand Rapids: Eerdmans, 1983) 74.

6 Descartes quoted in Arthur Pontynen. *For the Love of Beauty: Art, History, and the Moral Foundations of Aesthetic Judgment* (New Brunswick: Transaction, 2006) 230. Pontynen is useful for tracking the meaning and history of the decline of beauty in the west.

7 Hume as quoted in, Ekbert Faas *The Genealogy of Aesthetics*. (Cambridge University Press, 2002) 131.

8 Charles Harrison and Paul Wood. *Art in Theory 1900-1990*. (Oxford: Blackwell, 1998) 573.

9 The most ready source for these articles is Lesley Walmsley, ed. *C.S. Lewis Essay Collection and Other Short Pieces* (London: Harper Collins, 2000). The writings are "Christianity and Culture," "A letter to the Editor of Theology," and "Peace Proposals for Brother Every and Mr. Bethell." Due to the different sources in which these articles are found, and the fact that they are short, page numbers have been omitted from the citations.

10 He defines it at the start of "Christianity and Culture." It is worth pointing out here that while Lewis challenges the value of culture after his conversion he does not challenge how he defines it. One of the problems, examined below, is the problem of reducing culture to the aesthetic.

11 "Christianity and Culture."

12 Ibid.

13 Ibid. For example, Lewis quotes St. Jerome's idea that the pig slop the prodigal son had to eat was, "*cibus daemonum . . . carmina poetarum, saecularis sapientia, rhetoricorum pompa verborum*." ("Food of demons, songs/poems of poets, worldly wisdom, verbiage of rhetoricians.") As seen below, however, there are other church fathers that Lewis may have considered.

14 Ibid.

15 Ibid.

16 "Christianity and Culture." Can one be a gentleman without goodness? Perhaps more to the point, what is a gentleman who is not good? The separation of perfection from the Ideal, or the aesthetic from the Beautiful, is a problem and one that Lewis must surely have recognized. He does not discuss it in regards to arts and letters but in other writings, examined below, he approaches it. This separation is a key concept in understanding much about the Modern and Postmodern worldviews.

17 Ibid.

18 Ibid.

19 Peter J. Schakel. *Imagination and the Arts* (Columbia: University of Missouri Press, 2002), p.188.

20 Schakel, *Imagination*, p. 2.

21 Arthur Pontynen and Rod Miller. *Western Civilization at the American Crossroads* (Wilmington: ISI Books, 2010) p. 480. Lewis's understanding and use of reason and imagination went through stages. Early on, particularly in the 1930's, he engaged his friend, Owen Barfield, in The Great War, pitting his reason against Barfield's imagination. In *Reason and Imagination in C.S. Lewis:A Study ofTill We Have Faces* (Grand Rapids: Eerdmans, 1984), Schakel carefully traces the history in Lewis's thinking and suggests a synthesis in his later works. According to Schakel, moving Lewis away from his strict use of reason may have been his well known debate with G.E.M. Anscobe (which some scholars suggest he lost), his relationship with Joy Davidman, and his subsequent subjective reflections upon his own life in *Surprised by Joy.* Schakel sees the shift at the end of Lewis's life as a positive reconciliation between reason and imagination. There are other ways of considering Lewis's writing in regards to how he uses reason and imagination. I am persuaded that Lewis's struggle is related to his understanding of the value of arts and letters, an understanding, I argue below, that is mistaken.

22 Schakel, *Imagination.* p. 171. Schakel is quoting from correspondence between himself and Doris T. Myers.

23 "Peace Proposals for Brother Every and Mr. Bethell."

24 Ibid.

25 Ibid.

26 Which technique is better than others? Not that technique has no bearing, but if criticism is reduced to discussing merely technique not much can be said. Did Jackson Pollock have good technique? What about Alan Ginsberg? Mark Rothko? There is another realm to be discussed in terms of artistic production and value: content.

27 "Christianity and Culture." Betham's quote from which Lewis takes his comment, "The utility of all these arts and sciences,—I speak both of those of amusement and curiosity,—the value which they possess, is exactly in proportion to the pleasure they yield. Every other species of preeminence which may be attempted to be established among them is altogether fanciful. Prejudice apart, the game of push-pin is of equal value with the arts and sciences of music and poetry. If the game of push-pin furnish more pleasure, it is more valuable than either."

28 This section in Lewis's writing is difficult to follow as one may read Lewis arguing hypothetically from the position of his opponents and the subsequent problems. If this is in fact the case, we may still take Lewis to task for giving too much ink in discussing pleasure and too little to wisdom.

29 All quotes are Lewis's from "Different Tastes in Literature," published in *C.S. Lewis Essay Collection and Other Short Pieces.*

30 Schakel, *Imagination*, p. 14. Lewis's quote is from *An Experiment in Criticism.*

31 C.S. Lewis. *An Experiment in Criticism* (Cambridge: Cambridge University Press, 1961) p. 130.

32 *An Experiment in Criticism,* p. 131. Lewis fears those who would use texts in this way, to prove their own power plays; the text is reduced to a mere bludgeon and, since there cannot be another use, is wielded with violence. The issues of violence and meaninglessness are commonplace in postmodern theory; an explanation of and a response to both are below.

33 *An Experiment in Criticism,* p. 134.

34 Schakel, *Imagination*, p. 11.

35 C.S. Lewis, editor. *George MacDonald: An Anthology of 365 Readings* (New York: Harper Collins, 2001). "If I were to deal with him as a writer, a man of letters, I should be faced with a difficult critical problem. If we define Literature as an art whose medium is words, then certainly MacDonald has no place in its first rank—perhaps not even in its second." Quote from page XXVIII.

36 Schakel, *Imagination*, p. 8.

37 *An Experiment in Criticism* p. 126.

38 Ibid. p. 141.

39 Lewis responded to this issue as early as 1939. Texts can only be reduced to the personal if that is all that exists. "Either there is significance in the whole process of things as well as in human activity, or there is no significance in human activity itself." "You cannot have it both ways. If the world is meaningless, then so are we; if we mean something, we do not mean alone." Quoted from, *The Personal Heresy* (London: Oxford University Press, 1939) pp. 29–30.

40 *The Personal Heresy,* p. 114.

41 On the other hand, at least one author has suggested that Lewis did not try to make generalizations, following another interpretive tradition. "Lewis undoubtedly agreed with Croce (and Vico) that a work of art can be understood and judged only within its historical context. He also agreed that no valid assertions can be made about 'art' or 'poetry,' only about paintings or poems." Lionel Adey. *C.S. Lewis' 'Great War' with Owen Barfield* (Victoria, British Columbia: University of Victoria, 1978) p. 34.

42 This is an uncharacteristically silly statement from Lewis; it requires that we assume all popular entertainment from different cultures to be of some kind of equal level of quality. As stated in the text, clearly art considered fine or popular can be of wildly different levels of quality.

43 "Neither view [postmodern nihilism nor minimalist metaphysics] can give desire an object worthy of our most profound sense of longing. Instead, we are faced with desires that result from accidents of evolutionary forces, guided, if by anything, by self-interest expressed quite often in violence." Michael P. Muth. 'Beastly Metaphysics: The Beasts of Narnia and Lewis's Reclamation of Medieval Sacramental Metaphysics.' *C.S. Lewis as Philosopher: Truth, Goodness and Beauty.* David Baggett, Gary R. Habermas, Jerry L. Walls, eds. (Downers Grove, Illinois: Intervarsity Press, 2008) 244.

44 Arthur Pontynen. *For the Love of Beauty: Art, History, and the Moral Foundations of Aesthetic Judgment* (New Brunswick: Transaction, 2006) p. 45.

45 "Christianity and Literature." There are other timely and valuable contributions in this essay surrounding arts, originality, and genius.

46 C.S. Lewis. *The Four Loves* (London: Harcourt Brace Jovanovich, 1960) p. 180.

47 Mary H. Allies, trans. *St. John Damascene On Holy Images* (London: Thomas Baker, 1898) pp. 10-17

48 Wladyslaw Tatarkiewicz, *History of Aesthetics: Medieval Aesthetics* (Bristol: Thoemmes Press, 1999) p. 54. The quote is from Tatarkiewicz in regards to Augustine's concepts of Beauty.

49 Pontynen, p. 154

C.S. Lewis, Objectivity, and Beauty

JERRY ROOT

C.S. Lewis's view of beauty and the arts cannot be separated from his view of truth and objectivity. He actually believed that one could possibly make objective statements about what was and what was not beautiful. Of course one could also make misjudgments as well. Since this is so, it is essential, in any attempt to understand Lewis in these matters, to gain some background about Lewis's view of objectivity generally, before applying it to beauty and art specifically.

LEWIS WAS AN OBJECTIVIST

Lewis was an objectivist, that is, he believed that there are objects that exist independent of what one thought of them. These objects, whether they be material objects empirically perceived, or objects of thought held by definition and perceived intellectually, could be accurately thought about. This possibility is because independent knowers also exist, who are capable of thought. Furthermore, these knowers can think accurately or inaccurately about those objects and make reasonable statements about beauty and art that are not always arbitrary. Lewis does not deny the existence of the subjective that is, the existence of knowers and feelers; but, he does deny that anything can be properly known or felt without respect for these objects. Subjectivism, or the subjectivistic, in this regard, is understood to mean the projection of individual predilection onto an object without particular obligation to that object or sensing any responsibility to the thing itself. Lewis believed, rather, that the subject, or the knower, must always surrender to the dictates of that which can be known. For Lewis, truth was not reality *per se*; truth was what people thought about reality when they thought accurately about it.[1] For Lewis truth was found when there was coherence between reality and thought and that such a coherence was achievable, though this achievement would never be absolute, always approximate. One could have a sure word about some things but not necessarily a last word about anything. The sure word prevented Lewis from being a relativist; the inability to find a last word preserved Lewis from arrogance. Any truth known could be plumbed deeper still as well as be applied to questions yet unasked. One may or may not agree with Lewis in these matters; nevertheless, it is necessary to understand Lewis's ideas about objectivity if one would grasp his ideas about beauty and art.

Lewis's views about objectivity appear in applied form throughout his published work. His literary critical studies demand that he make judgments about literary art and his objective approach is certainly applied in these texts. His Christian apologetics lead him to make judgments about truth in religion and his objectivist approach is evident there as well. In fact, in both Lewis's pre-Christian writing as well as his post-conversion writing this objectivism is in evidence; but it is most explicitly set forth and developed in his book, *The Abolition of Man.*[2] The occasion for Lewis writing this book came when he received, for review, a copy of a grammar text for sixth form students (that would be the equivalent of the American 11th and 12th grade). Lewis was shocked to find subjectivist assumptions, held by the authors, laced throughout the book. Long before post modernists were concerned about deconstructing texts to find embedded assumptions and values, Lewis sets out to deconstruct this text. He calls it *The Green Book*, but it was actually titled, *The Control of Language* by Alec King and Martin Ketley.[3] And, for his critique of the book, Lewis gives the authors fictitious names, Gaius and Titius. Lewis's response to *The Green Book* is chronicled in *The Abolition of Man* and it is there he sets forth, in detail, his objectivist values and underscores his thoughts about objectivity; and, it must be remembered, it is these that guide him in making judgments in matters of beauty and art.

THE ARGUMENT OF *THE ABOLITION OF MAN*

Gaius and Titius begin their books with a story of the poet, Samuel Taylor Coleridge, on vacation with William Wordsworth and his sister Dorothy.[4] They were touring along the river Clyde and came upon the Cora Linn Waterfall. Two other tourists were there as well and one of them called the waterfall "pretty" while the other called it "sublime." Coleridge mentally endorsed the one who called it sublime, believing that this was the more accurate description of the two. At this point the writers of *The Green Book* take issue with Coleridge's endorsement. They claim he had no right to make such a judgment as the tourists were actually saying nothing about the waterfall but, merely, something about their own feelings. Lewis, at this point, takes Gaius and Titius to task and anyone making a clear thinking judgments would see why. First, Coleridge believed that the waterfall really existed and was independent of any judgments that might be made about it. Second that its existence, as well as all of its qualities, were important if any statement about it, that could be construed as making sense, might be made. Lewis once wrote, "An accusation always implies a standard."[5] And, in this case, the actual waterfall provided an independent standard by which the judgments of the tourists and Coleridge, as well as Gaius and Titius, could be measured. Without the independent object, in this case the waterfall, any judgments about it would be meaningless and self-referential; furthermore, if the judgment was forced, the judge becomes a tyrant. Lewis believed such standards could apply to beauty and art as well, but we are getting ahead of ourselves.

When Gaius and Titius say the tourists were merely making statements about their feelings, there is embedded in these writers' assumptions that one's sentiments operate independent of any significant contextualization, they are not in response to any objective state and therefore one description about feelings is as good as any other. Lewis takes issue with this as well, arguing that emotional states can be in harmony with reality. Therefore it can be expected that one would be solemn at a funeral out of respect for the honor of the one who died and out of deference to the grieving friends and family. A person giddy and full of laughter at such an occasion would be rightly considered out of place. Similarly, a person morose at a birthday party would act in a manner incongruous with the festive nature of that gathering. It may be that the morose member of the party heard bad news on the way to the party and certainly the sadness would be congruous with the bad news. Nevertheless, an appropriate response to the negative circumstance, with respect for those at the party, might be to call and ask to be excused from the party because of an unexpected situation. This would allow the one who was sad to have space to grieve, without spoiling the fun for those who had legitimate occasion to be happy. Lewis makes it clear that emotions, like reason, operate in response to objective circumstances and that Gaius and Titius were wrong about this fact; and they were wrong for judging Coleridge in this matter of the waterfall.

A deeper concern for Lewis is that Gaius and Titius, while denying Coleridge any right to make a judgment between the two statements made by the tourists, still make a judgment themselves as they dismiss Coleridge for making a judgment. In essence, they said he had no right to distinguish which of the tourists had spoken most accurately. Since Gaius and Titius do this, then by what standard do they make their judgments about Coleridge? When they deny judgment to Coleridge, who clearly used the waterfall itself as his point of reference, by what objective standard do they make their judgment against Coleridge? If they have no objective standard, yet they still make a judgment, then they appear to be hypocritical. Having rejected objective reality they are reduced to personal preferences which are little more than self-referential. The question is, why should their preferences be preferred over anyone else's? All sense is sacrificed to anarchy, and, again, if one party amasses power the anarchy could possibly become a tyranny. Furthermore, if one has respect for the independence of an object, then fair-minded judgments can be made about those objects and their validity determined based on how closely the judgment might be measured by the thing itself. Certainly this consideration has merit in making judgments about beauty and art.

Furthermore, in *The Abolition of Man*, Lewis, aware of the dangers of subjectivism, keeps to the course of objectivity. He calls this objective approach to judgments (in matters of reason, morality, beauty, and the sentiments) the *Tao* and defines it as "the doctrine of objective value, the belief that certain attitudes are really true, and others really false, to the kind of thing the universe is and the kind of things we are".[6] Lewis's embedded ontology—that reality exists and it is independent of our thoughts about it—implies that truth is not reality; but rather, truth is what I think about reality when I think accurately about it. Furthermore, the real world of objects, perceived empirically, or the real world of ideas, grasped and perceived by the reason through definition and inferences drawn coherently from those definitions, is Lewis's means of validating a truth claim. Of course, Lewis is far more sophisticated than this and has a rather robust epistemology, nevertheless, for the purposes of this discussion about beauty and art it is enough to understand Lewis's objectivist approach in these matters.[7] Coleridge, as well, clearly thought as Lewis did, and joins many others like them as well. For Lewis this possibility of confirming a thought or a judgment by means of the *Tao* is no small matter. Lewis writes that, "Only the Tao provides a common human law of action which can over-arch rulers and ruled alike. A dogmatic belief in objective value is necessary to the very idea of a rule which is not tyranny or an obedience which is not slavery."[8] Throughout the book, Lewis drives home the point that unless you believe that nature exists independent of your best thoughts about it, you will make a muddle of any kind of judgment about the real world. As an aside, it must be noted that Lewis's ideas here must not be confused for Enlightenment, or Modern, notions about objectivity and the capacity of Reason to come to an absolutized grasp of reality by which all debate would cease. Lewis's notions of reality are far too complex than that and his notions of man's capacity to know is far less sanguine. Lewis did not have some inflated view that man could settle all disputes and that some cultures could arise above the rest and assert their culture's sense of beauty above all others. Nevertheless, he did believe that whatever art or sense of beauty was enjoyed by any culture, objective standards would apply and be particularized to the applications of creativity and artistic endeavor in that unique context. Lewis was no colonialist in regards to art and beauty.

LEWIS'S OBJECTIVE STANDARDS CAN BE APPLIED TO BEAUTY

Lewis believed that one could apply the standard of the Tao—that is, the standard of objectivity—to beauty and art and he stated this explicitly, noting: "And there is really no reason why we should not do the same about standards of beauty [that is, apply objective standards]. There is no reason why our reaction to a beautiful landscape should not be the response, however humanly blurred and partial, to something that is really there."[9] In this regard, Lewis makes a distinction between what he calls *Admirable Beauty* and *Enjoyable Beauty*. Admirable Beauty is objective, it is that aspect of beauty intrinsic to things about which it can be accurately said they are beautiful. This admirable quality is present whether or not we happen to notice it. And Enjoyable Beauty is that subjective capacity in one whereby he or she can perceive Admirable Beauty and appreciate its loveliness. The subjective appreciation must be guided by the object itself as manifest in the glories of nature, or the beauties of a work of art. Lewis writes,

> The sense by which the picture "deserves" or "demands" admiration is rather this: that admiration is the correct, adequate or appropriate, response to it, that if paid, admiration will not be "thrown away," and that if we do not admire we shall be stupid, insensible, and great losers, we shall have missed something. In that way many objects both in Nature and in Art may be said to deserve, or merit, or demand, admiration.[10]

Admirable Beauty, therefore, according to Lewis is synonymous with objective beauty because it is intrinsic to the thing itself. This being the case, to admire the thing as it truly is, as best one is able, is a just act for it renders to the thing its due. To fail to admire that to which admiration is due may be an act of injustice, or simply the consequence of ignorance, or insensitivity.

Many years ago I declared, with great insensitivity, that I thought the artist Picasso was an idiot! My wife, hearing the comment, gave me a perturbed glance and then asked what I knew of Picasso or his art. Embarrassed, I had to admit that I knew next to nothing about his work. She responded, "Then the first thing we must do is renegotiate who the idiot might be here and then seek to determine whether or not that idiot is educable." She had recently finished a course on the art of Picasso and the Chicago Art Institute was having a special show of Picasso's art. So, we went to the museum and looked at many Picasso pieces, and I was amazed. Years later we had the good fortune to visit the Picasso Museum in Barcelona, Spain and I was even more delighted by this great artist. Why was I able to make a change from being dismissive of Picasso to appreciating his work? First, I had to admit I was wrong. Second, I needed someone who understood his art and was patient enough to take the time to help me break free of my prejudices. Third, I needed to lay aside those prejudices (could I use the word "repent" of those prejudices?), and try and see the art itself without projection. Or as Lewis says, I needed to receive the work of art and not try to do anything with it; simply receive it.[11] Judgments ought to be reserved until one truly understands the thing being judged. Consequently, expert opinion in matters of beauty—that is someone who has spent time trying to understand a thing of beauty and knows why it is beautiful—can be of help to another who has not yet developed the capacity to notice the excellences of a work of art. This is the reason why my wife, in the example of Picasso, could help me to appreciate Picasso in ways I could not. It is difficult to take seriously anyone who is dismissive of a thing of beauty before they have even made the first attempts to see and understand. Lewis knew this. The authors of *The Green Book* held no credit for Lewis as they did not even understand the philosophical and epistemological issues at play when it came to Coleridge and the tourists at the waterfall.

Similarly, philosopher Mortimer Adler recognized the place of experts and the value of their opinions in helping others to see and perceive the objective qualities in a thing of beauty. He wrote,

> Men differ in the degree to which they possess good perception—and sound critical judgment—even as objects differ in the degree to which they possess the elements of beauty. Once again in controversy concerning the objectivity or subjectivity of beauty, there seems to be a middle ground between the two extreme positions, which insists upon a beauty intrinsic to the object but does not deny the relevance of differences in individual sensibility.[12]

Without some objective features present in a sunset, or a rose, or the curl of a wave before it breaks on the shore, without an artist's capacity to capture with his or her materials anything that merits the pronouncement that it is a beautiful painting, or sculpture, or symphony, all discussion about beauty turns to nonsense. Judgments about beauty have a built in assumption that there is something objective that is on display and that it can be perceived by most who give careful attention to the thing itself.

In further developing the application of Lewis's ideas about beauty and artistic judgment more ought to be considered. Of course, if there are objective standards of beauty it is not only fair to ask what they are, it is essential to ask this if discussions about beauty are to have merit beyond personal preferences. In this regard, Thomas Aquinas is helpful. He wrote in the *Summa Theologica* that, "Beauty includes three conditions: integrity or perfection, since those things which are impaired are by the very fact ugly; due proportion or harmony; and lastly, brightness, or clarity, whence things are called beautiful which have an elegant color."[13] Aquinas mentions integrity, proportion and clarity as three objective characteristics in a thing whereby one could call it beautiful. Of course, one must not suppose that this list is exhaustive. If there could be three qualities or characteristics by which one might call a thing beautiful, there might equally be more than a hundred and three. Furthermore, most of us do, in fact, make judgments about beauty with respect for these three facets.

Integrity seeks to notice that a work of art properly captures something of the essence of the thing itself; that is, it has integrity. When we go to buy a Christmas tree we have an idea of *treeness.* This idea can simply be informed by the collective experience of Christmas trees gathered over a lifetime and the ideal tree, that is the beautiful one, is the composite of all those past Christmas trees one has seen; that is, the ideal tree is a generalization. If this is the case then we may be driven by an Aristotelian understanding of the idea of a beautiful tree. Or, perhaps we have gained our understanding of *treeness* from the Platonic ideal as it has come down from some archetype and is now embedded in our imaginations and our conscious. We see a tree and we are reminded of this ideal. We go to the Christmas tree lot and select a tree with something in mind and we look for the tree that most captures this ideal. However these things come to us is less important than the fact that they do. And to perceive a thing of beauty is, in part, to notice its integrity within the class of objects from which it is drawn. Furthermore, the artist, given the level of perception and skill with his or her materials is able to make a true, generalized, statement about the object through the work of art. One must be careful here, however. Most often objective statements about beauty are not as simple as saying two plus two equals four; and this is certainly so relevant to the matter of integrity. There is a painting by Marcel Duchamp called *Nude Descending a Staircase*. The painting looks nothing like a nude; but what Duchamp clearly captured in the portrait was *descent*. And to the degree in which Duchamp captured this descent his painting exhibited integrity, and this might have been missed by someone merely looking for a portrait of a nude. There is beauty in Duchamp's work and it is a delight to behold and even inspires awe. Duchamp, the artist, who saw the beauty allows the observer of his painting to see what he saw; and had he not painted it others might have missed it. Similarly, in Lewis's fiction he is able to portray, by means of literary art, with integrity, the beauty of a child's love for God, as when Lucy in Narnia longs to bury her face in Aslan's mane; or, with integrity, the beauty of an adult's love for God by means of Reepicheep's intense longing to go to Aslan's country.

Aquinas points to proportion as another characteristic of beauty. Proportion can be observed in the interplay between the sections of a painting and the balance and symmetry achieved by the variety of the components in a work of visual art. The same could be said as well about a piece of musical composition. So too, it is one of the things a poet pays attention to in his composition as he works with a variety of rhyme schemes and meter. In fact, there are standards of proportion common to certain varieties of poetry whereby we can distinguish a sonnet, a Haiku, a ballad, and lyric or narrative poetry from one another. And, here again, the artist may see subtleties perhaps missed by the untrained eye or ear but the skilled artist calls attention to these beauties and awakens others that they also might see what the artist sees. We become riveted to the thing itself and in noticing we are elevated by the experience. Furthermore, Aquinas speaks of clarity, use of color, or texture as objective features that also contribute to the substance a beautiful object and make possible accurate judgments about it.

It is because of these objective features in the thing itself that Lewis believed the tourists at the waterfall could make statements about the waterfall and Coleridge was able to legitimately endorse the one he felt most robust and full in its description. Lewis's belief about objectivity generally has application to statements of beauty specifically. To believe with Lewis that this is so does not make one an art critic of credit. It is a start in the right direction but training and practice as well as care and study are necessary lest one overstate a position carelessly. I cannot, with credit, say that Prague is the most beautiful city in the world because I've not been to every city and therefore my statement falls short of any kind of substance. I can say Prague is the most beautiful city I've ever seen. This may be fair minded but someone clearly has the right to ask me two questions to see if my statement has credit. First, I should be asked, "What cities have you seen"? If I have only seen slums and tenements, my judgment is of no significance. But if I have seen Paris, Florence, Quebec City, San Francisco, Seattle, Charleston, Vancouver, or Santa Barbara, then my statement about Prague takes on more significance. But a second question must also be asked if my claim is to have merit. That question is, "What is your standard of beauty and how do you apply it to cities?" This question, too, must be answered substantively or I am reduced to self-referential comments that are unconvincing and lack authority. A thing of beauty may have objective, admirable features but knowing this is so will not guarantee a flawless application of the principle. Nevertheless, the more one is able to deepen an understanding of the objective features of a thing of beauty the more one increases the capacity to take disinterested, not utilitarian, pleasure and enjoyment from that object.

PERCEPTION OF BEAUTY OUGHT TO LEAD TO A SENSE OF AWE, WORSHIP, AND THANKSGIVING

Lewis wrote a short paragraph asking his readers to consider the difference between gratitude and adoration. He wrote, "Gratitude exclaims, very properly: 'How good of God to give me this.' Adoration says: 'What must be the quality of that Being whose far-off and momentary coruscations are like this!' One's mind runs back up the sunbeam to the sun."[14] I remember when I first read those words, it was during the time when Voyager, the first interplanetary space probe, was speeding past Saturn, the most mysterious planet in our solar system. Photographs were taken and sent back to earth. Then, it was discovered that of the network of Saturn's rings, one of the outer ones, the F-ring, was braided. Using Lewis's word I caught myself asking, "Wow! What must God be like that He chose to braid the outer ring of Saturn even though no human eye had seen it until then?" I've asked physicists for an explanation and in my hearing they have yet to come up with a concrete, coherent explanation for this braided ring. So far I've heard five probable explanations and each contains something that refutes the others. I am sure physicists will eventually explain this extraordinary phenomenon. In the mean time I just ask, "What must God be like that he braided the outer ring of Saturn?" And a friend of mine once observed, "Yeah, and we don't even know if God just braided it for the picture."

There are research ships that park themselves in the Pacific Ocean above seas that descend miles; and, into those depths they dangle cameras on tethers deeper than the light of the sun can reach and they capture pictures of fish painted neon bright. Why do fish at those depths have any color at all is a question I would like answered. It certainly cannot be to attract a mate, there is no sunlight that reaches into those depths (and one would assume no sight) at those depths either. I suppose the real question is, "How do fish at those depths even find each other to mate and reproduce other fish?" That itself is a mystery. Furthermore, the coloration of the fish cannot be for camouflage in order to hide from predators. Every time I think about it, I just think, "Wow! What must God be like that He painted fish neon bright in the bowels of the ocean, even though no human eye might ever see it?" It is a thing of beauty and it does evoke wonder.

Having once lived in Southern California, I loved to see palm trees silhouetted against an auburn sunset sky, or a mountain range silhouetted against an auburn sunset sky. Then I moved to the Midwest and I came to love a cornfield silhouetted against an auburn sunset sky. There is beauty there if one would willingly distill it out. But, we could have lived on a planet with neither sunrises nor sunsets; then one day, on our darkened planet we could have gotten word from on high that there would be one sunset. We could have lined every west coast of every continent and island on our globe and regaled our progeny with the glory of that great event by writing of it in our journals. But, what must God be like that He has made our planet a perpetual kaleidoscope of both sunrises and sunsets? There is no escaping the fact that there are sunsets so glorious that even careless eyes stop and stare to take in the glory. A sadness falls over the heart of those who witness it as it dissolves before them. They need not grieve too deeply; God is so liberal with His glory, he will give another on another evening still to come. God, it appears, is prodigal in his distribution of beauty and glory.

One star twinkling in the night sky should be enough to awaken awe and wonder in the mind and heart of every right thinking and right feeling individual. But, what must God be like that He glittered the night sky with stars and moons and suns and galaxies and comets and shooting stars and Northern Lights that pulsate and coruscate in reds and greens and blues and whites? Those who have seen the Aurora Borealis are not quick to forget the experience; it lingers long in the memory. I remember my first sight of them; I stood with others on a ski dock on a lake way up in the north woods of Wisconsin and we sang songs of praise and worship long into the night until they disappeared. A proper response to a thing of beauty is not merely an act of worship an adoration, it is also an act of justice, for it renders to the thing its due.

What must God be like that He made delicate things like hummingbirds and butterflies and flower petals and peacock feathers? G. K. Chesterton once observed that "One elephant with a trunk looked odd; but, every elephant with a trunk looked like a plot!" There is much beauty in the universe and some of it is unique, some of it is common; and, as Lewis suggests, all of it seems to indicate something about the hand that made the universe where we live and therefore, beauty gives just cause to worship. Even so, there remain complexities that must yet be accounted for; not all in the world sparkles with obvious strains of beauty. And Lewis will not let his readers forget. One must also ask, "What must God be like that He allows AIDS babies to be born in Africa; earthquakes in Haiti; and Tsunamis in Japan?" If beauty is objective then so is ugliness and the despairing, and this too must be given account and made sense of in a world where God exists. Nevertheless, Lewis reminds his readers, "If our religion is something objective then we must never avert our eyes from those elements in it which seem puzzling or repellent; for it will be precisely the puzzling or the repellent which conceals what we do not yet know and need to know."[15] Furthermore, it is not only the pastors and theologians who can help the lay person see and makes sense of such things; the artist also might see through these calamities and bring to light both the bad and the beauty that can emerge from the rubble of such tragedies. Winters do break into springs; a mother's labor pains do give way to birth; some cracks do allow light to shine through, and the Crucifixion is followed by Resurrections.

LEWIS'S APPLICATION OF OBJECTIVE STANDARDS TO JUDGMENTS OF LITERARY BEAUTY

It is one thing for Lewis to believe that objective beauty exists, in theory; but can he apply his beliefs in this matter to some specific form of art and thereby exhibit what he means? If so, what might this look like? It is one thing for Lewis to write about objectivity but how would his ideas translate into an actual application in the realm of his own expertise of literary art and criticism? While it is possible to come up with numerous examples in works such as Lewis's *A Preface to Paradise Lost*, or his masterful work, *The Allegory of Love*, as well as his magisterial *English Literature in the Sixteenth Century Excluding Drama*, examples are also found in a host of critical essays on authors as diverse as Tasso, Shakespeare, Jane Austen, William Morris, Rudyard Kipling, and Charles Williams. But turning attention to one particular work may suffice to give light on Lewis's application of his objectivist commitments when engaging in literary criticism and literary judgment. Clearly, one will have to make allowances when applying Lewis's ideas to studio art, music, dance, photography, sculpture, architecture, and a score of other artistic expressions; nevertheless, a clever person will not fail to find a viable, natural segue to other artistic fields. An explicit work where Lewis makes positive claims about the possibility of making objective artistic judgment is *The Personal Heresy*.

THE PERSONAL HERESY

The Personal Heresy began as a challenge Lewis made in the public arena in an article he wrote in *Essays and Studies*, an annual journal, published by the English faculty at Oxford University.[16] For background, E. M. W. Tillyard, who at the time was the Master of Jesus College, Cambridge, wrote that *Paradise Lost* was actually about the state of Milton's mind at the time he wrote the poem.[17] Lewis took issue with this and said that Milton's work was actually about the poem and not the state of the author's mind. In fact, Lewis argued that an attempt at analysis of the author's mind would be an exercise in unverifiable judgments that likely amount to nothing more than the critic's own projections onto the author of the text. Furthermore, this alleged criticism of the author's mind, since it is never present, removes the discussion from the text which is readily available; attention, therefore, is focused away from the objective and directed towards the hypothetical. Lewis remarks that criticism must be about texts themselves; this way if a critic's judgment is valid or invalid the text may be referenced in order to establish or disestablish a claim. The text is objective, and Lewis rightly observes that when looking at a text the one thing we do not see is the author; we see what the author sees we do not see him. Consequently, Lewis cleverly observes, we make of the author a pair of spectacles and avoid making a spectacle of him or her.[18]

Tillyard responded the next year, also in *Essays and Studies*, and a debate followed in print through three issues of the journal. In the end, Tillyard and Lewis thought the discussion deserved fuller treatment and eventually they published the book *The Personal Heresy*. If for no other reason the book should be read by all who want an example of serious, respectful, academic debate with no rancor; a debate that produces light not heat and understanding is benefitted. Both authors are capable of making points and conceding points for both demonstrate a level of security and confidence in their field and in their knowledge of that field as well as having appreciation for their opponent's command of the discipline. It must be noted, in an age of growing incivility and the readiness to dismiss points of view contrary to our own, *The Personal Heresy* is a model of collaborative scholarship benefitted by respectful opposition. It is itself, a thing of beauty given its internal integrity, proportion, and texture and clarity. However, Lewis does seems to get the upper hand in the debate as he keeps driving home the point that the critic must keep to the text as the final court of appeal in literary judgments; if this is not done, one is left with mere subjectivistic claims devoid of any objective veracity. Nevertheless, at this point, Tillyard rightly challenges Lewis to go further than merely stating claim to what poetry cannot be, and to state positively what poetry is. The world owes a debt to Tillyard for pushing Lewis to set forth his case. Furthermore, what follows, in fact, reveals an example of how Lewis applies his beliefs about objectivity and beauty in the case of literature. Furthermore, Lewis's example of objective judgment about literary texts can be modified for application to judgments about beauty generally. Lewis's ideas are consistent with what he would later write about objectivity in *The Abolition of Man*. Furthermore, Lewis sets forth principles regarding literary judgments which have the possibility of wider application. Of course, there is always the possibility an application may fall short of an objective standard. Nevertheless, *an abuse does not nullify a proper use*. If objective judgments can be made at all, if questions of Beauty can be settled, then National Parks *can* be established and guarded to protect natural wonders in which all can take delight. Museums can be built to preserve works of art for the pleasure of the many. Furthermore, Orchestras can be expected to play beloved classical pieces that have stood the test of time. And, therefore, we should, in fact, expect that guiding principles might be discerned that explain why some things have a beauty that gives pleasure, is awe inspiring, and is generally undeniable and reasonable. There are rules to reason as there are rules to the game of chess; knowing the rules does not guarantee one wins the game each time he or she sits at the board to play. Skill and application of the rules is also important. Lewis believes objective judgments are possible in matters of beauty and art because something is present to the senses and it can be talked about. Furthermore, these descriptions and discussions can be modified and refined through careful appeal to the objects themselves. Whatever scoliosis occurs in any given judgment it might yet be adjusted to the plumb line of reality. This adjusted understanding can be the work of one, over time; or, the work of a community adding perspective and angles of vision, in a given discussion; or, it can be the work of generations, revealing an enduring quality of beauty in some objects that seem to transcend time and place. Consequently, this also leaves room for expert opinion. A person more skilled in the application of those rules can help others, who have not yet seen, gain a clearer vision of what is before them.

So, how did Lewis set forth his principles for literary judgment regarding texts, in response to Tillyard, and how might these be applied to judgments of beauty? First, Lewis defined his terms. "By poetry I mean, as the renaissance critics meant, imaginative literature whether in prose or verse."[19] Lewis says more than once that poetry is an art or skill.[20] What's more, Lewis rightly notes that "A skill is defined by its instruments"[21] or it could be said that a particular art is defined by its materials. Stone is the instrument of sculpture. Pigment and oil is the instrument of some kinds of painting. As Lewis observes, in the case of literary art the instrument is language. Language can be used for purposes other than poetry, that is, in philosophy, commerce, science, etc., therefore, a poet must use language in a particular way. The skill of the poet (as the skill of any artist with regard to his or her materials) provides another objective basis of valuation. Has the artist applied his skills well? This has nothing to do with the artist's character, motives, or intentions. A craftsman may be well intended even where his skill may be lacking. Furthermore, an artist with poor character may be brilliantly skilled. We may not care for the lifestyle of the artist; but, as Lewis made clear, the judgment is not about the artist but the art.

If the material of the poet is language and language can be used in a variety of ways, Lewis seeks to focus attention on the particular ways language might be used by the artist. Comparing poetic use with scientific use, Lewis sees each form of language modifying common conversation in one of two divergent ways. The scientists might say, "It is twice as cold as yesterday." To be even more precise, he constructs a mercury thermometer and places a graduated scale beside the mercury vessel whereby the rise and fall of the mercury lends itself to the quantification of ever more precise measurement. In this way the scientist uses language to quantify the measurable; but the words are likely to have no value to the French Polynesian who has no experience of anything like Alpine forms of winter weather with its frigid temperatures, ice, and snows. The meteorologist's words indicating that it is five degrees below freezing may be accurate but they have little meaning to the ears of the Polynesian. On the other hand, the poet seeks to modify common language in a way that allows the reader to feel something of the quality of the experience of cold; it felt like "a smack in the face".[22] Science "escapes from the sensuous altogether into the world of pure quantities;" whereas, poetry uses its tools (extra-logical elements of language—rhythm, vowel-music, onomatopoeia, associations; one might also add use of metaphors, similes, and analogy), "to convey the concrete reality of experiences."[23] Lewis adds that those who do this comparatively well, with the materials they have, may be regarded as the better artists with respect to those materials. Here again the judgment is both comparative and objective.[24] By this qualitative appeal to the senses the artist calls into action the sensory capacities of the observer and thereby also awakens an emotional response in the observer as well.

While Lewis here has given some basis (certainly not all) for making some judgments regarding beauty and art; he seeks to prevent the false notion that ambiguity in these matters might be eliminated. Furthermore, Lewis warns against the temptation to assert, in any literary judgment, that it is a last word of all that might be said of a given literary work. He writes,

> It is therefore not usually possible, and it is never necessary, to say of a composition in any absolute sense, "This is poetry": what we can say is, "This is further in the poetical direction than that." But as, in ordinary terminology, we mean by a tall man or a rich man one who is taller or richer than most, so by a poem we mean a composition which communicates more of the concrete and qualitative than our usual utterances do. A poet is a man who produces such compositions more often and more successfully than the rest of us.[25]

This warning has application to any artistic expression, for no work of art has fully revealed or exhausted the complexities of the object. No artistic endeavor could ever be said to be a last word. There may be much to appreciate about a work of art or a thing of beauty; but careful study will reveal wonders yet. And these discoveries can be objective when tethered to the object.

A poem or other literary work can be about any topic one might discuss in ordinary conversation. Nevertheless, Lewis says, "Of any utterance, whether conversational or poetical, our first demand is that it should be interesting."[26] That which makes something interesting may, perhaps, be similar to what makes something beautiful; that is, it has integrity, proportion, and clarity. Furthermore, it may awaken curiosity and hopefully leads to some degree of pleasure and perhaps even awe. Lewis says also, that it "should have a desirable permanent effect on us if possible—should make us either happier, or wiser, or better."[27] Lewis asserted that great poetry, for example, preserves what is worth repeating. Therefore, he writes, "the best judge of poetry is he who can best judge of human utterances."[28] Here Lewis stops short of going much further, and does not give a definition of who this best judge might be. Nevertheless, he adds, "There is no essential qualification for criticism more definite than general wisdom and health of mind. To make such wisdom effective, many conditions may be necessary, such as a good knowledge of language [the poet's instrument, and here it might be added the artist's skill with his materials] and a wide experience of poetry."[29] Consequently, Lewis, who believed judgment on these matters is possible because of his objectivist commitments, leaves room in his thinking for ever more refined judgments.

While *The Personal Heresy*, as an embodiment of Lewis's objectivist commitments in matters of art and beauty, comes early in his academic career, one can see that he still holds to this course late in his life as well; this is evident in what he wrote in *Studies in Words*.[30] While this book was written to give the definitions of a select number of words and demonstrate changes in the meanings of those words over time; Lewis acknowledges in the *Preface* that his "words are studied as an aid to more accurate reading and chosen for the light they throw on ideas and sentiments."[31] Clearly Lewis wants those making critical judgments about texts to have at their disposal all the resources that will allow for a close read of texts. Literary judgment must be rooted in the texts themselves as all aesthetic judgments must also be connected to the objects being described. Further, in this regard, Lewis makes it clear that negative judgments about a text merely need to begin with the word *bad*. And he adds, "The only good reason for ever departing from that monosyllable when we condemn anything is to be more specific, to answer the question 'Bad in what way?'"[32] Equally it could be said good criticism should begin with the word "good" and after this it is the burden of the critic to say in what way something is good. This can only be done with an appeal to the text itself; that is by an objective appeal to a particular thing that is what it is regardless of what the critic thinks of it. If the critic's judgments are to be considered fair, then there must be objective validation for the judgment "good." Certainly this can be applied to all types of art and all questions of beauty. Lewis believed this and he assumes the truth of it right up to nearly his last book.

CONCLUSION

Lewis's argument in *The Personal Heresy* is coherent both with his argument in *The Abolition of Man* and his claims in *Studies in Words*. In summary: 1) his judgments are rooted in the objectivity of the text. 2) He defines his object and does not compare or contrast that object with items that do not fit the definition or classification. 3) He is sensitive to qualities within the text itself relative to the literary form such as rhythm, word-music, richness of metaphors, capacity to utilize the memory and experience of his readers. 4) He does not suggest a final kind of judgment; he offers a sure word, validated in the object itself and is therefore open to further revision and clarification. He keeps niggling at the object to understand it more. With respect to the variety of arts and artistic expressions these ideas have their applications.

It is to be expected that Lewis's ideas are themselves not last words about beauty and art. In fact, if what Lewis suggests is true then debate is to be expected. Lewis would invite it, for he was constantly open to revising and refining his grasp of virtually everything he studied. He appreciated the benefits of conversation in these matters and had respect for the perspectives of others. Should someone challenge him however, he would expect that the challenge be validated objectively. This was perhaps most vividly attested to when once, in a debate with a man who disagreed with Lewis's objectivism, he was challenged, "How do you know there isn't a blue cow on that piano right now?" Lewis responded, "In what sense blue?"[33] Without appeal to an object the claims, "Beautiful!" or, "This is great art!" have no meaning. Furthermore, the idea that beauty, or great art, is arbitrary is also false. Nevertheless, the claim that beauty is objective does not solve all problems. Demonstrating in what way the beauty exists or establishing the claim that the art ought to be appreciated is far more difficult. Lewis would likely leave that to his betters; but, if head way in the discussion is to be made in a reasonable fashion, respect for the object itself must not be neglected.

ENDNOTES

1 A fuller exposition of Lewis's ideas regarding beauty and literary judgment can be found in C.S. Lewis, *An Experiment in Criticism* (Cambridge: Cambridge University Press, 1961). Note especially, chapter three, "How the Few and the Many use Pictures and Music." And a more developed discussion of Lewis's grasp of the relationship between truth and reality can be found in chapter two of *C.S. Lewis and a Problem of Evil: An Investigation of a Pervasive Theme* by Jerry Root (Eugene, Oregon: Princeton Theological Monograph, 2009).

2 One might also consult, "On Ethics," "The Poison of Subjectivism," and "De Futitlitate" for more on Lewis's objectivist commitments. These essays can be found in C.S. Lewis, *Christian Reflections*, Walter Hooper, editor. (Grand Rapids, Michigan: Eerdmans, 1967).

3 King, Alec, and Ketley, Martin, *The Control of Language* (London: Longmans, Green and Co., 1942).

4 The account of this vacation is found in Dorothy Wordsworth, *The Grassmere Journals, 1803*.

5 C.S. Lewis, "De Futilitate" *Christian Reflections* (Eerdmans: Grand Rapids, Michigan 1967), 65-66.

6 C.S. Lewis, *The Abolition of Man* (San Francisco: Harper Collins, 1974), 16.

7 If a reader would want to understand Lewis's approach to epistemology, he or she would do well to consult *Christian Reflections* p. 41 where Lewis discusses the check and balance of authority, reason, and experience. See also C.S. Lewis, *The Discarded Image* (Cambridge University Press: Cambridge, 1964) 189. And also, Jerry Root, *C.S. Lewis and a Problem of Evil: An Investigation of a Pervasive Theme* (Cambridge, England: James Clarke & Co., 2009). See pages 32-39 for an exposition of Lewis's epistemology.

8 Lewis, *The Abolition of Man*, 43.

9 Lewis, "De Futilitate," *Christian Reflections*, 71.

10 C.S. Lewis, *Reflection on the Psalms* (Orlando, Florida: Harcourt, 1986), 92.

11 In Lewis's *An Experiment in Criticism*, he says that there are two types of readers: those who use literary art and those who receive it. Those who use art tend to manipulate the art to their own purposes and often disrespect the art as it is in itself; those who receive art in its various forms learn to see it and appreciate it as it is. Lewis writes in that book, "In coming to understand anything we must reject the facts as they are for us in favor of the facts as they are." See page 138.

12 Mortimer Adler, *Six Great Ideas* (New York: Simon and Schuster), 114.

13 Thomas Aquinas, *Summa Theologica*, First Part, Question 39, Article 8. *Great Books of the Western World*, Vol. 19 Thomas Aquinas: I. Robert Maynard Hutchins, Editor in Chief (Chicago: Encyclopedia Britannica, 1952) 211.

14 C.S. Lewis, *Letters to Malcolm: Chiefly on Prayer* (London: Geoffrey Bless, 1964), 118.

15 C.S. Lewis, *The Weight of Glory: and Other Addresses* (New York: Macmillan, 1949), 7.

16 C.S. Lewis, "The Personal Heresy in Criticism." *Essays and Studies: by Members of The English Association.* Volume XIX, Collected by D. Nichol Smith (Oxford: Clarendon Press, 1934), 7-28.

17 E.M.W. Tillyard, *Milton* (Chatto & Windus: London. 1930). Tillyard actually wrote: "No one reading through Paradise Lost with any degree of seriousness can help asking with what the poem as a whole is most truly concerned, what were the feelings and ideas that dominated Milton's mind when he wrote it." (P. 1). And later Tillyard writes, "It is strange how little, till quite recently, critics have concerned themselves with the meaning of Paradise Lost. The style, the versification, the celestial geography, the thought, who is the hero: all these have concerned the critics far more than what the poem is really about, the true state of Milton's mind when he wrote it." (P. 201). Both quotes above are taken from the Peregrine Books edition, 1966. Lewis's remarks come from *The Personal Heresy* (London: Oxford University Press, 1939) and can be found on P. 2.

18 C.S. Lewis and E.M.W. Tillyard, *The Personal Heresy: A Controversy*. (London: Oxford University Press, 1939). See pages 12, 13, 99.

19 *Ibid.* 108.

20 *Ibid.* 103 and 107.

21 *Ibid.* 107.

22 *Ibid.* 108.

23 *Ibid.*

24 It must be noted that Lewis also develops these ideas in his essay, "The Language of Religion" in *Christian Reflections*, edited by Walter Hooper (Grand Rapids: Eerdmans, 1967), 129-41.

25 *Ibid.* 108-09.

26 *Ibid.* 119.

27 *Ibid.*

28 *Ibid.* 116.

29 *Ibid.* 116.

30 C.S. Lewis, *Studies in Words* (Cambridge: Cambridge University Press, 1960) (Pagination above is referenced from the second edition; while this edition was prepared, by Lewis, for publication, before Lewis's death in 1963, it did not see print until 1967.)

31 *Ibid.* vii.

32 *Ibid.* 327.

33 ROUTLEY, Erik Routley, "A Prophet" *C.S. Lewis at the Breakfast Table*, James Como, editor (New York: Macmillan, 1979), 35.

C.S. Lewis on the Transformative Power of (Theory-Free) Literature

DAVID ROZEMA

Each man can judge competently the things he knows, and of these he is a good judge.
—Aristotle, Nicomachean Ethics I.3

In the world of literary studies, it might well be argued that the last 100 years have been the age of the critic. In the wake of the new theories of Man proposed by Darwin, Marx and Freud, literary criticism has grown exponentially since the end of the 19th Century to the point that there may now be more critics of literature than writers of it. Adding to the fray, we now have—under the influence of Nietzsche, Heidegger, and Sartre—the further ironically complicating notion that meaning is necessarily indeterminate. The indeterminacy of what *this* means has produced an even wider platform for those wishing to "do criticism," and has considerably spiced things up for those striving to retain their places of honor in the pantheon of secondary sources. It is certainly true that the number of novelists, poets, playwrights, and screenwriters has also increased in recent times, but the fame of a critic (like the popularity of whatever theory is in fashion) is generally more fleeting than the fame of the authors whose works they critique, making the critics' circle both more inclusive and more volatile in the marketplace of what is known as "research" in the arts and humanities.

One of the chief reasons for this drastic shift has been the nearly wholesale acceptance of theory-driven criticism by the professors of literature at colleges and universities. One would be hard pressed to find an English department in America (or elsewhere) today in which literature is not read through the lens of one or another theoretical perspective. There are several deleterious consequences of this development: it draws attention away from the ideas and characters (or subjects) which the author portrays and places it instead on the psychological history of the author, the sociological history of his or her time and place, and the anthropological tendencies of this or that "culture" in which the work was composed; it has the tendency to make the critique of literature more of a science (complete with theories and a method) than an art; it contributes to the proliferation of footnotes and bibliographies which serve to verify one's qualifications as a *bone fide* member of the tribe.[1] But by far the worst consequence is the way in which this theory-driven criticism nullifies—or at least drastically inhibits—the transformative power that a work of literature can have on the soul of the individual.

In this essay I want to do what I can to help defend a theory-free reading and critique of literature, to further explicate the pernicious effects of theory-driven criticism, to rehabilitate the primacy of the art itself, and to evoke (or reawaken) that pleasure in reading which most modern criticism is incapable of doing.[2] However, since I am neither the best nor the first author to carry out these tasks, my main contribution will consist of pointing to my betters who have already done so.

For, as bleak as things are (if the description I've given above is accurate), amidst the flurry of books and authors and professors purporting to offer the critical keys to understanding this or that work of literature, one can still find voices calling in the wilderness. There are those who still call us to repent of this misplaced primacy of the critic and urge us to look to the literature itself for what we need. They are the ones who themselves feed on the literature. One of the sanest and sweetest of these voices is that of C.S. Lewis. In his masterful and prophetic monograph, *An Experiment in Criticism*, Lewis offers an antidote to the fashionable form of criticism—judging works of literature through the lens of a particular theory—with this "experiment":

> Literary criticism is traditionally employed in judging books. Any judgment it implies about men's readings of books is a corollary from its judgments about the books themselves. Bad taste is, as it were by definition, a taste for bad books. I want to find out what sort of picture we shall get by reversing the process. Let us make our distinction between readers or types of reading the basis, and our distinction between books the corollary.[3]

Lewis then accordingly draws a distinction between "the few and the many"—the few being the "literary" and the many being the "unliterary." The distinction between these two types is not merely a difference in what they read (e.g., Dante vs. the women's magazines), but rather in the activity itself. Although both types of people could be said to be reading, the use of the same word for both cases easily misleads us into supposing that the difference is only one of *degree*, and not a difference *in kind*. As Lewis points out, the way in which the few read and like (or dislike) what they read is vastly different from the way in which the many read and like (or dislike) what they read. "The differences leap to the eye," he says. "In the first place, the majority never read anything twice," while the few who love literature "will read the same work ten, twenty or thirty times during the course of their life." "Secondly, the majority, though they are sometimes frequent readers, do not set much store by reading. They turn to it as a last resource. They abandon it with alacrity as soon as any alternative pastime turns up. It is kept for railway journeys, illnesses, odd moments of enforced solitude, or for the process called 'reading oneself to sleep'." We could now add to this list: for airports, for something to do while drinking your latté, or for the process called 'seeing if it's like the movie'. By contrast, "literary people are always looking for leisure and silence in which to read and do so with their whole attention." A third difference is that "to the literary, the first reading of some literary work is an experience so momentous that only the experiences of love, religion, or bereavement can furnish a standard of comparison. Their whole consciousness is changed.... But there is no sign of this among the other sort of readers." And, finally, the response to what they have read is vastly different. To the few, "what they have read is constantly and prominently present to the mind," providing "a sort of iconography by which they interpret or sum up their own experience. They talk to one another about books, often and at length." The many, on the other hand, "seldom think or talk of their reading."[4]

In an earlier essay ("On Different Tastes in Literature"), Lewis emphasizes the primacy of these last two criteria:

> In all this, surely, we find the symptoms of a real want for bad art, but of a want which is not even in the same species with men's want for good art. What the patrons of the bad art clearly desire—and get—is a pleasant background to life, a something that will fill up odd moments, 'packing' for the mental trunk or 'roughage' for the mental stomach. There is really no question of *joy*: of an experience with a razor's edge which re-makes the whole mind, which produces 'the holy spectral shiver', which can make a man (as the 'wind musique' made Pepys) feel 'really sick—just as I have formerly been when in love with my wife'.[5]

Lewis argues that it is this sort of momentous experience that initially and conclusively separates the "few" from the "many," and therefore serves as the initial qualification for someone to become a competent judge of literature (indeed, of any art). For the transformative experience is exactly what all art has the potential to evoke: if it *can* do this, then it *can* be (good) art. As Frost has said, "No discovery for the writer, no discovery for the reader." The discovery he has in mind is a discovery about the meaningfulness of a person's own life in light of the relationships he has to his particular place in creation and to his fellow human beings—his family, friends, ancestors, and enemies. Art can be defined as those creative works of people which have the potential to affect such an experience. The corollary, as Lewis says, is that "bad art" can never produce such experiences, not even in those people who have had them before and who are, therefore, open to such experiences. The relationships between these two kinds of readers and the things they read is asymmetrical: a good reader will look for the crucial experience in all the books she reads, but can only find it in the "good art," never the "bad art": a poor reader will not look for such an experience at all and, therefore, can never find it at all, not even in the "good art" which is capable of producing it. From the starting point of this kind of transformative experience in reading literature, the other differences between the few and the many—re-reading, setting great significance to reading, and reading with complete attention—follow: they are consequences of this initial difference. It is, in fact, the repeated and consistent practice of these activities that shape a reader into an increasingly better one, one who is more discerning, more exacting, and, at the same time, more sympathetic. For such a reader, one good story leads to another. And if, as Frost said, a good poem is a "momentary stay against confusion," then many good poems will, for a good reader, lead to a longer, more permanent stay.

What all of these differences clearly show, according to Lewis, is that "if *like* is the correct word for what [the unliterary majority] do to books, then some other word must be found for what [the literary few] do. Or, conversely, if [the literary few] *like* [their] kind of book, we must not say that [the unliterary many] *like* any book."[6] The word Lewis uses for what the literary "do to books" is *love* them. But this is a truly *appreciative* love, for the true reader loves reading literature for its own sake, and not for the sake of some further pleasure or goal. As Lewis so aptly illustrates with the visual arts and with music, the true lover of literature is one who "receives" it, not one who "uses" it as a means to some other end. People who read books for these other ends range from the status seeker, who reads only to impress others—and reads only those books that he thinks will do so; to the thrill seeker, who demands that there be what he calls 'action'; to the egoistic castle-builder, who reads in order to vicariously experience the pleasures of wealth, honor, success, or sensuality; and even to the person who is seeking a philosophy by which to live, and thinks the best place to find such philosophies is in literature. The users of literature neither know nor care about literary elements such as symbolism, imagery, sound, description, witty or implicative dialogue, or pacing. Not even whether or not it is a compelling *story*. The receivers of literature, on the other hand, look for and savor such things when they are well done. The user of literature looks only for what Lewis calls "the Event" and will soon discard as worthless any book that does not deliver the event(s) that will satisfy him. Not all the users of literature have depraved or vulgar motives for reading, but, as Lewis says, "'Using' is inferior to 'reception' because art, if used rather than received, merely facilitates, brightens, relieves or palliates our life, and does not add to it."[7] There can be no doubt that these other good ends are often attained through such an appreciative love of art—wisdom, encouragement, comfort, refreshment—and Lewis by no means diminishes the value of them. But if the readers' prime motive is a love for the art, the receiver of literature adds to her life by opening herself up to all the pleasure and goodness that might be found in a book—*any* book, *any* piece of literature.

As Lewis himself would be quick to acknowledge, this approach to literature and criticism has its parallel in Plato, to whom I now turn.

Midway through Book V of Plato's *Republic*, Socrates introduces the idea of the true philosopher (the "philosopher-king or -queen") in response to Glaucon's question of what it would take to make the ideal city a real city. Socrates proposes this idea also in response to the dismal failure of Glaucon and the other youths with whom he is conversing to reject or even question the suggestions he has made earlier in Book V (e.g., coed naked wrestling, selective breeding of humans, polygamy, population control through abortion and infanticide, and having children raised in "rearing pens"). From these failures, it is clear to Socrates that these young men are not thinking; their appetites have overruled their reason, and it's time to disabuse them of the notion that they are leadership material. So Socrates paints a picture of the true philosopher, the kind of person who would truly be fit to lead. This picture will ensure that none of them suppose they are wise yet, and either discourage them from seeking to rule, or encourage them to keep searching for the wisdom that would make them worthy of it. The primary characteristic of the true philosopher, Socrates says, is the very thing that defines the term—the "love of wisdom." Such a person must love all kinds of wisdom; he must not be picky, like a picky eater, but must hunger and thirst for all of it.[8] On the other hand, he must not be satisfied with opinions, but will want only what can truly be known, for knowledge is a far greater treasure and much more potent than mere opinion.

One of the illustrations Socrates uses to clarify this characteristic of the true philosopher is the wine lover. The wine lover, he says, loves all wine.

Let's stop here for a moment.

Is this true? Does the true wine lover love all wine?

What is a lover of wine? A wino—a drunkard; or a connoisseur? One who does not discriminate, or one who does? Does Socrates really think the wine lover is the one who loves all wine indiscriminately? Once again (and not for the last time) Socrates presents Glaucon (and Plato presents his readers) with a test, for matters are not as simple as they seem.

The true wine lover, most would agree, is the connoisseur, not the drunkard. But the connoisseur clearly does not love *all* wine, and the drunkard takes whatever (and as much as) he can get, no matter how poorly made. We might say—and truthfully enough in this case—that it's a matter of taste. But note that the difference between them is not that the connoisseur likes some wines while the drunkard likes others. They have no arguments about the aesthetics of taste. The latter makes no distinctions between wines whatsoever. The difference between them is that the connoisseur has *discriminating* taste, while the drunkard's taste is so indiscriminating as to be completely useless. We might as well say that the drunkard *has no taste*, for it's quite true that he does not drink his wine for the taste. He does not enjoy it for its own sake, but only for the sake of what it does to him. Anything which will produce the same effect will do just as well. He doesn't *taste* wine: he *consumes* it. He may very well have lost the ability to taste things. But even if he hasn't lost the ability, he might as well have, for, functionally speaking, he is tasteless. He is a 'user' of wines (and other things), not a 'receiver' of them. He does not love the wine for what it is. If he makes a choice between one wine and another, it will be a choice of the cheaper, not the better.

The connoisseur, on the other hand, is a 'receiver', not a 'user'. For a connoisseur is a true wine lover in the sense that she will, first of all, enjoy tasting wines, sensing each one's individual qualities and effects. She will also be open to both new and familiar sensations, from *any* wine and from *any* wine maker. She doesn't pre-judge the issue: the tasting is "blind"; she doesn't care who made it, how much it costs, the country of its origin or the process used to produce it. But, at the same time she will have a finely developed capacity for distinguishing these sensations, one from another, and of evaluating the effectiveness of each wine in producing the desired sensation. Unlike the drunkard, the connoisseur drinks for the taste and, very nearly, the taste alone. While the drunkard gulps it down, the connoisseur savors the wine while it is in the mouth, nearly forgetting to swallow—might not swallow at all if it weren't an involuntary function—and even after swallowing will speak of its aftertaste. The connoisseur is concerned to "cleanse the palate" before tasting the wine. It's true that both the drunkard and the connoisseur drink wine—they each put it in their mouths and swallow it—but that's as far as the similarity goes. You could hardly say that they are doing the same thing. The two activities are as different from each other as a two-year-old's banging on the piano and a virtuoso's performance of a Rachmaninoff concerto. And what the connoisseur does is clearly closer to what we'd call 'wine loving' than what the drunkard does.

Now, if the drunkard has no taste for the wine, then the connoisseur, at her best, *defines* such taste. That is, such a connoisseur would be a defining example of what wine tasting *is*—would be wine-tasting *par excellence*. In between these two extremes—the drunkard and the connoisseur—are a whole host of people who are more or less able to taste. For such a capacity to taste requires development; requires experience and training.

The point I want to stress in all this is that prior to the question of whether or not any particular wine is a good wine, is the question of whether or not the person tasting the wine has the functional capacity to taste it. So the lover of wine must be, first of all, a wise and loving *taster* of wine. We might even go so far as to say that unless you are a taster of this sort you are in no position to say whether what you're drinking is wine at all. To say that it is wine that you are drinking would be merely to express your opinion. Perhaps your only evidence was the label on the bottle, or the word of someone else. "Is this wine, or isn't it?" Only the true wine lover knows for sure.

So, now, does the true philosopher love all wisdom, just as the wine lover loves all wine?

Yes. For, just as the true wine lover loves all wines worthy of being called such, the true philosopher loves all wisdom worthy of the name. Everything else is just a pretender. It is not clear whether Glaucon agrees with Socrates on this point for these reasons, but we can be sure that Socrates himself is thinking of things this way, for he (famously) goes on to say that true knowledge—which he equates with wisdom—is only of the ideal Forms: Beauty, Truth, Goodness, Justice, etc. Debates over the so-called Platonic Theory of Forms have lasted as long as people have read Plato's dialogues, and I do not intend to enter into that discussion here.[9] I will say only this, without offering an argument: the introduction of theory is as harmful and misleading in philosophy as it is in literature. I do, however, wish to note a less controversial implication here: namely, that there is a distinction between those who know and respond to goodness, truth, and beauty, whenever and wherever they see them (or hear, taste, smell, or touch them), and those who do not know or do not respond to them. As the allegory of the cave shows us, such a capacity is a possibility for all human beings, but it becomes a reality only for relatively few. The road to wisdom is long and difficult.

As is the road to beauty, which is the road—less travelled, most assuredly—that must be taken by the critic, if he or she is to judge competently. This road begins, as we have seen, with an initial receptive love for language and story, opening the way for that first, most precious transformative experience in reading. From there, over the course of many readings and re-readings—literary voyages, some of which are riding the crests, others through the troughs—the true lover of literature gradually develops a finely-tuned capacity for making distinctions between literary works in terms of their effects on the passions, their artistic construction, and the depth of their reach in understanding the human condition. Such a person is functionally literate, a true reader, while others remain functionally illiterate, as the drunkard is functionally tasteless, even if he has not destroyed his taste buds. The true reader—teacher, critic—is, then, a fellow traveler, more seasoned; sharing the journey and the transformational experience as a gift, not only to and for himself, but to and for his fellow travelers as well.

So what, then, does a true reader, a true lover of literature, *do*? What *specific* habits, practices and features characterize such a person's reading? What does it mean to have the capacity to *read literature*?

It is when I look at Lewis's answers to these questions that I become worried. For if my own experience with literary critics and professors of literature is at all representative of the general state of literary studies, there are a great many of them who do not know how to read literature as literature. They read it as they would something else—an anthropological history, a psychological confession, an historical artifact, or a political tract—and, therefore, cannot help others learn to read it as literature. And without a chance to learn, there is no chance to love. I do not mean that literature is no longer read by these people or in departments composed of these people, only that it is no longer read *as literature*. The common view among this group—a group that includes theorists of many different varieties: New-Historicists, Freudians, Marxists, Feminists, Structuralists, Post-Stucturalists, Deconstructionists, and so on—is that a work of literature is an *artifact* or a *tool*: either an historical or "cultural" artifact, like an ancient arrowhead or cooking-pot, which at one time and in one place and for some people had a purpose, but now (even if "now" happens to be only a short time or distance away) is only an object of curiosity; or as a political instrument, like a tool which, despite its ornamentation, is used by an author (and the political faction he belongs to) to gain and retain political and psychological power over others.

Thus, in modern and postmodern times, a gap has appeared between social-scientifically oriented critics, teachers, and readers of literature; and the artists themselves. This is a gap that continues to widen, despite the apparent consonance between these groups. In reality many modern critics and teachers of literature have welcomed, or at least complied with, the "scientification" of their art and the "tribalization" of their objects: even many so-called poets. All alike have bowed to the modern pantheon of "the sciences of human behavior," following a false faith in the principle that people are what they are because the laws of nature have made them so. Whether these laws are genetic or social—whether the ideological limitations and aims of era, age, race, gender, class, and culture are social constructions, or the inheritances of nature—the common assumption is that these are inescapable forces: no author (and no reader) can write (or read) beyond them. Nevertheless, the ideological, pseudo-scientific view has many intellectual adherents, and the result has been the phenomenon of a widening gap between the *art* of literature and the so-called *science* of criticism. (In fact, a new "genre" of literature has sprung up out of this unartful approach to the interpretation of literature—a genre distinguished by the subjects typically portrayed—which we might call "victim literature.") This gap has extended, naturally, to students too: on the one hand there are now those—the majority—who learn to "interpret" literary works as artifacts or instruments, or as products or services, and, on the other hand, the minority who learn to *read* works of literature as art.

Both modernists (those who think all works of literature can or must be explained in terms the historical, social, or political forces that were operative upon the author) and postmodernists (those who think that there can or must be no determinate meaning to any work of literature) see a work of literature as an *object*. This leads to the supposition that we can distinguish a "text" from its "meaning." That is, what all of these theorists share is a common picture, a common illusion, fostered by constantly seeing the method of science before their eyes, studying works of literature as if they were phenomena, in need of explanation by means of theory, reducing works of literature to mere 'texts'. The result is a peculiar sort of illiteracy: there is no longer such a thing as reading literature, there is only "the interpretation of texts." Thus it is that many of the *literati* of our time are themselves functionally illiterate.

Well, what then does Lewis say about what good readers, lovers of literature do? First of all, they read in an open, receptive spirit, in anticipation of what the literary work itself, on its own, will do to them. The literary reader reads attentively, with an eye and an ear for the images, the sounds, the allusions, the apt descriptions, the stylistic phrasings, the character portrayals, the placing and pacing of the dialogue, and the storytelling. He reads, as Lewis says, "disinterestedly"—that is, unselfishly and unself-consciously—he "gets himself out of the way" when he reads. If he engages in "castle-building," it is not of the egoistic kind; he takes pleasure in the imaginative world that the author has created for him, not because this world serves his own (or anyone else's) ends or wishes, but because such a world, when he enters it, has the potential to enlarge, free, or transform him, perhaps—as is often the case with a good reader—even to transform his life into one of greater worth to others. A particular work of literature may or may not have such an effect, but the literary reader is receptive to the possibility. In virtue of his sympathetic soul and robust imagination he becomes a co-creator, maybe not equal to the author, but creatively subservient.

A corollary of this characteristic of good reading is that a literate reader will never rely on the critics to pass judgment on a literary work, but will read it and judge it for himself. As Lewis says, "We can find a book bad only by reading it as if it might, after all, be very good. We must empty our minds and lay ourselves open."[10] And this goes for any work, for a good reader gives the benefit of the doubt to the work, not to the critic. Critics, as Lewis points out, are at their best when they encourage and facilitate good reading. Evaluative criticism, he says, "stands or falls by its power to multiply, safeguard, or prolong those moments when a good reader is reading well a good book and the value of literature then exists *in actu*."[11] Furthermore, "[c]riticism normally casts a retrospective light on what we have already read. . . . If we have to choose, it is always better to read Chaucer again than to read a new criticism of him."[12] This goes even for the best critics, those who are themselves good readers.

But, as Lewis points out, there are a great many critics who are not good readers—not true lovers of literature at all. In his unfinished essay, "On Criticism," Lewis cites the indicators of unliterary critics and anticipates the deplorable state of literary criticism I have already mentioned. He writes this essay from the point of view of an author of literary works, explaining what he has learned about the faults of critics (and, of course, of other unliterary readers). He cites these faults in order to avoid committing them in his own critical reading and writing. The primary fault he cites is the kind of misreading which results from critics imagining "that they know a great many facts relevant to a book which in reality they don't know."[13] And this is where theories come in, for literary theories are given when there is something we don't know and when we suppose that the missing knowledge is crucially relevant to our understanding the book. Lewis mentions three forms of theorizing in which critics often mistake their conjectures for the truth about the work of art. In each case he points out not only that these conjectures are usually mistaken, but also that they are—even when they happen to be correct—irrelevant to a literary assessment of the work. (1) Theories about the history of the work; that is, guesses about how, why, and when the work was written based on the historical circumstances in which it was composed. Even in cases where the critical reviewer of a book might be expected to make accurate guesses about the history of a work's composition (if, for example, the reviewer and the author are contemporaries), "he seldom guesses right." And furthermore, "in all these conjectures the reviewer's error has been quite gratuitous. He has been neglecting the thing he has been paid to do, and perhaps could do, in order to do something different. His business was to give information and to pass judgment on it. These guesses about its history are quite beside the mark."[14] (2) General psychological theories applied to the author that are supposed to explain how and why the work was written and provide the key to interpreting it. These sorts of theories are especially insidious, as they usually assume unconscious forces to be the motives behind the author's work. "By definition [the author] is unconscious of the things [the psychological critic] professes to discover. Therefore the more loudly the author disclaims them, the more right the critic will be; though, oddly enough, if the author admitted them, this would prove the critic right too."[15] These sorts of theorists discount the author's conscious motives, especially "the plastic impulse," as Lewis calls it—"the impulse to make a thing, to shape, to give unity, relief, contrast, pattern ... the impulse which chiefly caused the book to be written at all. They have, clearly, no such impulse themselves, and they do not suspect it in others. They seem to fancy that a book trickles out of one like a sigh or tear or automatic writing."[16] (3) Particular psychological hypotheses about why a certain work or a certain part of a work was written as it was. For example, the critic may say of a passage that it is "labored" or that it is "an afterthought," and then proceed to give a hypothetical explanation of why this is so. "The trouble is," says Lewis, "that certain critical terms—*inspired, perfunctory, painstaking, conventional*—imply a supposed history of composition. The critical vice I am talking about consists in yielding to the temptation they hold out and then, instead of telling us what is good and bad in a book, inventing stories about the process which led to the goodness and badness."[17] It is a case of mistaking the efficient causes for the formal causes. As with the other forms of criticism, this sort of theorizing is of no use because it is irrelevant to judging the artistic worth of the work.

These forms of criticism are, it seems to me, even more prominent today than when Lewis wrote his essay. On the one hand, we see some critics applying a particular theory of interpretation *over all literature*. That is, they apply the theory *a priori*; not just on *particular* works of literature. To apply a theory universally like this effectively ignores the question of what an author consciously and deliberately intends. Even if the author admits, for example, that he or she intended the work to be a political tool, the admission would be nothing more than a confirmation of what a feminist or Marxist critic thinks is necessarily true in any case. A Freudian critic "knows" in advance what to look for in any novel or poem: the unconscious struggle between the desires of the id and the imperatives of the superego. Pragmatist theories that deny that any work of literature has a determinate (or determinable) meaning are also applied universally, dismissing (as irrelevant) the question of what an author consciously and deliberately means to do or to show. Furthermore, the universal application of a theory ignores or dismisses the distinction between the intentions, desires, passions, beliefs, and aims *of the author* and those *of the subject* (i.e., the person or object from whose 'point of view' the story or poem is written). Obviously, there can be many nested points of view, none of which necessarily tell us anything about the author's own point of view. To give an example, a novelist might include a character—or even write the entire novel from the point of view of a character—whose way of life *can* be best understood in terms of Freudian analysis. But this does not imply that the author himself can be best understood in those terms, or that the author is (consciously or unconsciously) affirming the truth, effectiveness, or universal application of such an analysis. In fact, the author may be indirectly showing just the opposite.

On the other hand, a critical theory may be applied *a posteriori*—i.e., to particular works of literature, and to particular characters or subjects in literature. Samuel Beckett's plays, for example, may be best understood as displaying the indeterminacy of meaning, or of the incommensurability of meanings between various characters. But if one applies this very same theory to the plays themselves, then it's a wonder why one would pay any attention to them at all—and why Beckett would write anything at all. It would be absurd to do so! Even if the characters within the plays portray lives lived in accordance with the theory, this does not (and, logically, *cannot*) imply that Beckett himself thinks such a theory is, or ought to be, true or beautiful or good. Nor does it imply that Beckett thinks all works of art ought to be interpreted in terms of that theory. Still, the application of theory at this level is less harmful than the *a priori* application, for it makes allowances for the differences between individual works of literature, as well as differences between authors and their literary subjects.

Clearly, much of modern literary criticism is of the first sort, the *a priori* universal application of a theory. That is, all works of literature are read through the lens of a certain pseudo-scientific theory in order to determine the "meaning(s)" (if any) of that work. There are, of course, all sorts of critical theories that are applied in this *a priori* manner, but the common element in all of them is, as we've seen, the use of a *theory*: you cannot read or think critically unless you have a "theory" by which to "interpret" the literature. Having so many different theoretical approaches to "understanding" works of literature has its advantages—it is certainly a boon to the job market for professors and critics of literature—but it ignores the possibility that the author is intentionally, creatively, and rationally *making art*, and that his rationale in making it is not to illustrate theory *x*. The author's meaning may be intentionally obscure, or ambiguous, or hidden, but that does not mean he does not know what he meant to say or show or make.

Furthermore, making the meaning of literature a matter for theory to decide also ignores the possibility that literature is, as Camus says, "a means of stirring the greatest number of people by offering them a privileged picture of common joys and sufferings,"[18] and that, as Solzhenitsyn says, "This art [of literature] can work a miracle: it can overcome man's detrimental peculiarity of learning only from his own experience, unaffected by others. From man to man, as he completes his brief spell on earth, art transfers the whole weight of an unfamiliar, lifelong experience with all of its hardships, its colors, its vitality, re-creating in the flesh an unknown experience and allowing us to possess it as our own."[19] But seeing a work of literature as simply an artifact or a tool will prevent it from working this miracle: only when it is experienced as *art*, as communicating something universal in the particular, something of eternal significance in the temporal—only then can we be said to be *reading* it for what it is.

And so, most importantly, there is something more that the theorists ignore by considering works of literature to be artifacts or tools. They ignore the importance of the literature's *affects*: its evocation of a reader's *passions*, and its capability to transform and shape those passions. It is because of this possible—and, in many cases all-too-actual—consequence of theory-driven criticism that Lewis suggests "a ten or twenty year's abstinence both from the reading and the writing of evaluative criticism."[20] The literature itself is both the end and the means of good reading, of literacy. For, as Lewis says,

> Literary experience heals the wound, without undermining the privilege, of individuality. There are mass emotions which heal the wound; but they destroy the privilege. In them our separate selves are pooled and we sink back into sub-individuality. But in reading great literature I become a thousand men and yet remain myself. Like the night sky in the Greek poem, I see with a myriad of eyes, but it is still I who see. Here, as in worship, in love, in moral action, and in knowing, I transcend myself; and I am never more myself than when I do.[21]

ENDNOTES

1 Notes: If any readers of this essay desire footnotes or endnotes, I have provided as few as possible, and most of which are just references.

2 What I say in this essay is specifically about literature and literary criticism. However, I suspect that the argument could be generalized to all the arts, more or less.

3 C.S. Lewis, *An Experiment in Criticism* (Cambridge: Cambridge University Press, 1961), 1.

4 Ibid., 2-3.

5 C.S. Lewis, *On Stories and Other Essays on Literature* (New York: Harcourt Brace Jovanovich, 1982), 121.

6 C.S. Lewis, *An Experiment in Criticism* (Cambridge: Cambridge University Press, 1961), 4.

7 Ibid., 88.

8 Plato, *Republic*, trans. G.M.A. Grube, 3rd edition. (Indianapolis: Hackett, 1992), 150.

9 I do enter this discussion in chapter 3 of an earlier book: Gene Fendt and David Rozema, *Platonic Errors: Plato, A Kind of Poet* (Westport, CT: Greenwood Press, 1998).

10 C.S. Lewis, *An Experiment in Criticism* (Cambridge: Cambridge University Press, 1961), 116.

11 Ibid., 121.

12 Ibid., 124.

13 C.S. Lewis, *On Stories and Other Essays on Literature* (New York: Harcourt Brace Jovanovich, 1982), 132.

14 Ibid., 133.

15 Ibid., 134.

16 Ibid., 134-5.

17 Ibid., 136.

18 Albert Camus, Nobel Prize Acceptance Speech (Stockholm: The Nobel Foundation, 1957).

19 Alexander Solzhenitsyn, Nobel Lecture, trans. F.D. Reeve (New York: Farrar, Straus and Giroux, 1972).

20 C.S. Lewis, *An Experiment in Criticism* (Cambridge: Cambridge University Press, 1961), 129.

21 Ibid., 140-1.

"The really important things": Music and Dance in C.S. Lewis

PETER J. SCHAKEL

C.S. Lewis's first friend, Arthur Greeves, was an accomplished pianist who also tried his hand at composing. His second friend, Owen Barfield, was a graceful dancer who considered dancing as a career. Lewis could not sing or play an instrument, and he could "dance no better than a centipede with wooden legs."[1] But he loved listening to music, live or recorded, and enjoyed watching others dance. The appeal of both to Lewis starts with appreciation of their aesthetic beauty. But their deeper appeal came from their aesthetic and imaginative impact as an image, or archetype, for the meaning they had collected over hundreds of years as authors Lewis loved dearly used them to depict a physical and metaphysical universe that Lewis emotionally longed for and spiritually lived in.

From his earliest years, music was one of the great pleasures of Lewis's life. Lewis does not say specifically when or how his education in music began, or what influenced the love of classical music which he and his brother shared from very early in their lives.[2] Presumably their father set an example by his own appreciation of music, as well as providing a gramophone and money for records. The boys attended concerts with their father, and corresponded with him about others that they couldn't attend jointly. Lewis wrote to his father on 2 February 1911, about a month after entering Cherbourg House in Malvern: "We had great fun this week, we went to the 'Messiah.' It was only an amateur performance, but still it was simply lovely," and his father wrote to him 17 December 1915, "I am sorry you are not home here tonight. John Harrison is singing the tenor of the Messiah and we might have gone."[3] Similarly, Lewis's father wrote to him 4 November 1912: "Next week we are promised an opera company. They are doing Carmen and Maritana and others that Warnie and you would rather like to hear. I am sorry that they did not postpone their visit till Xmas" (*Lewis Papers* 3.301).

Lewis and his brother, in their teens, were avid collectors of gramophone records. Lewis approached this interest with the thoroughness he would later devote to his scholarship: he received the monthly lists issued by various record companies—"gramophone catalogues were . . . one of my favorite forms of reading" (*SbyJ* 73)—and he ordered more records than he could afford to: "the bill is rather a staggerer . . . I am thinking of sending it out to my brother to pay."[4] He compared the performances on various records, and contributed to "The Leeborough Review," which Warren describes as consisting "almost entirely of reviews of new gramophone records."[5] He knew which records lasted longer than others (Odeon records "wear out in a month"—letter to Greeves, 1 June 1915; *CL* 1.127) and regularly asked Arthur about records he had purchased or would recommend ("Any new records?"—letter to Greeves, 22 May 1916; *CL* 1.183). But he also expressed concerns about the effects of relying too heavily on recorded music in developing one's knowledge and tastes: "Perhaps after all, the taste in music developed by a gramophone [sic] is a bad, artificial, exotic one" (letter to Greeves, 12 October 1915; *CL* 1.145); a gramophone "gives you opportunities of hearing things that you might otherwise never know: but . . . it teaches you to expect a standard of performance which you can't get . . . on the stage" (letter to Greeves, 8 February 1916; *CL* 1.164).

That early love of music appears throughout his long correspondence with Arthur Greeves, who shared many of Lewis's tastes in music. Lewis expresses his disappointment that his schoolmates at Malvern College show an "absolute lack of appreciation of anything like music or books" (5 June 1914; *CL* 1.159). Later in the year he finds the same to be true in Surrey as well: wherever he looks, it is only the few who can talk about "the really important things—literature, science, music & art" (20 October 1914; *CL* 1.84). The Kirkpatrick household, where Lewis was being tutored, was an exception. Mrs. Kirkpatrick was a good pianist who occasionally played for Lewis in the evenings, performing "some of Chopin's preludes, 'Chanson Triste,' Beethoven's Moonlight Sonata, Chopin's March Funebre, The Peer Gynt Suite & several other of our old favourites. Of course I do not know enough about music to be an authoritative critic, but she seemed to me to play with accuracy, taste & true feeling. So that there is added another source of attraction to Great Bookham" (letter to Greeves, 14 October 1914; *CL* 1.83-84). To Lewis in his younger years music was a really important thing, an art that reached to his emotional depths, that drove him "wild with delight" (12 October 1915; *CL* 1.145). In 1934 he tells Arthur about attending a concert of Beethoven, Debussy, Sibelius, and Elgar "which I enjoyed more than any I have ever heard" (26 December 1934; *CL* 2.151). The following year he writes that he has "seldom enjoyed anything more" than a magnificent performance of the *Ninth Symphony*: "How *tonic* Beethoven is, and how festal—one has the feeling of having taken part in the revelry of giants" (7 December 1935; *CL* 2.170). Ten years later he mentions being "greatly moved" by a gramophone performance of Gustav Holst's *The Planets* (26 December 1945; *CL* 2.693).[6]

His musical tastes ranged widely. He knew a great deal about opera and attended many performances, though his familiarity probably came mostly from records;[7] he mentioned, in addition to Wagner's works, *Faust, Carmen, Aïda, The Magic Flute,* and *Tosca.* The *Lewis Papers* include an essay Lewis wrote at Cherbourg House around 1912 (when he was thirteen) on Richard Wagner, which begins with a brief history of the development of the opera and how Wagner influenced its development.[8] In 1914 he sketches out the plot for an opera, *Loki Bound,* based on Norse mythology, for which Arthur was to have written the score (letter to Greeves, 6 October 1914; *CL* 1.75-78). He also liked and referred to a wide variety of orchestral music, and urged Arthur in 1935 to buy "big works (symphonies etc)" and "never play them except in their entirety" (letter to Greeves, 29 December 1935; *CL* 2.175). He describes at length, in two different letters, his enjoyment of Sunday evenings at the Kilns in the early 1930s, when, after a quiet supper, Lewis, Warren, Mrs. Moore, and Papworth the dog would gather in the study and listen to a complete symphony on Warnie's excellent gramophone—"I am sure one gains enormously by always hearing one symphony as a whole and nothing else" (letter to Greeves, 25 March 1933; *CL* 2.101; also 5 November 1933; *CL* 2.128).[9] "Violin solos were never much in my line," he informed Arthur (12 October 1915; *CL* 1.145), and he noted in his diary that "the organ is a thing I cannot learn to like."[10] But he was very fond of the piano as a solo instrument: "One sort of music still holds me as much, or indeed more than ever—piano music" (letter to Greeves, 15 February 1917; *CL* 1.277); urging Arthur to look up the Chopin piece he likes so well, the *21st Prelude,* he asks if it is not "the best music in the world" (18 July 1916; *CL* 1.216).

It may seem surprising that the Christian Lewis did not care for church music. "Hymns were disagreeable to me" (*SbyJ* 234). Hymn singing and organ playing, he wrote in 1956, "set my teeth on edge" (letter to Mrs. Halvorson, March 1956; *CL* 3.731). His preference was to attend "said" services, because for Lewis hymns were the "dead wood" of a service (letter to Eric Routley, 16 July 1946; *CL* 2.720). Lewis disliked hymns partly because, he said, the lyrics are not good poetry—they often are sentimental and "cheap" and frequently contain "confused or erroneous thought and unworthy sentiment."[11]—and because the airs, like those of certain popular songs, are "vile and ugly."[12] When Screwtape mentions the "shabby little book containing corrupt texts of a number of religious lyrics, mostly bad, and in very small print,"[13] he reflects closely Lewis's own view: "fifth-rate poems set to sixth-rate music."[14] He commented further that the English, unlike the Welsh and Germans, are not good singers (letter to Routley, 21 September 1946; *CL* 2.740)—therefore, the singing in English churches is not the offering of "our natural gifts at their highest to God," but people "shout[ing] their favourite hymns.... What I... chiefly desire in church are fewer, better, and shorter hymns; especially fewer."[15]

Beyond that he questioned the spiritual value of church music—whether it glorifies God or is only an aesthetic rather than truly spiritual aspect of worship. He had such an aesthetic experience when he, Arthur, and Maureen Moore attended a choral evensong at New College in 1922, at a time when he did not consider himself a Christian and listened to the music as if at a concert; he "enjoyed the music immensely, especially the psalms and Stanford's *Magnificat:* I wondered why I had never troubled to go before" (*All My Road* 71). He also feared that the way church music, whether highbrow or lowbrow, can alienate and divide a congregation may outweigh its potential benefits (letter to Eric Routley, 21 September 1946; *CL* 2.740). He acknowledged, however, that such difference in tastes can be an opportunity for exercising spiritual humility: it can "teach us humility and charity towards simple low-brow people who may be better Christians than ourselves. I naturally *loathe* nearly all hymns: the face, and life, of the charwoman in the next pew who revels in them, teach me that good taste in poetry or music are [sic] *not* necessary to salvation" (letter to Mary Van Deusen, 7 December 1950; *CL* 3.69).

Music was, however, important to Lewis's life in a sense closely related to religion. Music was an important source of the intense longings experienced throughout his life, for which he used the German term *Sehnsucht* (*SbyJ* 7). In the preface added to the third edition of *The Pilgrim's Regress,* Lewis distinguishes this from ordinary longings in two ways: first, that though the longing is acute and even painful, the mere wanting is felt to be somehow a delight; and second, that there is mystery about the *object* of this desire—the things that stir the longings are not what we in fact are longing for.[16] "The books or the music in which we thought the beauty was located will betray us if we trust to them; it was not *in* them, it only came *through* them, and what came through them was longing.... For they are not the thing itself; they are only the scent of a flower we have not found, the echo of a tune we have not heard, news from a country we have never yet visited."[17]

Music is one of the recurring images associated with such longing,[18] particularly the kind of music Samuel Pepys described as "so sweet that it ravished me and, indeed, in a word, did wrap up my soul so that it made me really sick."[19] Lewis mentions several such musical experiences in letters to Arthur Greeves. In response to hearing Mrs. Kirkpatrick play some preludes of Chopin, he writes: "Aren't they wonderful? ... They are so passionate, so hopeless, I could almost cry over them: they are unbearable" (*CL* 1.174). His next letter mentions how some combinations of words can give "a thrill like music" (*CL* 1.175). On Christmas Eve, 1929, "the glorious windy noise of the bells overhead, the firelight & candlelight, and the beautiful music of unaccompanied boys' voices, really carried me out of myself" (*CL* 1.852).

His spiritual autobiography *Surprised by Joy* tells the story of how Lewis slowly, step by step, learned that the longing is a desire for God implanted by God to draw us to him, a desire to be with God, in the presence of God, thus a longing for heaven. Not surprisingly, then, music is frequently associated with heaven and the longing for heaven. In *Mere Christianity,* explaining the imagery used for heaven in the Bible, Lewis writes: "Musical instruments are mentioned because for many people (not all) music is the thing known in the present life which most strongly suggests ecstasy and infinity."[20] In *The Pilgrim's Regress* John hears "the sound of a musical instrument ... very sweet and very short ... so high and strange that he thought it was very far away, further than a star" and sees "a calm sea, and in the sea an island." He experiences "a sweetness and a pang so piercing" that he longs to hear the music again and to go to that island (*PR* 24).

He undertakes a long journey in pursuit of his desire, and learns that the island can be reached only through death. What John longed for was heaven. Small wonder, then, that the tempter Screwtape warns Wormwood against "that detestable art which the humans call Music," which expresses joy and is, therefore, "disgusting and a direct insult to the realism, dignity, and austerity of Hell" (*SL* 57-58). "Music and silence—how I detest them both!" Screwtape fumes, and rejoices that great strides have been taken on earth toward replacing music with noise (*SL* 113-14).

The depth of music in Lewis's life and thinking is indicated by how frequently he used music in similes and metaphors throughout his writing. Only a few, varied examples can be cited here. He wrote to Arthur Greeves in 1915, "On Saturday I met the prettiest girl I have ever seen in my life. . . . [S]he is just like that grave movement in the Hungarian Rhapsody (or is it the 'dance'?) that I love so much" (letter to Greeves, 8 June 1915; *CL* 1.129). The early morning aromas on Malacandra "did to the sense of smell what high, sharp violin notes do to the ear."[21] Wine, Orual learns, can make sorrows "seem glorious and noble, like sad music."[22] Peggy's clothes, bath salts, and general voluptuousness "were a huge overture to an opera in which she had no interest at all."[23] The title "Transposition" is an important musical allusion, and references to music run throughout the sermon, as for example: "If you are making a piano version of a piece originally scored for an orchestra, then the same piano notes which represent flutes in one passage must also represent violins in another" (*Transposition and Other Addresses* 13-14).

Lewis frequently uses similes and metaphors involving music to clarify points in his literary criticism. Thus, for example, he says that looking for the "point" of a story "may prevent one from getting the real effect of the story in itself—like listening too hard for the words in singing which isn't meant to be listened to that way (like an anthem in a chorus)" (letter to Phyllida, 18 December 1953; *CL* 3. 388). Similarly, he comments that the medieval universe can be compared both to a great building and "to a fugue—the orderly and varied reiteration of the same 'subject.'"[24] To convey the difference between *danger* and *danger from giants,* he suggests: "turn it into music and you will feel the difference at once."[25] In comparing English poetry with Old French, he writes, "Ours is 'all instruments'; theirs is the 'lonely flute'" (*AofL* 135). The *Parlement of Foules,* he suggests, is "like Mozartian music" (*AofL* 174), and Spenser's *Epithalamion* is extraordinary because of its ability to express joy: "Music has often reached that jocundity; poetry, seldom."[26] A romance or fantasy story "is in a way more like a symphony than a novel. . . . The images are in every possible relation of contrast, mutual support, development, variation, half-echo, and the like, just as the musical themes are."[27]

Music appears prominently in Lewis's lyric poetry. It runs through his earliest collection, *Spirits in Bondage,* as a sustained motif, in titles—"French Nocturne," "Irish Nocturne," "Song of the Pilgrims," "Song," "Hymn (For Boys' Voices)," and "Lullaby"—and in the imagery and figures of many poems.[28] Later poems display the same interest, in titles—"Pindar Sang," "Evolutionary Hymn," "Science-Fiction Cradlesong,"

"Coronation March," "Angel's Song," "Evensong," and "Narnian Suite," with its subtitles "March for Strings, Kettledrums, and Sixty-three Dwarfs" and "March for Drum, Trumpet, and Twenty-one Giants"—and in action, imagery, and figures.[29]

References to music are prominent throughout Lewis's fiction, from *The Pilgrim's Regress* (the haunting sound of music that draws John into the woods and the songs of Mr. Halfways that evoke for John a vision of the Island, the avant-garde music of the Clevers in Eschropolis, and the songs of praise, worship, and encouragement sung on their journey by the pilgrims), to *Till We Have Faces,* which starts with the Fox attempting to teach fourteen young women to sing a Greek bridal hymn at the King's wedding (they sang "very badly" [*TWHF* 20]) and ends with the voice of the god, which Orual earlier described as sweet, "like a bird singing on the branch above a hanged man" (*TWHF* 182).

The use of music in the Ransom trilogy and in the Chronicles of Narnia is more frequent and sustained than it is elsewhere. On Malacandra the *hrossa* are great singers (*OSP* 186), and Ransom records the words of their song at Hyoi's funeral (213-15). He later recalls with longing "the sound of their singing"—"great hollow hound-like music from enormous throats, deeper than Chaliapin, a 'warm, dark noise'" (*OSP* 255)—and the haunting qualities of the funeral music: "They go down, singing, to the edge of the lake. The music fills the wood with its vibration, though it is so soft that I can hardly hear it: it is like dim organ music" (261).

Perelandra, with its operatic tone and movement, is filled with music: "You will see, if you look, how *operatic* the whole building up of the climax is in *Perelandra*" (letter to Charles A. Brady, 29 October 1944; *CL* 2.630).[30] Ransom awakes to hear Tinidril singing to herself in a low voice, and when she tells Ransom that she is the Mother of the planet, he seems not just to hear her voice, but "a phantom sense of vast choral music was all about him."[31] Perelandrian thunder is "like the playing of a heavenly tambourine" (*Per* 143). Ransom's body, as he prepares for physical conflict with the Un-man, is an "instrument . . . tuned up to concert pitch" (*Per* 176). Of his long period of convalescence, after destroying the Un-man, he remembers a song: "it floated through his sleep and was the first sound at every waking. It was formless as the song of a bird, yet it was not a bird's voice. As a bird's voice is to a flute, so this was to a cello: low and ripe and tender, full-bellied, rich and golden-brown" (*Per* 213).

And in *That Hideous Strength* the descent of the spirit of Mercury leads the St. Anne's group to "such talk—such eloquence, such melody (song could have added nothing to it)."[32] And later the spirit of Jupiter can be captured only faintly by such symbols as the pealing of bells and the blowing of trumpets, or the first beginning of music in the hall of a high king (404).

At least forty-five references to music appear in the Narnian Chronicles, in many different contexts, creating a wide variety of imaginative effects.[33] Music appears first when Tumnus the faun, in *The Lion, the Witch and the Wardrobe,* pulls a strange little flute from its case and begins to play for Lucy. The tune he plays moves her deeply: it makes her want to "cry and laugh and dance and go to sleep all at the same time."[34] In *The Lion, the Witch and the Wardrobe* music is associated with Aslan. When Mr. Beaver first mentions the name Aslan, each of the children feels something jump inside: "Susan felt as if some . . . delightful strain of music had just floated by her" (54). Later, as the two beavers and the three children approach the wonderful pavilion near the stone table, they hear music, made on stringed instruments by a group of Dryads and Naiads; it is the music that leads them to turn and see "what they had come to see," the great Lion (101). Near the end of the story, as Narnia celebrates the coronation of the four Pevensie children with a great feast, the music inside the castle Cair Paravel is answered by "the voices of the mermen and mermaids swimming close to the castle steps and singing in honour of their new Kings and Queens" (148).

Music occurs throughout *Prince Caspian,* including poignant memories of their previous visit, a year (or a thousand years) before. Susan recalls "the mer-people singing in the sea," and Lucy remembers "when we had the musicians up in the rigging [of the *Splendour Hyaline*] playing flutes so that it sounded like music out of the sky" (15, 93). As six mice carry the battered body of Reepicheep toward Aslan on a litter, "their leader piped on his slender pipe a melancholy tune" (173). In *The Voyage of the "Dawn Treader"* the sailors sing catches in the evenings, and Ramandu and his daughter greet the dawn with a high, almost shrill, very beautiful "early morning kind of song" (21, 172). And Digory's mother, in *The Magician's Nephew,* after she was healed by the Narnian apple, had the old piano tuned and "took up her singing again."[35]

Music is invoked or mentioned at least eighteen times in *The Silver Chair.* The music motif begins as Eustace and Jill, upon going through the door in the stone wall around Experiment House, see a blaze of sunshine and hear birds making a riotous noise: "but it was much more like music—rather advanced music which you don't quite take in at the first hearing—than birds' songs ever are in our world" (10). They are on Aslan's mountain, we learn at the end of the story, which *The Last Battle* tells us is connected to, or is the outskirts of, heaven. The intricate ("advanced") harmonies of the music—even, in the heavenly realm, of birds' songs—captures the nature of that place, with its sense of order, harmony, and joy.

The music motif continues as Jill floats down from the mountains of Aslan's Country toward Cair Paravel and hears "a sound of music" honoring the old, frail king as he boards the tall ship; then trumpets sound as the ship moves away from the quay (*SC* 24, 30). The Green Witch plays a musical instrument rather like a mandolin, and her music has a hypnotic power (148). As the children, Puddleglum, and the prince escape from the Underworld, Rilian "whistled as he rode, and sang snatches of an old song about Corin Thunder-fist of Archenland" (166). And the final paragraph of the book tells how Narnians, on hot summer days, would go down through that opening with ships and lanterns and "sail to and fro, singing, on the cool, dark underground sea" (208). In all these references except for the Witch's hypnotic strumming and "soft, musical laugh" (148), the presence of music signals freedom and well-being, while its absence accompanies bondage and disorder.

The use of abundant references to music in the Ransom books and the Chronicles of Narnia is one of Lewis's ways to weave into them qualities of the image constructed by the great thinkers of the Middle Ages, as Lewis describes in *The Discarded Image*, to enable them to comprehend the universe, "the medieval synthesis itself, the whole organisation of their theology, science, and history into a single, complex, harmonious mental Model of the Universe."[36] Its origins were not in the physical world but in books, as medieval thinkers drew upon *auctours* and wove what they borrowed into a new and intricate fabric (*DI* 5). The result was an "imagined universe" (13), a universe of triads and plenitude (43-44); a universe composed of the four elements (4); a universe filled not with inert spheres reflecting borrowed light but with living beings, "planets as well as gods" (105); a universe full of light and resonant with music, moving dancelike constantly in expression of and response to the "intellectual love" of God (112, 115). It was a universe created—invented—by the imagination: the "supreme medieval work of art" (12). It was a work of the characteristically medieval "realising imagination,"[37] one which provides abundant close-up details to "make sure that we see exactly what [the artist] saw" (206). "Few constructions of the imagination seem to me," says Lewis, "to have combined splendour, sobriety, and coherence in the same degree" (216).

Lewis uses music in a dramatic and significant way to convey an image of the universe in the creation scene of *The Magician's Nephew*. In the absolute darkness of the unknown place they fall into, Digory, Polly, Uncle Andrew, and Jadis hear a voice begin to sing, "the most beautiful noise [Digory] had ever heard, . . . so beautiful he could hardly bear it." The voice was joined by other voices, more voices than one could count, singing "in harmony with it, but far higher up the scale: cold, tingling, silvery voices." A moment later the blackness overhead was blazing with thousands and thousands of stars. Digory was quite certain "that it was the stars themselves who were singing, and that it was the First Voice, the deep one, which had made them appear and made them sing" (87-88).

Two things seem striking about that passage in a book for children. One is the specific detail about music it employs. By assuming readers know about "harmony" and "scale," it affirms music as something that one should know about, and that can be experienced as almost unbearably beautiful. The other is the way the use of music enables Lewis to elaborate his creation story in ways that fire the imaginations of young readers, enabling them to hear the process as well as to visualize it step by step: "The Voice rose and rose, till all the air was shaking with it. And just as it swelled to the mightiest and most glorious sound it had yet produced, the sun rose" (*MN* 90). Then the lion sang a new song, "softer and more lilting than the song by which he had called up the stars and the sun; a gentle, rippling music. And as he walked and sang the valley grew green with grass," spreading out from the lion like a pool and running "up the sides of the little hills like a wave" (92). Then the song changed again: "It was more like what we should call a tune, but it was also far wilder. It made you want to run and jump and climb." This song made the ground swell into humps of different sizes and from each hump burst an animal, with vivid detail describing their emergence: "Butterflies fluttered. Bees got to work on the flowers as if they hadn't a second to lose. But the greatest moment of all was when the biggest hump broke like a small earthquake and out came the sloping back, the large, wise head, and the four baggy-trousered legs of an Elephant" (100, 101-2).

By having the lion *sing* the song of creation, Lewis has quietly, unobtrusively put young readers in touch with an ancient tradition regarding the universe. In western culture music has long served as an image of the orderliness and harmony of the universe, particularly through the music of the spheres, the perpetual "sweet, immeasurable sound" that keeps the concentric hollow globes circling the earth in an orderly way.[38] The image is grounded in Plato's adaptation of Pythagorean notions about the beauty and proportion of numbers to the physical universe: "On the upper surface of each circle is a siren, who goes round with them, hymning a single tone or note. The eight together form one harmony."[39] By association with the myth of Amphion's use of the lyre to erect a wall around Thebes, charming rocks and moving them into their proper places, music became also a symbol of creation, bringing order to what previously had been chaotic. Thus, in the divine creative act, the elements, scattered about "without form, and void" (Gen. 1:2), were drawn into order by the harmonizing power of music.

The opening of John Dryden's "A Song for St Cecilia's Day, 1687" expresses this myth powerfully:

From Harmony, from heav'nly Harmony
This universal Frame began.
When Nature underneath a heap
Of jarring Atomes lay,
And cou'd not heave her Head,
The tuneful Voice was heard from high,
Arise ye more than dead.
Then cold, and hot, and moist, and dry,
In order to their stations leap,
And MUSICK's pow'r obey.[40]

In Dryden's ode and Lewis's creation account, the beauty, orderliness, and harmony of music are integrally related to the deepest structures of the universe—not that those structures are like music, but that they are formed of music and by music. Written in an era when order, harmony, and especially purposefulness are widely denied in the nature of things, Lewis's story affirms them, not through philosophical argument or scientific demonstration, but through the imaginativeness of story and myth.

As music characterized the creation of Narnia, music also signals its dissolution, and that perhaps is as it should be: the harmony and order established by music now crumble into dissonance and disorder. The crumbling is signaled by a final note, the sound of the last trumpet: "Then the great giant raised a horn to his mouth.... After that—quite a bit later, because sound travels so slowly—they heard the sound of the horn: high and terrible, yet of a strange, deadly beauty."[41] This is the only reference to music in *The Last Battle*, and it too forms a connection to the myth Lewis is drawing upon. As the opening section of "A Song for St. Cecilia's Day, 1687" illuminates Lewis's handling of his creation story, so its concluding grand chorus, both Dryden's words and Handel's magnificent setting, illuminates his handling of Narnia's return to chaos:

> As from the pow'r of sacred Lays
> The Spheres began to move,
> And sung the great Creator's praise
> To all the bless'd above;
> So when the last and dreadful hour
> This crumbling Pageant shall devour,
> The TRUMPET shall be heard on high,
> The Dead shall live, the Living die,
> And MUSICK shall untune the Sky.

Samuel Johnson, an 18th Century writer whom Lewis loved and whom he resembles in several ways, found the image of music untuning the sky in the final lines "so awful in itself that it can owe little to poetry."[42] The account of night falling on Narnia is similarly powerful and disturbing. What makes it bearable, perhaps, especially for young readers, is that these are not the final words of the story. Night is followed by light, and the characters move further up and further in, to the real Narnia which is the true object of their desires.

Dance played a much smaller role in Lewis's life than music did. He had no fondness for it as a participatory activity. In his late fifties, he recounted with deep feeling his unpleasant memories of childhood dances:

> It was the custom of the neighborhood to give parties which were really dances for adults but to which, none the less, mere schoolboys and schoolgirls were asked.... To me these dances were a torment... the discomfort of one's Eton suit and stiff shirt, the aching feet and burning head, and the mere weariness of being kept up so many hours after one's usual bedtime. Even adults, I fancy, would not find an evening party very endurable without the attraction of sex and the attraction of alcohol; and how a small boy who can neither flirt nor drink should be expected to enjoy prancing about on a polished floor till the small hours of the morning, is beyond my conception. (*SbyJ* 46-47)

Nor did he always enjoy viewing it as a spectator: in 1923 Lewis wrote in his diary that he had turned down a free seat at a folk dancing, because "I really [do] not understand that sort of thing: I could be said to like dancing only as a girl who picnicked in a ruin could be said to like architecture" (*All My Road* 240). Thus, he wrote earlier, after watching a young woman dance, "She seemed good to me but I know nothing of dancing" (*All My Road* 88). But he did enjoy Barfield dancing in a ballet program in 1922: "What struck me particularly was Barfield's dancing in the rowdier passages: a terrific, infectious gaiety about him and you'd think he cd. never be tired" (*All My Road* 34).[43]

Despite his lack of enthusiasm for Dance as a social activity, references to dance occur throughout Lewis's works. Dancing appears frequently as a metaphor, though less frequently than music does. For example, in *The Allegory of Love* he writes, "In Montgomerie we seem to hear the scrape of the fiddle and the beat of dancing on the turf: in Googe, the ticking of a metronome" (259). In *The Great Divorce* the sound of the gigantic waterfall was "like giants' laughter: like the revelry of a whole college of giants together laughing, dancing, singing, roaring at their high works."[44] Numerous figurative examples appear in the Chronicles of Narnia: "'What is it, Aslan?' said Lucy, her eyes dancing and her feet wanting to dance"; "the reflections of the sunlit water dancing on the ceiling of her cabin"; "The water danced brightly in the early sunlight"; "The waterfall keeps the pool always dancing and bubbling and churning."[45] Attempting to convey to Arthur Greeves the effect of reading the *Paradiso,* he describes it in part as "like a slow dance" (13? January 1930; *CL* 1.857). In *Till We Have Faces,* as Orual reaches the top of the holy mountain, an inner voice seems to ask her, "Why should your heart not dance?" and the beauty of all that is around her makes her feel as if she had misjudged the world: "it seemed kind, and laughing, as if its heart also danced" (104); in the following chapter, Psyche asks her the same question (113).

Lewis's most meaningful figurative use of dance is as a metaphor for community, including the divine nature as a community.[46] Lewis, attempting in *Mere Christianity* to clarify the difficult and abstract doctrine of the Trinity, says that "the words 'God is love' have no real meaning unless God contains at least two Persons," since love is an activity between different individuals. Then he continues: "in Christianity God is not a static thing—not even a person—but a dynamic, pulsating activity, a life, almost a kind of drama. Almost, if you will not think me irreverent, a kind of dance" (138). Groping for a way to express the inexpressible, Lewis turns to an image which has divine associations for him because of its archetypal overtones, and which readily unites his understanding of God with the Western cultural myth. That it should even occur to him to compare God to a dance can be understood from Plato. Plato emphasizes that the act of creation involves correspondences between the world and its pattern, and the creation and the Creator. If creation can be viewed as a dance, so too, by correspondence, can the Creator: Lewis simply follows through and concretizes what is implicit in the *Timaeus.*[47] And in doing so he relates the nature of God to the attributes of the world view dance has traditionally imaged: dance is active, orderly, and hierarchical, and Lewis deliberately attaches those qualities to God.

Dancing as a social activity occurs or is mentioned at least thirty times in the Chronicles of Narnia. Tumnus tells Lucy, in *The Lion, the Witch and the Wardrobe,* about midnight dances when the Nymphs and Dryads "came out to dance with the Fauns" (12). Such a midnight dance takes place in *Prince Caspian,* with Fauns dancing and Caspian, and then even the dwarf Trumpkin, joining in (67). On a different night Lucy sees the trees move in and out through one another "as if in a complicated country dance" (114). Later, Bacchus and Silenus lead a romp across the countryside freeing those who have been held by the constraints of Miraz (165-70). Still later Bacchus, Silenus, and the Maenads join in "a magic dance of plenty" (177). Aravis in *The Horse and His Boy* dances before her father (31), and Shasta, after he becomes Prince Cor, complains that he will have to be educated and learn "reading and writing and heraldry and dancing" (178). And in *The Last Battle* Jewel the Unicorn tells Jill about whole centuries in which "notable dances and feasts" were "the only things that could be remembered" (84). These allusions bring dance before readers repeatedly, but mostly unobtrusively, as a beautiful and meaningful artistic expression, suitable for boys and men as well as girls and women.

Lewis uses dance in the Chronicles not just as an activity human beings use for enjoyment or to express joy. In the western cultural tradition dance, like music, has been used since classical times as an image of order and harmony in the universe.[48] Dance too is part of an ancient creation myth. Seventeenth-century poet Andrew Marvell's retelling of how Amphion constructed the walls of Thebes illustrates the easy transition from the one myth to the other: "The rougher Stones, unto his Measures hew'd,/ Dans'd up in order from the Quarryes rude."[49] Such use of dance as a cosmological symbol, like the use of music, can be traced to Plato, who, in the *Timaeus,* described how the Creator fashioned the world after its eternal pattern:

> When all things were in disorder God created in each thing in relation to itself, and in all things in relation to each other, all the measures and harmonies which they could possibly receive....
>
> The fixed stars were created, to be divine and eternal animals, ever-abiding and revolving after the same manner and on the same spot; and the other stars which reverse their motion.... Vain would be the attempt to tell all the figures of them circling as in dance,... and to say which of these deities in their conjunctions meet, and which of them are in opposition, and in what order they get behind and before one another.[50]

Used recurrently in the middle ages, especially in Neoplatonic writers, the image received its finest articulation in Sir John Davies's poem *Orchestra,* published in 1596; Lewis wrote of it, "Davies's *Orchestra* gives us the right picture of the Elizabethan or

Henrican universe; tingling with anthropomorphic life, dancing, ceremonial, a festival not a machine."[51] Davies's narrator, Antinous, urging Penelope to dance with him, gives this explanation of the origin of dancing:

> *Dauncing* (bright Lady) then began to be,
> When the first seedes whereof the world did spring,
> The Fire, Ayre, Earth and Water did agree,
> By Loves perswasion, Natures mighty King,
> To leave their first disordred combating;
> And in a daunce such measure to observe,
> As all the world their motion should preserve.
>
> Since when they still are carried in a round,
> And changing come one in anothers place,
> Yet doe they neyther mingle nor confound,
> But every one doth keepe the bounded space
> Wherein the daunce doth bid it turne or trace:
> This wondrous myracle did Love devise,
> For Dauncing is Loves proper exercise.[52]

It is to this tradition that Doctor Cornelius refers when he assures Caspian that the stars Tarva and Alambil are not going to collide: "Nay, dear Prince, . . . the great lords of the upper sky know the steps of their dance too well for that" (*PC* 40). This tradition is invoked when Ramandu, the star "at rest" in *The Voyage of the Dawn Treader,* anticipates his reentry into "the great dance" (*VDT* 175).

The appeal in such images of dance, for Lewis, is the world view dance affirms. It assumes that the universe is a *cosmos,* a harmonious system, and that human life, as an integral part of that whole, also has order, unity, and meaning. The universe is not engaged in "modern shuffling" (*THS* 404)—unpatterned and individualistic; rather, it echoes the stately movement of the chorus in a Greek tragedy or the stylized formality of the country dance in an Austen novel: "The ladies and gentlemen ranged as two long rows facing one another, whilst the couples at the extreme ends danced down the set."[53] Lewis accepted that world view—he responded to such imagery with an empathy impossible for most of his colleagues at Oxford and for the modern world as a whole.

Some of the most meaningful passages employing such universal imagery are ones where Lewis combines music and dance, echoing his own thought that the fullest image for capturing the medieval Model is "a dance, a festival, a symphony, a ritual, a carnival, or all these in one."[54] Music and dancing combine as central images in the unfinished poem which Walter Hooper entitled *The Nameless Isle,* Lewis's retelling of *The Magic Flute.* The story reaches its climax as the dwarf, by playing on the golden flute and dancing, brings the marble statues and the marbled lady back to life.[55] Similarly, in the poem "Pindar Sang," the poet sang "Light as a flight of tumbling birds / Was the dipping and soaring of his syllables" while the chorus of beautiful young men "danced his ode" (Lewis, *Poems* 15).

In *The Great Divorce*, as Sarah Smith approaches, she is accompanied by bright Spirits who danced and scattered flowers and a band of singers and musicians: "If I could remember their singing and write down the notes," says the narrator, "no man who read that score would ever grow sick or old" (97). And as she walks away, bright spirits come forward to receive her, singing a paraphrase of Psalm 91 (109-10). Similarly, in *Perelandra* following Tinidril's first resistance of the Un-man's advances, Ransom senses the triumphant celebration of the planet, or the universe, "festal revelry and dance and splendour poured into him . . . in such fashion that it could not be . . . thought of except as music" (121).

In *That Hideous Strength* two bookend-like passages highlight the interrelated significance of music and dance: in the first, near the end of Ransom's initial meeting with Jane, as they discuss obedience and marriage, Ransom says, "But you see that obedience and rule are more like a dance than a drill—specially between man and woman where the roles are always changing" (181). The dance metaphor draws together a key theme of the novel. Mark and Jane's marriage serves as a paradigm of the larger struggle of independence against authority throughout the novel: a struggle which involves the St. Anne's group and the N.I.C.E. as well as Jane and Mark personally. Mark and Jane must learn that obedience is different from servility and that authority is different from arbitrary tyranny, and then learn that "equality is not the deepest thing" (179). Jane before meeting Ransom would have been deeply offended by this impingement upon her independence. But her response after meeting Ransom was a joy best expressed in music: "She reflected with surprise how long it was since music had played any part in her life, and resolved to listen to many chorales by Bach on the gramophone that evening" (184).

The second passage in *That Hideous Strength* occurs as the Oyarsas of Viritrilbia, Perelandra, Malacandra, Lurga, and Glund descend on St. Anne's to impart their powers to Merlin, to prepare him for the decisive confrontation with Belbury. As the Glund-Oyarsa, King of Kings, the Oyarsa of Jupiter, approaches, the members of the company at St. Anne's waiting in the kitchen respond to his coming with a festive combination of music and dance:

> Arthur—the only musician among them—was bidden to get out his fiddle. The chairs were pushed back, the floor cleared. They danced. . . . It seemed to each that the room was filled with kings and queens, that the wildness of their dance expressed heroic energy, and its quieter movements had seized the very spirit behind all noble ceremonies. (404)

And in the Blue Room above, Ransom and Merlin are "momentarily caught up into the *Gloria* which those five excellent Natures perpetually sing" (405), making their contributions to the music of the spheres.

Even more festive than the dancing in the kitchen is a combination of music and dance in *The Silver Chair*, as Jill Pole emerges from the Underworld and finds herself back in Narnia. The first sound she hears is "the music of four fiddles, three flutes, and a drum" and the first sight she makes out is the Great Snow Dance (185). Fauns and dryads were "doing a dance—a dance with so many complicated steps and figures that it took you some time to understand it.... Circling round and round the dancers was a ring of Dwarfs.... As they circled round they were all diligently throwing snowballs,... . throwing them through the dance in such perfect time with the music and with such perfect aim that if all the dancers were in exactly the right places at exactly the right moments, no one would be hit. This is called the Great Snow Dance and it is done every year in Narnia on the first moonlit night when there is snow on the ground" (185-86). The placement and effect of the dance are striking: the Underworld from which Jill is emerging had been a totally repressive regime, where a tyrant allowed no freedom and citizens (or slaves) forgot how to "make a joke or dance a jig" (172). There was order, but it was the mechanized orderliness of a forced march, not the voluntary interactive patternings of a dance. The first thing Jill sees as she emerges is a dance that epitomizes Narnian society, a perfect blending of order and freedom. "Jill felt she could have fainted with delight; and the music—the wild music, intensely sweet and yet just the least bit eerie too, and full of good magic... —made her feel it all the more" (186).

An even more magnificent combination of music and dance appears in the final chapter of *Perelandra*. Near the end of his stay on Perelandra, Ransom, confused by the complexity of all that he has experienced since his arrival on the planet, doubting for the moment the coherence of things, fearing that all is mere chance or chaos, is introduced to the nature of the universe itself. The passage begins as a litany, a series of beautifully poetic speeches in which the voices of Ransom, Tor, and Tinidril (the King and Queen of the planet), and the oyarsas of Perelandra and Malacandra "followed one another—if, indeed, they did not all take place at the same time—like the parts of a music into which all five of them had entered as instruments" (246). The twenty sections of the litany celebrate the Dance and the Lord of the Dance. Christ is the center of the Dance, but is constantly moving so that the center is everywhere and everywhere is the center:

> Each grain is at the centre. The Dust is at the centre. The Worlds are at the centre. The beasts are at the centre. The ancient peoples are there. The race that sinned is there. Tor and Tinidril are there. The gods are there also. Blessed be He!
>
> Where Maleldil is, there is the centre. He is in every place....

> Each thing was made for Him. He is the centre. Because we are with Him, each of us is at the centre. (249)[56]

The dancing figures are used to emblematize hierarchy and wholeness, on the one hand:

> In the plan of the Great Dance plans without number interlock, and each movement becomes in its season the breaking into flower of the whole design to which all else had been directed. Thus each is equally at the centre and none are there by being equals, but some by giving place and some by receiving it. . . . Blessed be He (250),

and correspondence, relation, and truth, on the other:

> All that is made seems planless to the darkened mind, because there are more plans than it looked for. . . . Set your eyes on one movement and it will lead you through all patterns and it will seem to you the master movement. But the seeming will be true. Let no mouth open to gainsay it. There seems no plan because it is all plan: there seems no centre because it is all centre. Blessed be He! (251).

After hearing in the melodic litany about the orderliness and harmony of all things, Ransom is afforded a glimpse of the Great Dance to which Doctor Cornelius and Ramandu referred:

> What had begun as speech was turned into sight, or into something that can be remembered only as if it were seeing. He thought he saw the Great Dance. It seemed to be woven out of the intertwining undulation of many cords or bands of light, leaping over and under one another and mutually embraced in arabesques and flower-like subtleties. Each figure as he looked at it became the master-figure or focus of the whole spectacle, by means of which his eye disentangled all else and brought it into unity—only to be itself entangled when he looked to what he had taken for mere marginal decorations and found that there also the same hegemony was claimed, and the claim made good, yet the former pattern not thereby dispossessed but finding in its new subordination a significance greater than that which it had abdicated. (251-52)

Ransom is shown, not what the universe looks like, but the Truth about what it actually *is* like, the same Truth medieval people sought in the imaginative Model they constructed. As Lewis shows in *The Discarded Image*, that Model delighted them (216), it satisfied them: "Other ages have not had a Model so universally accepted as theirs, so imaginable, and so satisfying to the imagination" (203). It held great significance for them, "as a manifestation of the wisdom and goodness that created it" (204). Thus they recreated it again and again in their art, because "their minds loved to dwell on [it]" (202-3). And C.S. Lewis likewise sought to recreate that Model in the images of his fiction, and to convey to 20th Century minds and hearts some of that same delight and satisfaction it engendered in the Middle Ages.[57]

ENDNOTES

1 Lewis, *Letters to Malcolm: Chiefly on Prayer* (London: Geoffrey Bles, 1964), 121.

2 His love of music began long before his discovery of Wagner: "My general appreciation of music was not, at first, much altered [by his discovery of Wagner]," he wrote in 1955. "'Music' was one thing, 'Wagnerian music' quite another." (*Surprised by Joy: The Shape of My Early Life* [New York: Harcourt, Brace & World, 1955], 75—subsequent references will be cited parenthetically and abbreviated *SbyJ*).

3 Lewis, *The Lewis Papers,* 3.228 and 5.40—eleven single-spaced typescript volumes of family papers assembled, edited, typed, and bound by Lewis's brother Warren. The original is in the Wade Center, Wheaton College (Illinois), with a copy in the Bodleian Library, Oxford. Subsequent references will be abbreviated *Lewis Papers*.

4 Letter to Arthur Greeves, 7 March 1916; *The Collected Letters of C.S. Lewis,* ed. Walter Hooper, 3 vol. (London: HarperCollins, 2000-2007), 1.171. Subsequent references will be cited parenthetically and abbreviated *CL*.

5 *Lewis Papers* 3.259. One issue of "The Leeborough Review" is reproduced in an appendix to the *Lewis Papers* (11.248-50).

6 In *Spenser's Images of Life,* ed. Alastair Fowler (Cambridge: Cambridge University Press, 1967), Lewis quotes appreciatively a sentence from Mendelssohn: "The thoughts which are expressed to me by music that I love are not too indefinite to be put into words, but on the contrary too definite" (115).

7 Lewis wrote to Joan Lancaster on 9 September 1954, "I've never seen Aida, but I've known the music since I was a small boy: and how good it is" (*CL* 3.505). On 8 November 1916 he wrote to Arthur Greeves, "I should give anything to be at home for these operas" (*CL* 1.248) and discussions of operas appear in that letter and his next two letters to Greeves.

8 *Lewis Papers* 3.233-35. From the time he discovered the *Ring of the Nibelung* through a review in a magazine, Wagner held a special place in Lewis's life, for his music and for the aura of Northernness his work conveys. In Lewis's letters to Greeves and elsewhere he mentions going to London on numerous occasions to attend performances of one or all of its parts. "I will by no means join in the modern depreciation of Wagner. He may, for all I know, have been a bad man. He may (though I shall never believe it) have been a bad musician. But as a mythopoeic poet he is incomparable" ("The Funeral of a Great Myth" [mid 1940s?], *Christian Reflections,* ed. Walter Hooper [Grand Rapids, Mich.: Eerdmans, 1967], 84).

9 The "excellent gramophone" Lewis mentioned on 25 March 1933 was replaced just five days later by an even better one. Warren noted in his diary on 30 March 1933, "This afternoon my long expected new gramophone arrived by [road] in charge of two men, who set it up in the study where we tested it with a Debussy, a bit of the Pastoral symphony, and a chorus from Beethovens Mass. I am delighted with it. . . . After supper [Lewis, Mrs. Moore] and I sat cosily in the study and I played them the Pastoral Symphony and a sonata of Bach" (W. H. Lewis, *Brothers and Friends: The Diaries of Major Warren Hamilton Lewis,* ed. Clyde S. Kilby and Marjorie Lamp Mead [San Francisco: Harper & Row, 1982], 100). Jill Freud, who stayed at the Kilns the summer of 1943, recalls such evenings: "Almost every Sunday night the brothers listened to a complete symphony on Major Lewis's old gramophone. It had a large, wooden, handmade horn. The sound was good and he was proud of it;

no one else was allowed to use it" ("Part B: With Girls at Home," *In Search of C.S. Lewis*, ed. Stephen Schofield [South Plainfield, N.J.: Bridge Publishing, 1983], 57).

10 Lewis, *All My Road Before Me: The Diary of C.S. Lewis 1922-1927,* ed. Walter Hooper (London: HarperCollins, 1991), 255. Subsequent references will be cited parenthetically and abbreviated *All My Road.*

11 Lewis, "Christianity and Culture" (1940), *Christian Reflections* 13; "Christianity and Literature" (1939), *Christian Reflections* 2.

12 Lewis, *An Experiment in* Criticism (Cambridge: Cambridge University Press, 1961), 25.

13 Lewis *The Screwtape Letters* (London: Geoffrey Bles, 1942), 16. Subsequent references will be cited parenthetically and abbreviated *SL.*

14 Lewis, "Answers to Questions on Christianity" (1944), *God in the Dock: Essays on Theology and Ethics,* ed. Walter Hooper (Grand Rapids, Mich.: Eerdmans, 1970), 62. On May Day, 1930, Warren and Lewis climbed to the top of Magdalen tower and at dawn heard the choisters sing "a Latin hymn which was very effective and a beautiful tune: why on earth don't they sing these hymns in church?" (*Lewis Papers* 11.11).

15 Lewis, "On Church Music" (1949), *Christian Reflections* 95, 96.

16 Lewis, *The Pilgrim's Regress: An Allegorical Apology for Christianity Reason and Romanticism* (1933), new and revised edition (London: Geoffrey Bles, 1943), 7-8. Subsequent references will be cited parenthetically and abbreviated *PR.*

17 Lewis, "The Weight of Glory" (1941), *Transposition and Other Addresses* (London: Geoffrey Bles, 1949), 24.

18 Corbin Scott Carnell, *Bright Shadow of Reality: C.S. Lewis and the Feeling Intellect* (Grand Rapids: Eerdmans, 1974), 87-91.

19 Samuel Pepys, *Diary,* entry for 27 February 1668, as quoted by Lewis in his sermon "Transposition" (1944), *Transposition and Other Addresses* 11. See *The Diary of Samuel Pepys*, ed. Robert Latham and William Matthews, 10 vol. (Berkeley: University of California Press, 1970-1983), 9.94.

20 Lewis, *Mere Christianity* (London: Geoffrey Bles, 1952), 108.

21 Lewis, *Out of the Silent Planet* (London: Bodley Head, 1938), 255. Subsequent references will be cited parenthetically and abbreviated *OSP.*

22 Lewis, *Till We Have Faces: A Myth Retold.* (London: Geoffrey Bles, 1956), 233. Subsequent references will be cited parenthetically and abbreviated *TWHF.*

23 Lewis, "The Shoddy Lands," *Of Other Worlds: Essays and Stories*, ed. Walter Hooper (London: Geoffrey Bles, 1966), 105.

24 Lewis, "Imagination and Thought in the Middle Ages" (1956), *Studies in Medieval and Renaissance Literature,* ed. Walter Hooper (Cambridge: Cambridge University Press, 1966), 57.

25 Lewis, *The Allegory of Love* (Oxford: Clarendon Press, 1936), 135. Subsequent references will be cited parenthetically and abbreviated *AofL.*

26 Lewis, "Edmund Spenser," *Major British Writers,* ed. G. B. Harrison, 2 vol. (New York: Harcourt, Brace & World, 1959), 1.96.

27 Lewis, *Spenser's Images of Life* 116. Likewise, Spenser "can be as prosaic as Wordsworth: he can be clumsy, unmusical, and flat" (*AofL* 318), and Virgil's hexameters are "more like the slow movement of the Seventh Symphony and less like the *Walkürenritt*" ("Metre" [1960], *Selected Literary Essays,* ed. Walter Hooper [Cambridge: Cambridge University Press, 1969], 284).

28 Lewis, *Spirits in Bondage: A Cycle of Lyrics* (1919), ed. Walter Hooper (San Diego: Harcourt Brace Jovanovich, 1984): see the "Prologue" and the poems numbered 2, 3, 4, 5, 7, 12, 17, 18, 21, 22, 25, 29, 31, 33, 35, 38, and 39.

29 See Lewis, *Poems,* ed. Walter Hooper (London: Geoffrey Bles, 1964), pages 11, 14, 16, 17, 19, 24, 27, 30, 32, 41, 46, 50, 57, 67, 71, 74, 76, 81, 82, 90, 94, 97, 104, 105, 114, 115, 123, 124, 133, and 136.

30 Nearly two decades later, Donald Swann and David Marsh collaborated on an operatic version of *Perelandra.* Lewis heard the first performance of it on 29 June 1963 and said "it moved him to tears" (see Swann, *Swann's Way: A Life in Song,* ed. Lyn Smith [London: Heinemann, 1991], 202, and William Phemister, "Fantasy Set to Music: Donald Swann, C.S. Lewis and J.R.R. Tolkien," *Seven: An Anglo-American Literary Review* 13 [1996]: 65-82).

31 Lewis, *Perelandra* (London: Bodley Head, 1943), 74. Subsequent references will be cited parenthetically and abbreviated *Per.*

32 Lewis, *That Hideous Strength* (London: Bodley Head, 1945), 397. Subsequent references will be cited parenthetically and abbreviated *THS.*

33 One such context is the use of music in figures of speech. A few examples: the sound of Susan's horn was "loud as thunder but far longer, cool and sweet as music over water" (*Prince Caspian: The Return to Narnia* [New York: Macmillan, 1951], 82—subsequent references will be cited parenthetically and abbreviated *PC*). Aslan's roar "deep and throbbing at first like an organ beginning on a low note, rose and became louder . . . till the earth and air were shaking with it" (*PC* 129). The giant cook's snore in the House of Harfang is more welcome to Jill, Eustace, and Puddleglum than any music (*The Silver Chair* [New York: Macmillan, 1953], 112-13—subsequent references will be cited parenthetically and abbreviated *SC*). Once they get below the earth, they march across a mild, soft, sleepy place: "It was very sad, but with a quiet sort of sadness like soft music" (*SC* 122).

34 Lewis, *The Lion, the Witch and the Wardrobe* (New York: Macmillan, 1950), 12-13. Subsequent references will be cited parenthetically and abbreviated *LWW.*

35 Lewis, *The Magician's Nephew* (New York: Macmillan, 1955), 164. Subsequent references will be cited parenthetically and abbreviated *MN.* The importance of music is reinforced by its inclusion in the education of Prince Caspian and Prince Cor: Prince Caspian learned "sword-fighting and riding, swimming and diving, how to shoot with the bow and play on the recorder and the theorbo" (*PC* 46), and Shasta as Prince Cor will have to learn "reading and writing and heraldry and dancing and history and music" (*The Horse and His Boy* [New York: Macmillan, 1954], 178—subsequent references will be cited parenthetically and abbreviated *H&B*). Both are being given the Narnian version of the education of a Renaissance gentleman; music is one of the four subjects of the quadrivium because it teaches order and harmony. See H. R. Lyon, ed., *The Middle Ages: A Concise Encyclopedia* (London: Thames and Hudson, 1989), 277; Donald Leman Clark, *John Milton at St. Paul's School* (New York: Columbia University Press, 1948), 3; and especially Paul A. Olson, *The Journey to Wisdom* (Lincoln: University of Nebraska Press, 1955), 194-99.

36 Lewis, *The Discarded Image: An Introduction to Medieval and Renaissance Literature* (Cambridge: Cambridge University Press, 1964), 11. Subsequent references will be cited parenthetically and abbreviated *DI.* See also J.A.W. Bennett, "Grete Clerk," *Light on C.S. Lewis,* ed. Jocelyn Gibb (1965; rpt. New York: Harcourt Brace Jovanovich, 1976), 48.

37 In *The Discarded Image* Lewis contrasts the "realising imagination" of the middle ages with the "transforming imagination" of Wordsworth and the "penetrative imagination" of Shakespeare. One of the appeals of medieval literature, for Lewis, was its abundant detail and its grounding in reality. The vividness of medieval writers, he says, comes from "their devout attention to their matter and their confidence in it. They [do not try] to heighten it or transform it. It possesses them wholly. Their eyes and ears are steadily fixed upon it, and so—perhaps hardly aware how much they are inventing—they see and hear what the event must have been like" (206, 208).

38 Lewis, "Imagination and Thought in the Middle Ages" 52.

39 Plato, *The Republic*, book 10 (617a): *The Dialogues of Plato*, trans. B. Jowett, 3d ed., 5 vol. (New York: Macmillan, 1892), 3.334. The medieval world, wrote Lewis, was "resonant with music" (*DI* 112). On traditional ideas about music, see John Hollander, *The Untuning of the Sky: Ideas of Music in English Poetry, 1500-1900* (Princeton: Princeton University Press, 1961).

40 *The Works of John Dryden,* vol. 3: *Poems 1685-1692,* ed. Earl Miner (Berkeley and Los Angeles: University of California Press, 1969), 201. The ode, commissioned by the Musical Society for the annual celebration of the patroness of music on 22 November 1687, was set to music originally by G. B. Draghi, then more tellingly by George Frideric Handel in 1739. The Draghi setting is available in a recording by the Playford Consort and Parlay of Instruments; many recorded versions of the Handel are available.

41 Lewis, *The Last Battle* (New York: Macmillan, 1956), 142. Subsequent references will be cited parenthetically and abbreviated *LB*.

42 Johnson, "Dryden," *Lives of the English Poets* (1779-81), ed. George Birkbeck Hill, 3 vol. (Oxford: Clarendon Press, 1905), 1.440.

43 Two days later Lewis mentions that their friend Leo Baker was "trying to persuade Barfield to go on the music hall stage." And later in the week Lewis wrote that he had "congratulated [Barfield] on his dancing" and added, "he is quite seriously thinking of the 'Halls'" (*All My Road* 35, 37-38).

44 Lewis, *The Great Divorce* (London: Geoffrey Bles—The Centenary Press, 1946), 45.

45 *Prince Caspian* 165; *The Voyage of the "Dawn Treader"* (New York: Macmillan, 1952), 54-55—subsequent references will be cited parenthetically and abbreviated *VDT*; *The Horse and His Boy* 43; *The Last Battle* 2.

46 See Gilbert Meilaender, *The Taste for the Other: The Social and Ethical Thought of C.S. Lewis* (Grand Rapids: Eerdmans, 1978), 48-51, and Paul S. Fiddes, "On Theology," *The Cambridge Companion to C.S. Lewis,* ed. Robert MacSwain and Michael Ward (Cambridge: Cambridge University Press, 2010), 90-95. Charles A. Huttar has suggested to me that Lewis's use of the metaphor may have been influenced by Charles Williams: "The 'sweet reasonableness' of Christ is always there, but it is always in a dance and its dancing hall is from the topless heavens to the bottomless abyss" (*He Came Down from Heaven* [1938; rpt. Grand Rapids: Eerdmans, 1984], 69).

47 Plato, *Timaeus* 29-30: *The Dialogues of Plato* 3.450.

48 On Lewis's use of dance and the backgrounds he drew upon, I am indebted to Roland M. Kawano, "C.S. Lewis and the Great Dance," *Christianity and Literature* 26 (1976): 20-38, and an unpublished paper "The Celestial Dance" by Sarah E. Thomson.

49 Andrew Marvell, "The First Anniversary of the Government under O.C.," lines 51-52, *Poems and Letters*, ed. H. M. Margoliouth, 2 vol. (Oxford: Clarendon Press, 1927), 1.104.

50 Plato, *Timaeus* 69 and 40: *The Dialogues of Plato,* 3.491 and 3.459.

51 Lewis, *English Literature in the Sixteenth Century Excluding Drama*, vol. 3 of the Oxford History of English Literature, ed. F. P. Wilson and Bonamy Dobrée (New York: Oxford University Press, 1954), 4.

52 Davies, "Orchestra, Or a Poeme of Dauncing," stanzas 17-18: *The Poems of Sir John Davies*, ed. Robert Krueger (Oxford: Clarendon Press, 1975), 94-95.

53 Constance Hill, *Jane Austen: Her Homes and Her Friends* (1901), 3d ed. (London: John Lane, 1923), 58.

54 Lewis, "Imagination and Thought in the Middle Ages" 60.

55 In 1922 Lewis wrote in his diary, "I . . . looked into a book on Mozart and read the story of the *Magic Flute* which I found very suggestive. . . . I thought curiously of how this might be used for a big poem some day" (*All My Road* 112; see also 115-16 and 125). The result is *The Nameless Isle* (*Narrative*

Poems, ed. Walter Hooper [London: Geoffrey Bles, 1969], 105-27): see Charles A. Huttar, "A Lifelong Love Affair with Language: C.S. Lewis's Poetry," *Word and Story in C.S. Lewis*, ed. Peter J. Schakel and Charles A. Huttar (Columbia: University of Missouri Press, 1991), 86.

56 Compare this passage from the second section of T. S. Eliot's "Burnt Norton" (1936; the first of the *Four Quartets*): "At the still point of the turning world . . . there the dance is. . . . And do not call it fixity, / Where past and future are gathered. . . . Except for the point, the still point, / There would be no dance, and there is only the dance" (Eliot, *The Complete Poems and Plays 1909-1950* [New York: Harcourt, Brace & World, 1952], 119). Helen Gardner suggested that Eliot borrowed from the dance of the Tarot figures in Charles Williams's 1932 novel *The Greater Trumps* (*The Art of T. S. Eliot* [1950; rpt. New York: E. P. Dutton, 1959], 161), and Eliot acknowledged his general indebtedness to Williams. Lewis surely had read all of Williams's novels and is not likely to have forgotten Williams's dance image.

57 Parts of this essay are a revision of material that appeared earlier in my book *Imagination and the Arts in C.S. Lewis* (Columbia: University of Missouri Press, 2002). Chapters 6 and 7 contain other relevant material for which there wasn't space here.

Aesthetics vs. Anesthesia: C.S. Lewis on the Purpose of Art

CHARLIE W. STARR

My astonishing claim is this: Most of evangelical Christianity for the last hundred years (and longer) has gotten art and culture all wrong, but, as per usual, C.S. Lewis gets it right. We don't know what culture is for, we don't know what art is for, and we keep asking the wrong people: theologians. When we want to overcome a sickness, we go to a doctor. When we want to fix a leak, we call a plumber. We ask the experts and get the right answers. Why don't we do the same with art? We turn to Christians to find Christian answers, and rightly so. But if we want to know about art, theologians are not the experts to ask. Artists, on the other hand, frighten us. We trust so little of what they do, and they're a little weird to begin with, even the Christian ones. What we need is a Christian artist (perhaps a writer) with a background in theology—someone with the intellectual discipline of a philosopher and the critical eye, experience, and imagination of an artist. If such a *Jack*-of-all-trades were to exist, we'd call him C.S. Lewis.

I. IS ART UTILITARIAN?

With regard to the significance of the arts or culture in general, Lewis once concluded that "culture,[1] though not in itself meritorious, was innocent and pleasant, might be a vocation for some, was helpful in bringing certain souls to Christ, and could be pursued to the glory of God."[2] Though he valued culture, Lewis did not see it as a final good—an end unto itself. It is true that Lewis saw a connection between art and knowledge. In *The Great Divorce*, for example, a painter who has just come into heaven is told that "When you painted on earth . . . it was because you caught glimpses of Heaven in the earthly landscape. The success of your painting was that it enabled others to see the glimpses too."[3] And such glimpses, as Lewis himself found in "inanimate nature and marvelous literature" evoke in us an experience of "intense longing,"[4] an "unsatisfied desire which is itself more desirable than any other satisfaction."[5] Lewis calls this desire "Joy,"[6] and Joy is a marker—a stab of desire whose object is not to be found on earth:

> Creatures are not born with desires unless satisfaction for those desires exists. A baby feels hunger: well, there is such a thing as food. A duckling wants to swim: well, there is such a thing as water. Men feel sexual desire: well, there is such a thing as sex. If I find in myself a desire which no experience in this world can satisfy, the most probable explanation is that I was made for another world.[7]

Lewis sees the intense desire he calls Joy as an "ontological proof" for the existence of heaven and God.[8] He says, "if we are made for heaven, the desire for our proper place will be already in us, but not yet attached to the true object . . . ."[9] The desire will, in fact, erupt out of earthly encounters of pleasure—encounters with beauty in nature, with sexual pleasure, and with the beauty of artistic texts, especially (for Lewis) the literature of myth and fantasy.[10] But each of these earthly objects, then, can be confused for the true, heavenly object, and must be seen as merely a signpost, a hint of the real thing.[11] But the implication for art is that it may potentially point us to the truth of God's existence. It did for C.S. Lewis.

That said, Lewis did not see the purpose of art to be the production of sermonic tropes or Christian propaganda. Even as viewers of art we shouldn't look to see if there is a hidden *Christian* message in a movie or book. On the contrary, "The first demand any work of any art makes upon us is surrender. Look. Listen. Receive. Get yourself out of the way."[12] Writing specifically about literature, Lewis claims that whatever edification we get isn't about finding truth in books: "To value them chiefly for reflections which they may suggest to us or morals we may draw from them, is a flagrant instance of 'using' [texts for our own purposes] instead of 'receiving'" [them for what they are].[13] Instead, great art is about a particular activity of imagination; it is about finding new ways of *seeing*—about seeing through the eyes of others:

> The nearest I have yet got to an answer [to the question of literature's value] is that we seek an enlargement of our being. We want to be more than ourselves. Each of us by nature sees the whole world from one point of view with a perspective and a selectiveness peculiar to himself . . . . We want to see with other eyes, to imagine with other imaginations, to feel with other hearts, as well as with our own . . . .My own eyes are not enough for me, I will see through those of others. Reality, even seen through the eyes of many, is not enough. I will see what others have invented . . . . [I]n reading great literature I become a thousand men and yet remain myself . . . . Here, as in worship, in love, in moral action, and in knowing, I transcend Myself; and am never more myself than when I do.[14]

In short, Lewis very specifically rejects any view that "literature is to be valued . . . for telling us truths about life"[15]; instead, he values literature apart from its utilitarian purposes. This flies in the face of much contemporary Christian thinking about art and culture, both on popular and intellectual fronts. On the popular front are well meaning Christians who accept the model of "culture war"—we are in a battle that must be fought by governing what our kids are exposed to and protesting against films, songs, and TV shows which are hostile to our point of view. On the intellectual front is an emphasis on "worldview analysis"—examining the worldviews behind artistic texts to point out there hidden assumptions or mine their truth value. And while both have their place, they fail to understand what art is for.

II. PROBLEMS WITH WORLDVIEW ANALYSIS

The one time Lewis says anything about what we call worldview analysis is in his essay, "Christianity and Culture." Here he agrees that, in a work of art,

> the real beliefs may differ from the professed and may lurk in the turn of a phrase or the choice of an epithet; with the result that many preferences which seem to the ignorant to be simply 'matters of taste' are visible to the trained critic as choices between good and evil, or truth and error....[16]

But he follows this recognition by raising several questions and cautions. One is whether a man who has "had a literary training" ought also to be a judge of the world-views he reveals. Is this not the purview of the philosopher?[17] Secondly, Lewis wonders if aspects of a negative analysis have less to do with ideas and more to do with taste.[18] I read Lewis here as saying that aesthetic sensibilities are often ignored in worldview approaches to art. But to Lewis, an artistic text like a book is

> both *Logos* (something said) and *Poiema* (something made). As Logos it tells a story, or expresses an emotion, or exhorts or pleads or describes or rebukes or excites laughter. As Poiema, by its aural beauties and also by the balance and contrast and the unified multiplicity of its successive parts, it is an *objet d'art*, a thing shaped so as to give great satisfaction.[19]

Next Lewis takes issue with an approach to art which spends so much time "reading between the lines" that it neglects "the obvious surface facts about a book."[20] Is it not possible, for example, that, despite a book's "dreadful latent materialism, it does set courage and fidelity before the reader in an attractive light, and thousands of readers will be edified... by reading it?"[21]

Lewis then questions an approach to art which removes any sense of its primary purpose:

> I agree ... that our leisure, even our play, is a matter of serious concern .... [However,] to do them at all, we must somehow do them as if they were not. It is a serious matter to choose wholesome recreations: but they would no longer be recreations if we pursued them seriously.... For a great deal (not all) of our literature was made to be read lightly for entertainment. If we do not read it, in

> a sense, 'for fun'... we are not using it as it was meant to be used, and all our criticism of it will be pure illusion. For you cannot judge any artefact except by using it as it was intended. It is no good judging a butter-knife by seeing whether it will saw logs.[22]

Finally Lewis offers the tentative suggestion that there might be

> two kinds of good and bad. The first, such as virtue and vice or love and hatred, besides being good or bad themselves make the possessor good or bad. The second do not. They include such things as physical beauty or ugliness, the possession or lack of a sense of humour, strength or weakness, pleasure or pain.[23]

Lewis sees potential problems with his categories, but I think it legitimate to apply them to the arts in this way: If I say a secular film is bad because it is filled with false ideas, foul language, gratuitous sex, and gory violence, and then I say a Christian film is bad because the production values are cheap, the script overly didactic, the story dull, and the acting poor, I am not using the word "bad" in the same way. The former is bad for reasons involving morality and truth; the latter is bad for reasons involving aesthetics and imaginative effect.[24] Worldview analysis will almost always leave these latter considerations out of the equation.

An even stronger argument to be gleaned from Lewis regarding the problems of worldview analysis has to do with the nature of "meaning." "What does it mean?" is a question we ask all the time, often about the symbols and images we encounter in books, songs, and movies. But do we ever ask, "What does *meaning* mean?" Usually when we ask for the meaning of a word, a line in a song, or a symbolic image, we want an explanation in words. In *The Empire Strikes Back*, Luke journeys down into his own cave of knowledge and confronts Darth Vader. He cuts Vader's head clean off only to find his own face looking back at him. When my daughter first saw this scene she asked me what it meant. I told her, "It means Luke's worst enemy is himself. He has to fight his own fear and doubt before he can face the real Darth Vader. What happened in the cave was a dream or vision." I explained the meaning in words. But movies mean more than the words in them. Their magic is in the meanings they communicate *beyond* words. Their truth is in their images and experiential quality.

In a little known essay called "Bluspels and Flalansferes," Lewis helps us search for the meaning of *meaning*:

> [I]t must not be supposed that I am in any sense putting forward the imagination as the organ of truth. We are not talking of truth, but of meaning: meaning which is the antecedent condition both of truth and falsehood, whose antithesis is not error but nonsense.... For me, reason is the natural organ of truth; but imagination is the organ of meaning. Imagination, producing new metaphors

> or revivifying old, is not the cause of truth, but its condition.[25]

An obscure statement at best, what Lewis argues here, among other things, is that meaning is not the same thing as truth, the one belonging to the faculty of imagination, the other to the faculty of reason.

He discusses one major implication of this dichotomy in his essay, "Myth Became Fact," where he makes a connection between "myth" and "reality" and then a separation of "reality" from "truth": "What flows into you from the myth is not truth but reality (truth is always about something, but reality is that *about which* truth is)."[26] Reality (or fact) is what is; truth is a proposition *about* fact. Next, Lewis describes our earthly existence as a "valley of separation,"[27] or abstraction, arguing that "Myth is the mountain whence all the different streams arise which become truths down here in the valley; *in hac valle abstractionis*."[28] Lewis is saying that meaning can be abstract language statements like my explanation of Luke's internal struggle in *Empire Strikes Back*. But it can also be experiential and can precede language.

The context of the "Myth Became Fact" essay is the epistemological dilemma of thinking versus experiencing. To know by thought is to withdraw ourselves from reality. To know by experience is to be so caught up in the real that we can't think about it clearly. Consider how we can laugh at a joke or think about why it's funny, but we can't do both at the same time. More importantly, our very ability to know is hampered by this bifurcation: "'If only my toothache would stop, I could write another chapter about Pain.' But once it stops, what do I know about pain?"[29] We can't study pleasure while having sex, "repentance while repenting," nor humor while we're laughing hysterically, but "when else can you really know these things?"[30]

In order to understand how limiting this dilemma really is, Lewis suggests we think about the myth of Orpheus and Eurydice. Orpheus was allowed to lead Eurydice by the hand, but the moment he tried to turn around and see her, she disappeared. If we focus on the myth, the abstract concept of thinking versus experiencing is suddenly "imaginable." If I take what Lewis is saying and explain it in abstract, allegorical statements, then "experience" is Orpheus holding Eurydice's hand, "thinking" is her disappearing when he turns around to get a clear look at her, and the "myth," apart from this explanation, is an image of these ideas which acts on our imagination *like* an experience. Lewis goes on to note that our response might be that we've never seen the meaning just described in the myth of Orpheus and Eurydice. To this he replies, "Of course not. You are not looking for an abstract 'meaning' at all."[31] If we were looking for abstract meanings in the myth, it would stop being a myth to us and become an allegory (as I just made it above). Lewis says that, in receiving the myth as a myth,

> You were not knowing, but tasting; but what you were tasting turns out to be a universal principle. The moment we *state* this principle, we are admittedly back in the world of abstraction. It is only while receiving the myth as a story that you

experience the principle concretely.[32]

In other words, when we take a meaning out of a myth, we turn it into an abstract statement, an idea. When we leave the meaning in the myth and do not try to turn it into language statements, the meaning remains (or at least mimics) a concrete experience. Through myth, ideas can be experienced concretely. Lewis gives a hint that this occurs in the imagination, a mode of thinking that shares qualities of both reason and experience.

When we receive myth as story, we are experiencing a principle concretely. Only when we put the experience into words does the principle become abstract. But if we can know a principle either concretely or by abstraction, then meaning can be either concrete or abstract. This agrees with the statement in the "Bluspels" essay that meaning is the necessary antecedent to truth.[33] Some meanings are abstract propositions—word statements like my explanation of the scene from *Empire Strikes Back*. But there are other kinds of meanings which can only be grasped in the experiential imagination. Such meanings, the kind we get in myth for example, come prior to abstraction and apart from language. From them we do not get truths *about* reality but *tastes* of reality itself.

Lewis makes this mythic connection very specifically in connection to film. Though he had something of a love/hate relationship with movies, Lewis once made the profoundly positive statement that myth can be rendered through film. Myth is a communication which is not in the words used to communicate it but in the form of the myth itself. Lewis explains this in his introduction to *George MacDonald: An Anthology*:

> We all agree that the story of Balder is a great myth, a thing of inexhaustible value. But of whose version—whose *words*—are we thinking when we say this? For my own part, the answer is that I am not thinking of anyone's words. [. . .] What really delights and nourishes me is a particular pattern of events, which would equally delight and nourish if it had reached me by some medium which involved no words at all—say by a mime, or a *film*.[34]

Lewis suggests the idea of myth as a mode of languaging even more clearly in *A Preface to Paradise Lost* saying, "giants, dragons, paradises, gods, and the like are themselves the expression of certain basic elements in man's spiritual experience. In that sense they are more like words—the words of a language which speaks the else unspeakable."[35] Myth communicates meaning apart from words. And the same thing can be said for film.

In "On Fairy-Stories," Lewis's colleague J.R.R. Tolkien rejects the then widely held idea that myth is a "disease of language" and argues instead that the opposite is more the case.[36] M. Night Shyamalan argues a similar point in his film *Unbreakable*. There he sees language as originating in pictures. Says the expert in comic art: "I believe comics are a last link to an ancient way of passing on history. The Egyptians drew on walls. Countries all over the world still pass on knowledge through pictorial forms. I believe comics are a form of history that someone, somewhere, felt or experienced."[37] Though we may not think much of comic books revealing the hidden nature of the universe, Shyamalan is making a point that can be verified and is so by Lewis's friend and fellow Inkling Owen Barfield whose book *Poetic Diction* influenced Lewis's epistemology greatly.

In *Unbreakable,* Shyamalan offers a theory of myth, of a concrete picture language that precedes modern language forms in which sign abstracts the signified. The image form, surviving in a kind of collective human unconscious, intrudes itself into contemporary culture through comic art. What it reveals is an archetypal pattern of the hero, Joseph Campbell's "monomyth."[38] Shyamalan further intuits a quality of communicating which Barfield uncovers in his *Poetic Diction.*[39] A careful study of linguistic history reveals that a strong distinction between sign and signified, between the literal and the figurative, is new to human thinking. For people before the modern era (even up through the medieval period), to name a thing was to invoke it; speech had physical consequences in the world; words were what they signified; metaphorical meanings were possible because their connective representation was in some way literal. Film resonates with Barfield's view of past language. What it says is what it is, and what it shows is what it means. In the past, words *were* more like pictures, in fact more like physical actions.

Barfield suggests, for example, the metaphor, "I have no stomach for that."[40] This phrase is used to express our dislike for a thing. It is figurative . . . mostly. When I say, "I have no stomach for modern art," I'm not saying I get nauseous when I look at an abstract painting. However, if I say "I have no stomach for horror films," I am not only expressing my dislike for them, I am also saying that the blood, gore, and suspense in them *do* make me nauseous. Here is an example of a phrase that is both literal and figurative at the same time. Barfield claims humanity used to both think and use language this way constantly. Speech and action were much closer to each other than in our own day.

Well just as myth is a form of *languaging* and an expression of concrete thought, so film too is a mode of *languaging* which communicates to us like a physical action, as a concrete experience, and it is able to do so either without language or by converting language into experiential form. An example of film communicating as form without word can be seen in the early Tim Burton movie, *Edward Scissorhands.* In the middle of the movie, we see a long shot of the street on which Edward's adoptive family lives. Husbands simultaneously walk out to their cars from the various homes to begin the morning commute. They get in the cars at the same time, pull out of their driveways at the same time, and drive off after a bit of hesitation and jockeying for road space. There are no words, only pleasant, *Leave It to Beaver-esque* music. But here's what's really strange: the houses and the cars are all painted pastel colors. From a greater distance the street might look like an Easter basket. The colors are all solid, no two tones: whole houses and cars painted pink, or blue, or yellow, or green pastel.[41] Actions, sights, and sounds—all of them deliberate, intended. And without language, meaning is communicated in this scene. We certainly *can*, in this instance, put the meaning into words: "Suburbia is a world of conformity and façade." But the point is that we get the meaning *without having to* put it into words. Film communicates in a mythic fashion, often with meanings which cannot be abstracted into worldview analysis.

One more example: think of some favorite song, the kind that "blows you away" the first time you hear it. It moves you. You connect to it. It evokes feelings and thoughts you can't quite describe. Recall next how a month or two (or six) later you actually bother to pay attention to the lyrics, and you finally figure out what the song was saying. In one sense you knew all along what the song was about. You understood meanings in it that couldn't be put into words—meanings in the music itself or in the way a certain phrase touched your heart or connected with memories. The analysis of the lyrics was your reasoning self becoming aware of abstract, propositional meanings that your experiential self had not encountered. To use Lewis's terminology, you first *tasted* the song, then you came to *know* it. But to abandon the taste—the meanings which still cannot be put into words even after some analysis—is to abandon meanings which are certainly there.

The very nature of meaning in art is that many of its meanings will not be philosophically reduceable. In an essay called "The Language of Religion," Lewis points out that, far from being able to quantify reality in terms of the specialized languages of science or theology, most of experience can only be communicated with plain or poetic language: "Now it seems to me a mistake to think that our experience in general can be communicated by precise and literal language.... The truth seems to me the opposite ...."[42] Even a theologically accurate phrase like "Jesus Christ is the Son of God" is a metaphor.[43] It is true, but it is not literal. The relationship had between Christ and the Father in the Trinity is not the exact same as the relationship had between a man and his son. There was a time in which my son did not exist. Then he came into existence. But the First and Second Persons of the Trinity have co-existed eternally. We may attempt to convert the metaphor into a theological abstraction like, "There is between Jesus and God an asymmetrical, social, harmonious relation involving homogeneity,"[44] but in doing so the meaning will be all but lost to us. Lewis concludes that the "very essence of our life as conscious beings, all day and every day, consists of something which cannot be communicated except by hints, similes, metaphors, and the use of those emotions ... which are pointers to it."[45] If life itself is seldom reduceable to the abstract language of philosophy and theology, how much more must our approach to the arts be one which recognizes meanings that cannot be stated in any terms—or, at best, in poetic terms—let alone the terms of worldview analysis. Human knowing simply doesn't operate that way, and human art belongs more to the realms of concrete experience and analogical imagination.

For Lewis, meaning is *connection*, the perception of a relationship. But we can't think of meaning as solely an explanation in words. When we break out of that thinking, we begin to see art's purpose and methods. Art communicates experiences more than abstract truths and meanings more than philosophical positions. The meanings in art may be born of language, and such meanings may be translate into truth statements. But many of the meanings will exist apart from language. Many of them will be mythic, analogical, experiential, emotional, unconscious, semi-conscious, without clear definition, and even accidental.

Here, then, is the problem for worldview analysis: if the only thing we look for in examining an art form is a series of abstract, philosophical truth statements, we are missing both the power and purpose of art. I am not saying we should forget about examining worldviews in art (and neither did Lewis in "Christianity and Culture"). I am saying that worldview analysis *tends* to look for philosophical thought systems and nothing else. Students taught this approach to art end up with a myopic critical vision. Furthermore they end up spending their time "using" art instead of "receiving" it with the result that art stops being what Lewis says it should be most: "for fun."[46]

Imagine reducing the art of cooking to mere nutrition. We certainly need to know about it in order to be healthy, but if the joy of taste is sacrificed to nutritional facts, then food is reduced to a burden our taste buds must merely endure. Food needs to have flavor! And art needs to delight and to give us tastes of the real. This means it should first be approached experientially and imaginatively before it is ever viewed philosophically.

III. ART'S PURPOSES

None of this is to say that Lewis completely rejects the "using" of art in education. Though he primarily values art apart from its truth-bearing potentials, he nevertheless strikes a balance for us between our desires to enjoy art for what it is on the one hand and use it for edification on the other:

> The purpose of education has been described by Milton as that of fitting a man "to perform justly, skillfully, and magnanimously all the offices both private and public, of peace and war." ... Aristotle would substantially agree with this, but would add the conception that it should also be a preparation for leisure .... Vocational training, on the other hand, prepares the pupil not for leisure, but for work; it aims at making not a good man but a good banker, a good electrician, a good scavenger, or a good surgeon. You see at once that education is essentially for freemen and vocational training for slaves .... If education is beaten by training, civilization dies.[47]

Christian thinking about the arts—here I mean the thinking of American, Protestant,

Conservative, Evangelical Christianity—has suffered from pragmatism and didacticism. Rather than "enjoy" or "appreciate" art, we "use" it like dishes and cars to serve functions we consider important. What Lewis is saying is that, if art can serve the Kingdom of God, it is a good thing, but art created *for the purpose of* spreading the Kingdom of God (which is to say, art created for any purpose other than what art is for) will generally be bad, that is, inartistic. To use Lewis's terms, art thus becomes vocational, training beats education, and civilization (as it might be influenced by Christians) dies. Bad Christian art ends up defeating its own purposes. It doesn't reach anyone, and it quickly fades into obscurity.

Imagine a young man who wants to be a missionary doctor but who is so completely interested in spreading the gospel that he doesn't work hard at first becoming a good physician. Suppose that, with a little bit of training and a lot of funding from equally zealous Christians, he manages to get out to a third world country and practice medicine. In the field he tries his best as a doctor, but he just isn't very good at it—perhaps he is especially bad at administering anesthesia—and the consequences are dire. Of course he won't have any success in reaching people for Christ when he has failed them first at what he claimed to be—a physician.

Sound ridiculous? Yet this is exactly what goes on in Christian film making all the time: people zealous to spread the gospel, who don't know enough about making movies, produce celluloid sermons instead of real films. But before a movie can teach truth it must first be what films are: stories that enlighten, engage, show beauty, entertain, capture our imaginations, and put us through experiences. It is by happy coincidence and thanks to Lewis's unusual spelling of the word "anaesthetics"[48] that I learned the words "aesthetic" (the study of beauty), and "anesthetic" (the thing we most want the doctor to give us when going under the knife) come from the same root word, having to do with feeling or sensation. I am convinced that much of modern Christianity suffers from an anesthetic view of art. The result is Christian art which bores us to sleep.

Contrary to an anesthetic, utilitarian view of art, Lewis, like his friend Tolkien, valued the making of fairy tale stories (for example) especially when produced as an act of "sub-creation," of doing on a finite level what God did infinitely at the creation.[49] The purpose of such sub-creation is not to make something to be used for other purposes, but to participate in pleasure and worship in acting out in ourselves the Divine impulse of creativity given us as bearers of the image of God.[50] Applied to the arts in general, the point is that we make art for the delight of making. That act alone is sufficient reason for a book's, painting's, or movie's existence—it is made out of delight, out of a God given desire to imitate Him. It is an act of worship.

But the by-product of such activity is art that *can* have an effect on our civilization. Lewis concludes that, to be truly effective in affecting culture, we must stop making the affecting of culture our first goal:[51] "We must attack the enemy's lines of communication, [this is true. But w]hat we want is not more little books about Christianity, but more little books by Christians on other subjects—with their Christianity latent."[52] Recall Lewis's statement that leisure and play are of serious concern, but we cannot approach them too seriously.[53] Here he is saying the same thing about art. Unless we are doing it in our leisure, with a sense of play, and out of our God given creative (or sub-creative) impulses, it will not be good art. All we have to do is think of the difference between *The Passion of the Christ* and *Facing the Giants* for the point to become obvious. Admittedly, it is also counter-intuitive. But this, according to Lewis, is because we live in a fallen world in which play is frivolous:

> Dance and game *are* frivolous, unimportant down here; for "down here" is not their natural place. Here they are a moment's rest from the life we were placed here to live. But in this world everything is upside down. That which, if it could be prolonged here, would be a truancy, is likest that which in a better country is the End of ends. Joy is the serious business of Heaven.[54]

And art, then, can perhaps only be serious when it is created in play.

IV. THE MORAL IMAGINATION

Once again, though Lewis believed literature and other arts were not meant to be "used" for their truth value but "received" for their experiential delight, he did acknowledge the important relationship between art and moral development.

In an essay called "Horrid Red Things," Lewis argues that one of the things Christians must do to reach "modern" people is to "try to teach them something about the difference between thinking and imagining."[55] He illustrates:

> I once heard a lady tell her daughter that if you ate too many aspirin tablets you would die. "But why?" asked the child. "If you squash them you don't find any horrid red things inside them." Obviously, when this child thought of poison she not only had an attendant image of "horrid red things", but she actually believed that poison was red. And this is an error . . . . [However,] If I, staying at the house, had raised a glass of what looked like water to my lips, and the child had said, "Don't drink that. Mummie says it's poisonous," I should have been foolish to disregard the warning . . . .There is thus a distinction not only between thought and imagination in general, but even between thought and those images which the thinker (falsely) believes to be true.[56]

You see, the little girl clearly knew that poison was a bad thing, but she also thought that it was red. She had a right idea and a wrong image. And this wrong image could clearly lead the little girl to someday taking poison, not because she thinks poison good, but because the object she's about to swallow doesn't *look* poisonous to her.

Lewis presents this dichotomy again in *The Screwtape Letters* where a newly converted Christian is floundering in a sea of images confused with ideas. Elder demon

Screwtape writes to his pupil Wormwood about how best to tempt his patient:

> At his present stage, you see, he has an idea of 'Christians' in his mind which he supposes to be spiritual but which, in fact, is largely pictorial. His mind is full of togas and sandals and armour and bare legs and the mere fact that the other people in church wear modern clothes is a real—though of course an unconscious—difficulty to him.[57]

Consider how the American church today, without quite knowing how it was working, has had some success in reversing this trend through converting the classical worship service into the contemporary celebration of song and music. Removing the *images* that got in the way of belief—stained-glass stuffiness, hardened pews and faces, boring liturgy and pasted smiles—the church in the last thirty years has been able to draw people to the truth of Christ, not by restructuring Christian content, as liberal Christianity attempted to do, but by reconstructing the imaginative art forms (primarily in music and architecture) by which it is presented.

Lewis saw this exact need. At the writing of the Narnia books, there were those who believed that Lewis began by asking himself how he could share Christ with children which he thought best doable through fairy tales. Then he supposedly drew up a list of Christian truths he wanted to share with kids and put them into allegories. Says Lewis,

> This is all pure moonshine. I couldn't write in that way at all. Everything began with images; a faun carrying an umbrella, a queen on a sledge, a magnificent lion. At first there wasn't even anything Christian about them; that element pushed itself in of its own accord. It was part of the bubbling.[58]

Notice how Lewis here follows his own advice regarding the earlier point that we should not make art for the purpose of affecting culture, but rather culture will be affected if we make good art.

More important to the current point is what Lewis says came after the "bubbling," after he recognized that fairy tales were the best *form* he could find for all the creative energy he was about to unleash on paper:

> I thought I saw how stories of this kind could steal past a certain inhibition which had paralysed much of my own religion in childhood. Why did one find it so hard to feel as one was told one ought to feel about God or about the sufferings of Christ? I thought the chief reason was that one was told one ought to. An obligation to feel can freeze feelings. And reverence itself did harm . . . .But supposing that by casting all these things into an imaginary world, stripping them of their stained-glass and Sunday school associations, one could make them for the first time appear in their real potency? Could one not thus steal past those watchful dragons?[59]

Lewis achieved this in Narnia and the church has begun to do the same in our culture, making some inroads in music if still falling short in literature, film, and other art forms.

The point is a simple one: human beings pursue knowledge of the real through two modes of thought: reason and imagination. The first deals in abstract language and propositional statements. The second deals in images and concrete (even vicarious) experiences. Both matter for knowing, but imagination has been ignored or reduced in importance since the Enlightenment, and imagination is *definitely* more important in moral education than is reason.

This is Lewis's point in *The Abolition of Man*:

> St. Augustine defines virtue as *ordo amoris*, the ordinate condition of the affections in which every object is accorded that kind and degree of love which is appropriate to it. Aristotle says that the aim of education is to make the pupil like and dislike what he ought. When the age for reflective thought comes, the pupil who has been thus trained in 'ordinate affections' or 'just sentiments' will easily find the first principles in Ethics: but to the corrupt man they will never be visible at all and he can make no progress in that science. Plato before him had said the same. The little human animal will not at first have the right responses. It must be trained to feel pleasure, liking, disgust, and hatred at those things which really are pleasant, likeable, disgusting, and hateful . . . .All this before he is of an age to reason; so that when Reason at length comes to him, then, bred as he has been, he will hold out his hands in welcome and recognize her because of the affinity he bears to her.[60]

In plainer words: an imaginative understanding of goodness—one gleaned from story, song, beauty, an education that ties real qualities of the real to the feelings they ought to invoke—must precede a reasoned knowledge of moral precepts. Or, to use my anesthesia metaphor, a true aesthetic recognizes that good art teaches us how we ought to feel about things—objects, places, experiences—while bad art anesthetizes us to the good which ought to govern us. Lewis calls the products of such bad education, "Men without Chests."[61] I might call them patients etherized on an operating table.[62]

Teach second graders the Ten Commandments all you want; it's the story of Elijah and the prophets of Baal that they'll hold onto when someone questions commandment one before them. Lewis says that "no justification of virtue will enable a man to be virtuous. Without the aid of trained emotions the intellect is powerless against the animal organism."[63] If reason is to rule the appetites, it can only do so through the power of a third element, an imaginative sense of what's *right* or *ought to be* or (the technical term that I use), *cool*.

Coolness is what drew many of us to Christ. Whether it was the experience of a weekend long Christian Rave, the raucous joy of an Alt-Band concert praising God, the fantasy story by Lewis or Tolkien that drew our curiosity, the wise mentor, the high school friend who seemed to have it all together, the hip youth minister or the tattooed-and-pierced coffee house friend who *showed* the *beauty* or *nobility* of Christ to us *before* we ever thought Christianity might be true—that was what drew us first.

In the passage on the creation of the Narnia stories above, Lewis connects story to stealing "past watchful dragons," that is to recovering right moral sensibilities through imagination as well as envisioning Christianity by the same. His own poster child for the failure of abstract, storyless ethical education which leaves imagination and right response to experience out of the equation appears in his Narnia novel, *The Voyage of the Dawn Treader*. It begins, "There was a boy called Eustace Clarence Scrubb, and he almost deserved it."[64] Eustace is the worst kind of child Lewis could imagine: one raised by "modern" parents. Eustace hates fairy-tales, preferring books of information containing "pictures of grain elevators or of fat foreign children doing exercises in model schools."[65] Eustace is pretentious, petty, spiteful, and selfish. He is cruel to animals (even talking ones), steals water on a sea voyage when low supplies demand strict rations, acts a coward while hiding behind the self-righteousness of claiming to be a pacifist, and complains when the only girl on the voyage gets the only private cabin.

Eustace's problem is that he hasn't read any imaginative books like fairy-tales or adventure stories and so hasn't received proper moral instruction. He doesn't even recognize a dragon when he sees one because "he had read none of the right books."[66] Upon approaching a dragon's cave, Eustace is confused by what he finds there. Says Lewis: "Most of us know what we should expect to find in a dragon's lair, but, as I said before, Eustace had read only the wrong books. They had a lot to say about exports and imports and governments and drains, but they were weak on dragons."[67] Later in the novel, Eustace's cousin Edmund is able to solve a mystery because he is the "only one of the party who had read several detective stories."[68] In other words, his imagination has been trained through the experience of fiction so that, in his thinking, he is capable of seeing what others cannot.

What Eustace most needs is to experience reality so that he can know with his heart and not just his head; however, because he is too far gone into the abstract, theoretical shadow world of facts, figures, and practical applications, he needs more than just a dose of reality. He needs a higher reality, a world of the fantastic far more real than his own. He gets Narnia. Eustace is pulled into Narnia where, having learned before only in the abstract, about lifeless things, he can now learn by concrete experience of the really real. It takes becoming a dragon himself, and then being "undragoned" by Aslan, but Eustace does finally learn what his cold, analytical heart had been missing.

Art can be analyzed for its philosophical underpinnings and used to teach. It can glorify God, speak truth, and be used to build His Kingdom. It can even be used for moral development and instruction. But it can be used for none of these purposes if they become our primary reasons for making art or receiving it. C.S. Lewis is clear:

we make art out of pleasure, for play, out of our leisure, and because we bear the creative impulse of a creative God. And we read, view, and listen to art because it's fun, it gives us new experiences, it delights our imaginations, and it gives us greater vision. It doesn't drug us to sleep; it wakes us to the full.

ENDNOTES

1 Of the various topics which could be discussed under the umbrella of cultural analysis, I here intend, following Lewis's lead, to focus on art.

2 C.S. Lewis, "Christianity and Culture," in *Essay Collection and Other Short Pieces*, ed. Lesley Walmsley (London: Harper Collins, 2000), 85.

3 C.S. Lewis, *The Great Divorce: A Dream* (San Francisco: Harper Collins, 1973), 83.

4 C.S. Lewis, *The Pilgrim's Regress: An Allegorical Apology for Christianity Reason and Romanticism* (Grand Rapids: Eerdmans, 1943), 202.

5 C.S. Lewis, *Surprised by Joy: The Shape of My Early Life* (New York: Harcourt Brace Jovanovich, 1955), 17-18.

6 Ibid, 18.

7 C.S. Lewis, *Mere Christianity* (Westwood, NJ: Barbour & Co., 1952), 115.

8 Lewis, *Regress*, 205.

9 C.S. Lewis, "The Weight of Glory," in *Essay Collection and Other Short Pieces*, ed. Lesley Walmsley (London: Harper Collins, 2000), 98.

10 Lewis, *Regress*, 203.

11 Ibid.

12 C.S. Lewis, *An Experiment in Criticism* (Cambridge, UK: Cambridge University Press, 1961), 19.

13 Ibid, 82-83. See, especially, all of chapter eight for Lewis's discussion on the connections and disconnections between art and reality and art and truth.

14 Ibid, 137, 140-41.

15 Ibid, 130.

16 Lewis, "Culture," 86.

17 Ibid, 86-87.

18 Ibid, 87.

19 Lewis, *Experiment*, 132. See also page 82.

20 Lewis, "Culture," 88.

21 Ibid, 89.

22 Ibid, 90.

23 Ibid, 91.

24 See below for why these elements matter.

25 C.S. Lewis, "Bluspels and Flalansferes: A Semantic Nightmare," in *Selected Literary Essays*, ed. Walter Hooper (Cambridge: Cambridge University Press, 1969), 265.

26 C.S. Lewis, "Myth Became Fact," in *Essay Collection and Other Short Pieces*, ed. Lesley Walmsley (London: Harper Collins, 2000), 141.

27 Ibid, 141*n*.

28 Ibid, 141. The Latin means, "in this valley of separation."

29 Ibid, 140.

30 Ibid.

31 Ibid, 141.

32 Ibid.

33 Lewis, "Bluspels" 265.

34 C.S. Lewis, *George MacDonald: An Anthology* (London: Fount Paperbacks, 1946), 26-27. Emphasis added.

35 C.S. Lewis, *A Preface to Paradise Lost* (London: Oxford University Press, 1942), 57. See also, "On Three Ways of Writing for Children": "For Jung, fairy tale liberates Archetypes which dwell in the collective unconscious, and when we read a good fairy tale we are obeying the old precept, Know thyself. I would venture to add to this my own theory, not indeed of the Kind as a whole, but of one feature in it: I mean, the presence of beings other than human which yet behave, in varying degrees, humanly: the giants and dwarfs and talking beasts. I believe these to be at least (for they may have many other sources of power and beauty) an admirable hieroglyphic which conveys psychology, types of character, more briefly than novelistic presentation and to readers whom novelistic presentation could not yet reach.* Consider Mr [sic] Badger in The Wind in the Willows—that extraordinary amalgam of high rank, coarse manners, gruffness, shyness, and goodness. The child who has once met Mr Badger has ever afterwards, in its bones, a knowledge of humanity and of English social history which it could not get in any other way" (C.S. Lewis, "On Three Ways of Writing for Children," in *Essay Collection and Other Short Pieces*, ed. Lesley Walmsley [London: Harper Collins, 2000], 27). * Emphasis added.

36 J.R.R. Tolkien, "On Fairy-Stories," in *Essays Presented to Charles Williams*, ed. C.S. Lewis (Grand Rapids: Eerdmans, 1968), 48.

37 Bruce Willis, Samuel L. Jackson and Robin Wright, *Unbreakable*, directed by M. Night Shyamalan (Burbank: Touchstone, 2000).

38 Joseph Campbell, *The Hero with a Thousand Faces* (Princeton, NJ: Princeton University Press, 1973), 3-46.

39 Owen Barfield, *Poetic Diction: A Study in Meaning* (Middletown: Wesleyan University Press, 1973), 45-92.

40 Barfield, *Diction*, 80.

41 Johnny Depp and Winona Ryder, *Edward Scissorhands*, directed by Tim Burton (Los Angeles: Twentieth Century Fox, 1990).

42 C.S. Lewis, "The Language of Religion," in *Essay Collection and Other Short Pieces*, ed. Lesley Walmsley (London: Harper Collins, 2000), 263.

43 Ibid, 262.

44 Ibid.

45 Ibid, 265.

46 Lewis, "Culture," 90.

47 C.S. Lewis, "Our English Syllabus," in *Rehabilitations and Other Essays* (London: Oxford University Press, 1939), 81-82.

48 C.S. Lewis, "26 October 1955," in *Collected Letters 3*, 667.

49 See especially Tolkien, "Fairy," 74-75, 86-89.

50 Lewis, "Three," 509.

51 See below for Lewis's own example of how the Narnia books came into being.

52 C.S. Lewis, "Christian Apologetics," in *Essay Collection and Other Short Pieces*, ed. Lesley Walmsley (London: Harper Collins, 2000), 150. Lewis also says, "It is not the books written in direct defense of Materialism that make the modern man a materialist; it is the materialistic assumptions in all the other books. In the same way, it is not books on Christianity that will really trouble him [the

anti-Christian]. But he would be troubled if, whenever he wanted a cheap popular introduction to some science, the best work on the market was always by a Christian" (Ibid).

53 Lewis, "Culture," 90.

54 C.S. Lewis, *Letters to Malcolm: Chiefly on Prayer* (San Diego: Harcourt Brace Jovanovich, 1964), 92-93.

55 C.S. Lewis, "Horrid Red Things," in *Essay Collection and Other Short Pieces*, ed. Lesley Walmsley (London: Harper Collins, 2000), 128.

56 Ibid, 128-29.

57 C.S. Lewis, *The Screwtape Letters* (New York: Collier Books, 1942), 12-13.

58 C.S. Lewis, "Sometimes Fairy Stories May Say Best What's To Be Said," in *Essay Collection and Other Short Pieces*, ed. Lesley Walmsley (London: Harper Collins, 2000), 527.

59 Ibid, 527-28.

60 C.S. Lewis, *The Abolition of Man: Reflections on Education with Special Reference to the Teaching of English in the Upper Forms of Schools* (New York: Collier Books, 1947), 26-27.

61 Ibid, 34.

62 To paraphrase Lewis's least favorite line from Eliot's "Prufrock" (T. S. Eliot, "The Love Song of J. Alfred Prufrock," in *The Norton Anthology of Poetry*, 5th ed., eds. Margaret Ferguson, Mary Jo Salter and Jon Stallworthy [New York: Norton, 2005])—see C.S. Lewis, "A Confession," in *Poems*, ed. Walter Hooper (San Diego: Harcourt Brace, 1992), 1 where Lewis waxes poetic on his inability, after twenty years of looking at evenings, to see how any of them might "suggest / A patient etherized upon a table . . . " (lines 4-5).

63 Lewis, *Abolition*, 33-34.

64 C.S. Lewis, *The Voyage of the Dawn Treader*, (New York: Harper Collins, 1952), 1.

65 Ibid, 2.

66 Ibid, 89.

67 Ibid, 92.

68 Ibid, 131.

Christ, Culture, and C.S. Lewis

WILL VAUS

In his attitude as a Christian toward the arts, literature, and culture, C.S. Lewis maintained a position somewhere between the Anabaptist separatist approach to culture and the Calvinist transformation approach. Lewis seems to fit within the "Christ above Culture" approach articulated by H. Richard Niebuhr in his classic work *Christ and Culture*. Angus Menuge summarizes this position as follows:

> According to this view what is needed is not blank affirmation or rejection of culture for Christ but a synthesis of Christ and culture. It is pointed out that culture cannot be all bad because it is founded on the nature created good by God, and that although nature and culture are fallen, they are still subject to God. The view emphasizes that good works are carried out in culture, yet are only made possible by grace, so that the kingdom of grace impinges on the kingdom of the world from above. Only through grace can we love our neighbor, yet only in culture can we act on that love. On this view, "We cannot say 'Either Christ or culture,' because we are dealing with God in both cases," yet we must not say "'Both Christ and culture,' as though there were no great distinction between, them." For in His promises, Christ goes beyond culture, drawing us to the Father in heaven, but in His commands He directs us to act in culture . . .[1]

With that summary in mind, let us examine what Lewis had to say about the Arts.

RELATIONSHIP OF CHRISTIANITY TO THE ARTS

In *Mere Christianity* Lewis writes that Christianity "was never intended to replace or supersede the ordinary human arts and sciences: it is rather a director which will set them all to the right jobs, and a source of energy which will give them all new life, if only they will put themselves at its disposal."[2] Furthermore, Lewis writes that the arts are not merely to be subsumed by the Church as such. "Christian literature comes from Christian novelists and dramatists—not from the bench of bishops getting together and trying to write plays and novels in their spare time."[3]

So, what is art, from Lewis's perspective? Art and philosophy are but clumsy imitations of the business of heaven: the soul's never-completed attempt to communicate its unique vision to other people.[4]

What, then, is the purpose of art? Lewis generally sees a very humble role for the arts in society. In writing to his friend, Dom Bede Griffiths in 1940 Lewis says,

> I do most thoroughly agree with what you say about Art and Literature. To my mind they can only be healthy when they are either (a) admittedly aiming at nothing but innocent recreation or (b) definitely the handmaids of religious or at least moral truth. Dante is alright and Pickwick is alright. But the great serious irreligious art-art for art's sake-is all balderdash; and incidentally never exists when art is really flourishing. In fact one can say of Art as an author I recently read said of love (sexual love I mean), 'It ceases to be a devil when it ceases to be a god'. Isn't that well put? So many things—nay every real thing—is good if only it will be humble and ordinate.[5]

Thus, art itself, to Lewis's mind, is good, so long as it remains humble and ordinate. In other words, art must take its proper, or ordinate position, under God.

GOD IS THE GREAT ARTIST

Lewis believes that God is the great Artist with a capital "A." Furthermore, we, as human beings, are God's great artwork. In *The Problem of Pain* Lewis writes:

> We are, not metaphorically but in very truth, a Divine work of art, something that God is making, and therefore something with which He will not be satisfied until it has a certain character. Here again we come up against what I have called the 'intolerable compliment.' Over a sketch made idly to amuse a child, an artist may not take much trouble: he may be content to let it go even though it is not exactly as he meant it to be. But over the great picture of his life-the work which he loves, though in a different fashion, as intensely as a man loves a woman or a mother a child—he will take endless trouble—and would, doubtless, thereby give endless trouble to the picture if it were sentient. One can imagine a sentient picture, after being rubbed and scraped and re-commenced for the tenth time, wishing that it were only a thumb-nail sketch whose making was over in a minute. In the same way, it is natural for us to wish that God had designed for us a less glorious and less arduous destiny; but then we are wishing not for more love but for less.[6]

HUMANS AS SUB-CREATORS

If God is the great artist, then according to Lewis, and his friend J.R.R. Tolkien, human beings are created by God to be sub-creators. John Wain, a member of the Inklings, once recorded the following remarks by Lewis:

> Since the Creator has seen fit to build a universe and set it in motion, it is the duty of the human artist to create as lavishly as possible in his turn. The romancer, who invents a whole world, is worshiping God more effectively than the mere realist who analyses that which lies about him.[7]

Lewis's view of God as the master artist with human beings as sub-artists has profound implications for Lewis's understanding of what we normally call "artistic creation." Lewis avouches that creation as applied to human authorship is a misleading term. Human authors only re-arrange elements God has provided.[8] There is not a vestige of real creativity in human beings. Lewis invites us to try to imagine a new primary color, a third sex, a fourth dimension, or even a monster that does not consist of bits of existing animals stuck together. What happens when we try to imagine thus? Nothing happens because, strictly speaking, human beings create nothing.[9] An author's work never means to others quite what he intended, because the author is only re-combining elements made by God and already containing his meanings. Because of those divine meanings in the author's materials, it is impossible that the author should ever know the whole meaning of any of his own works. In fact, the meaning he never intended may be the best and truest meaning. Writing a book, Lewis insists, is much less like creation than it is like planting a garden or begetting a child. In all three cases, human beings are only entering as one cause into a causal stream, which works in its own way.[10]

The reality of God's creation and originality was so woven into the warp and woof of Lewis's everyday thinking that he consistently denied any originality for his own books. Consequently, Lewis made the following points about originality:

> Even in literature and art, no man who bothers about originality will ever be original: whereas if you simply try to tell the truth (without caring twopence how often it has been told before) you will, nine times out of ten, become original without ever having noticed it.[11]
>
> Human will becomes truly creative and truly our own when it is wholly God's, and this is one of the many senses in which he that loses his soul shall find it.[12]

Lewis traces these thoughts about originality back to the New Testament itself. In an essay entitled "Christianity and Literature" Lewis says:

> In the New Testament the art of life itself is an art of imitation: can we, believing this, believe that literature, which must derive from real life, is to aim at being 'creative', 'original', and 'spontaneous'. 'Originality' in the New Testament is quite plainly the prerogative of God alone; even within the triune being of God it seems to be confined to the Father. The duty and happiness of every other being is placed in being derivative, in reflecting like a mirror.[13]

This is the most fundamental difference, Lewis says, between the Christian and the non-Christian in their approach to literature, and I might add, in their approach to art. However, there is another difference. The Christian will take literature (and therefore art) a little less seriously than the cultured non-Christian. The Christian artist will feel less uneasy with a purely hedonistic standard for at least many kinds of work. The unbeliever is always apt to make a kind of religion of his aesthetic experiences. However, the Christian knows from the outset that the salvation of a single soul is more important than the production or preservation of all the epics and tragedies in the world. The Christian artist, unlike the Pagan artist, will tend to look at the receivers of his artwork as his superiors, rather than his inferiors. Furthermore, the Christian artist has no objection to comedies that merely amuse and tales that merely refresh, for he will realize, like Thomas Aquinas, that we can play, as we can eat, to the glory of God.[14]

MODERN VS. ANCIENT ART

What did Lewis think about modern art? As you might imagine, he was very skeptical of its value. In his own field of literature, Lewis did not care at all for the work of fellow poet T. S. Eliot. Lewis once wrote in a letter to a correspondent,

> Yes, I'm sick of our Abracadabrist poets. What gives the show away is that their professed admirers give quite contradictory interpretations of the same poem—I'm prepared to believe that an unintelligible picture is really a very good horse if all its admirers tell me so; but when one says it's a horse, and the next that it's a ship, and the third that it's an orange, and the fourth that it's Mt. Everest, I give it up.[15]

Thus, intelligibility was one difference Lewis saw between modern artists and older ones. A second difference Lewis could discern was regarding the artist's approach to his or her work. Lewis says,

> All the great poets, painters, and musicians of old could produce great work 'to order'. One who could not would have seemed as great a humbug as a captain who could navigate or a farmer who could farm only when the fit took him.[16]

A third difference Lewis saw between the modern and the ancient artist was regarded the relationship between artist and audience. He writes,

> Until quite recently—until the latter part of the last century—it was taken for granted that the business of the artist was to delight and instruct his public. There were, of course, different publics; the street-songs and the oratorios were not addressed to the same audience (though I think a good many people liked both). And an artist might lead his public on to appreciate finer things than they had wanted at first; but he could do this only by being, from the first, if

> not merely entertaining, yet entertaining, and if not completely intelligible, yet very largely intelligible. All this has changed. In the highest aesthetic circles one now hears nothing about the artist's duty to us. It is all about our duty to him. He owes us nothing; we owe him 'recognition,' even though he has never paid the slightest attention to our tastes, interests, or habits. If we don't give it to him, our name is mud. In this shop, the customer is always wrong.[17]

A fourth difference Lewis sees between much modern art and the more ancient variety is in the quality of the work:

> Many modern novels, poems, and pictures, which we are brow-beaten into 'appreciating,' are not good work because they are not work at all. They are mere puddles of spilled sensibility or reflection. When an artist is in the strict sense working, he of course takes into account the existing taste, interests, and capacity of his audience. These, no less than the language, the marble, or the paint, are part of his raw material; to be used, tamed, sublimated, not ignored nor defied. Haughty indifference to them is not genius nor integrity; it is laziness and incompetence. You have not learned your job. Hence, real honest-to-God work, so far as the arts are concerned, now appears chiefly in low-brow art; in the film, the detective story, the children's story. These are often sound structures; seasoned wood, accurately dovetailed, the stresses all calculated; skill and labour successfully used to do what is intended. Do not misunderstand. The high-brow productions may, of course, reveal a finer sensibility and profounder thought. But a puddle is not a work, whatever rich wines or oils or medicines have gone into it.
>
> 'Great works' (of art) and 'good works' (of charity) had better also be Good Work. Let choirs sing well or not at all.[18]

A fifth difference Lewis recognizes between much modern art and ancient art is in the very goal or purpose of the artwork:

> Until quite modern times—I think, until the time of the Romantics—nobody ever suggested that literature and the arts were an end in themselves. They 'belonged to the ornamental part of life', they provided 'innocent diversion'; or else the 'refined our manners' or 'incited us to virtue' or glorified the gods. The great music had been written for Masses, the great pictures painted to fill up a space on the wall of a noble patron's dining-room or to kindle devotion in a church; the great tragedies were produced either by religious poets in honour of Dionysus or by commercial poets to entertain Londoners on half-holidays.
>
> It was only in the nineteenth century that we became aware of the full dignity of art. We began to 'take it seriously' as the Nazis take mythology seriously. But the result seems to have been a dislocation of the aesthetic life in which

> little is left for us but high-minded works which fewer and fewer people want to read or hear or see, and 'popular' works of which both those who make them and those who enjoy them are half ashamed. Just like the Nazis, by valuing too highly a real, but subordinate good, we have come near to losing that good itself.[19]

A final difference Lewis notes between ancient and modern art has to do with novelty. Lewis's senior devil Screwtape writes to the junior devil Wormwood that the demand for continual novelty:

> . . . is valuable in various ways. In the first place it diminishes pleasure while increasing desire. The pleasure of novelty is by its very nature more subject than any other to the law of diminishing returns. And continued novelty costs money, so that the desire for it spells avarice or unhappiness or both. And again, the more rapacious this desire, the sooner it must eat up all the innocent sources of pleasure and pass on to those the Enemy forbids. Thus by inflaming the horror of the Same Old Thing, we have recently made the Arts, for example, less dangerous to us than, perhaps, they have ever been, 'lowbrow' and 'high-brow' artists alike being now daily drawn into fresh, and still fresh, excesses of lasciviousness, unreason, cruelty, and pride. Finally, the desire for novelty is indispensable if we are to produce Fashions or Vogues.[20]

As you can see, Lewis intensely disliked the fashion of art and literature in his day, primarily because he saw the arts veering away from the helpful purposes for which he believed God created them.

CHRISTIANITY & CULTURE

Given Lewis's perspective on the arts in the modern world, we must ask: what was Lewis's understanding of the proper relationship between the Christian and the surrounding culture? In March 1940, Lewis published in the journal *Theology* an article entitled "Christianity and Culture." In that article, he makes several perceptive points about the relationship between Christianity and the Arts.

Lewis begins by noting that there is no correlation between a person's response to art and their fitness for humane living.[21] A fine taste in poetry or music is not a condition of salvation.[22] In response to that, I think we all can breathe a sigh of relief.

Lewis goes on to note how:

> The 'sentimentality and cheapness' of much Christian hymnody had been a strong point in my own resistance to conversion. Now I felt almost thankful for the bad hymns. It was good that we should have to lay down our precious refinement at the very doorstep of the church; good that we should be cured at the outset of our inveterate confusion between psyche and pneuma, nature

and supernature.[23]

Art is not the most important thing in life. Lewis notes that the most important thing is: "The glory of God, and, as our only means to glorifying Him, the salvation of human souls."[24] That is the real business of life.

What, then, is the value of culture? Lewis turns first to the New Testament for an answer. There he finds several statements that speak against the value of culture. We are told in the New Testament that whatever is highly valued on a natural level is to be abandoned the moment it conflicts with the service of God.[25] Even blameless conformity to the Jewish law is considered as muck next to Christ, how much more so culture.[26] Furthermore, there are warnings against superiority. We are to become as children;[27] we are not to call one another Rabbi;[28] we are to dread reputation.[29] Few that are wise according to the flesh are called to be Christ-followers.[30] A man must become a fool by secular standards before he can attain real wisdom.[31]

However, Lewis also finds some Scripture favorable toward culture. Secular learning is embodied in the Magi, and not condemned. Talents in Jesus' parable might conceivably include talents in the arts. The miracle at Cana, by sanctifying an innocent, sensuous pleasure, could be taken to sanctify a recreational use of culture. Aesthetic enjoyment of nature was hallowed by Jesus' praise of the lilies. Some use of science was implied by St. Paul's demand that we should perceive the invisible through the visible.[32]

Lewis concludes his overview of New Testament attitudes toward culture by remarking that, on the whole, the New Testament seems, if not hostile, at least cold toward culture. We may still think culture innocent after reading the New Testament, but we are not encouraged to think it important.

However, Lewis goes on to cite the views of culture presented by other authors outside of Scripture. He cites the Anglican divine, Richard Hooker's statement that Scripture does not necessarily contain everything important or even necessary to life on earth.

Lewis examines the views of other classical authors regarding culture. Aristotle is positive toward culture, whereas Plato only tolerates that culture which conduces either to the intellectual vision of the good or the military efficiency of the commonwealth. Lewis notes that James Joyce and D. H. Lawrence would have fared ill in the Republic. Lewis notes how the Buddha, St. Augustine, Jerome, Thomas a Kempis, and the *Theologia Germanica* were anti-cultural.

Furthermore, Lewis says we shouldn't suppose that the values of imaginative literature have become more Christian since the time of the Early Church Fathers. Everything is questioned in Hamlet except the duty of revenge. In medieval romance, honor and sexual love are the true values, and in nineteenth century fiction, sexual love and material prosperity are the highest priorities. In romantic poetry, enjoyment of nature is one of the highest goods; this enjoyment of nature in romantic poetry ranges from pantheistic mysticism to innocent sensuousness. Romantic poetry also ranks "sehnsucht" very high on the list, a longing awakened by the past, the distant, and the imagined supernatural. In modern literature, the life of liberated instinct is the highest good. Lewis notes that the sub-Christian or anti-Christian values of literature do infect many readers.

On the other side of the argument, St. Gregory compares our use of secular culture to the action of the Israelites going down to the Philistines to have their knives sharpened. If we are to convert our heathen neighbors then we must understand their culture. On the Gregorian view, culture is a weapon, but it is a weapon that must be set aside as soon as we safely can.

Milton gives a glorious defense of the freedom to explore all good and evil through the arts, but this is based upon an aristocratic preoccupation with great souls and shows a contemptuous indifference to the mass of humanity.

John Henry Newman insisted on the beauty of culture for its own sake, but sternly resisted the temptation to confuse it with things spiritual. This leaves Lewis still wondering, "How much of one's time may a Christian legitimately spend upon culture, given that it is less than spiritual?"

Lewis came to the point of recognizing that he could no longer give to culture the status he had given it before his conversion. If any constructive case for culture is to be given, it will have to be of a humbler sort.

Lewis felt justified in continuing as a literary critic and a teacher of English literature after his conversion to Christianity because scholarly work was a way he could earn his living. On this score Lewis found the New Testament to be very encouraging.[33] Provided there is a demand for culture, and that culture is not actually deleterious, Lewis concluded that he was justified in making his living by it, especially since he did not feel fit for any other vocation.

Lewis came to believe that to counter bad culture it is appropriate for appropriately gifted Christians to become "culture-sellers." However, this does not authorize the Christian artist to engage in a "bait and switch" game in which the artist takes money to supply culture and actually uses the opportunity to provide something else—namely homiletics and apologetics. That, to Lewis's mind, is stealing. However, the mere presence of Christians among the culture-sellers will provide an antidote to bad culture.[34]

Is there, then, intrinsic goodness in culture for its own sake? Lewis answers this question by examining what culture has done for him personally. He notes that culture has given him an enormous amount of pleasure. Pleasure in itself is good, so long as it is not accepted in a way that violates the moral law. Often, as Newman saw, the enjoyment of culture can be an excellent diversion from guilty pleasure. To the non-Christian the values of honor, romantic love, pantheistic enjoyment of nature, and sehnsucht may all serve as a schoolmaster to lead one to Christ.

To sum up, Lewis's view of the relationship between Christianity and Culture is this:

> That culture is a storehouse of the best (sub-Christian) values. These values are in themselves of the soul, not the spirit. But God created the soul. Its values may be expected, therefore, to contain some reflection or ante-past of the spiritual values. They will save no man. They resemble the regenerate life only as affection resembles charity, or honour resembles virtue, or the moon the sun. But though 'like is not the same', it is better than unlike. Imitation may pass into initiation. For some it is a good beginning. For others it is not; culture is not everyone's road into Jerusalem, and for some it is a road out.[35]

For the non-Christian, culture may help to conversion. The cultured person is almost compelled to realize that reality is very odd and that ultimate truth must therefore have the characteristics of strangeness.

What good is culture, then, in the life of the Christian? Lewis says that if all cultural values are dim ectypes of the truth, then Christians can still recognize them as such. If we must rest and play, where better to do so than in the suburbs of Jerusalem? It is lawful to rest our eyes in moonlight—especially now that we know it is only sunlight at second hand. Not all people are called to glorify God directly in their vocation, as are ministers of the Gospel. All other Christians must glorify God at second hand, by offering their work to the Lord. Artistic work, if innocent, can be offered to the Lord just as the sweeping of a room can be so offered. The work of a charwoman and the work of a poet become spiritual in the same way—by being offered to the Lord.

ENJOYMENT OF ART

How is art to be enjoyed, according to Lewis? As we might expect, for Lewis "Culture" is irrelevant; what counts is real enjoyment of art. We shouldn't recommend a certain artist or author to another person because his or her work is "cultured" but because it is enjoyable.[36]

Lewis draws an important distinction between enjoying art because one finds it enjoyable and feigning enjoyment because one's friends approve of a certain kind of art. He says,

> A live dog is better than a dead lion. In the same way, after a certain kind of sherry party, where there have been cataracts of culture but never one word or one glance that suggested a real enjoyment of any art, any person, or any natural object, my heart warms to the schoolboy on the bus who is reading Fantasy and Science Fiction, rapt and oblivious of all the world beside. For here also I should feel that I had met something real and live and unfabricated; genuine literary experience, spontaneous and compulsive, disinterested. I should have hopes of that boy. Those who have greatly cared for any book whatever may

> possibly come to care, some day, for good books. The organs of appreciation exist in them. They are not impotent. And even if this particular boy is never going to like anything severer than science-fiction, even so,
>
> The child whose love is here, at least doth reap
> One precious gain, that he forgets himself.[37]

THE CHRISTIAN ARTIST

In the autumn of 1939, Lewis preached a sermon in Oxford entitled "Learning in War-Time." In that sermon, he asks the question: how can we carry on with learning when an all-important war is looming all around us? This, Lewis says, raises an even more serious question: how is it right, or even psychologically possible, for creatures who are every moment advancing either to heaven or to hell, to spend any fraction of the little time allowed them in this world on such comparative trivialities as literature or art, mathematics, or biology? Lewis says the bottom line is that we do spend time on things other than saving souls. Christianity does not exclude ordinary activities. We are to get on with our jobs. Scripture assumes we go to dinner parties. Jesus attended a wedding and provided miraculous wine.

> Under the aegis of His Church, and in the most Christian ages, learning and the arts flourish. The solution of this paradox is, of course, well known to you. 'Whether ye eat or drink or whatsoever ye do, do all to the glory of God.'
>
> All our merely natural activities will be accepted, if they are offered to God, even the humblest: and all of them, even the noblest, will be sinful if they are not.[38]

To paraphrase what Lewis says about philosophy and apply it to the arts: Good art must exist, if for no other reason, because bad art needs to be answered.[39]

ART THAT TEACHES

So then, is it the function of the Christian artist to use his artwork to teach others about Christianity? Possibly, says Lewis, so long as the art and the teaching are both done well. Lewis writes to a friend:

> I'm with you on the main issue—that art can teach (and much great art deliberately sets out to do so) without at all ceasing to be art. On the particular case of Wells I would agree with Burke, because in Wells it seems to me that one has first-class pure fantasy (*Time Machine, First Men in the Moon*) and third-class didacticism; i.e. I object to his novels with a purpose not because they have a purpose but because I think them bad. Just as I object to the preaching passages in Thackeray not because I dislike sermons but because I dislike bad

> sermons. To me therefore Wells and Thackeray are instances that obscure the issue. It must be fought on books where the doctrine is as good on its own merits as the art—e.g. Bunyan, Chesterton (as you agree), Tolstoi, Charles Williams, Virgil.[40]

ARTS IN THE CHURCH

I think we can also profitably learn from what Lewis wrote about arts in the Church, though he wrote on this subject only indirectly. I believe we can get at Lewis's ideas on this subject by looking at what he had to say about liturgy and about music, specifically, as used in church services.

In *Letters to Malcolm* Lewis asserted that laypeople should take what is given them in the liturgy of the Church and make the best of it—quite a humble perspective coming from one who greatly appreciated the arts. Lewis thought this task of the layperson would be easier if the liturgy of the Church of England was always and everywhere the same. He was not in favor of innovations. Novelty can only have an entertainment value. We don't go to church to be entertained but to use the service, to enact it. We are better able to worship and focus on God when we are so familiar with the service that nothing distracts our attention from the Lord. Every novelty prevents this; it focuses our attention on the service, or even on the one leading the service, rather than on God. Lewis claimed that his entire liturgical position boiled down to a plea for permanence and uniformity. He asserted that he would especially appreciate uniformity in the time taken by services. A lengthened service may throw the whole day into hurry and confusion for the layperson since he has less control over the hours of his business than the clergy do.

Any tendency to have a passionate preference for one type of service must be regarded simply as a temptation.[41] Lewis regarded a love of religious observances as a merely natural taste.[42] He himself denied being choosy about services. He claimed any form would do for him so long as he was given time to get used to it.[43] He contended that if we can't lay down our liturgical preferences at the door of the Church, along with all other carnal baggage, we should bring those preferences into Church with us to be humbled and modified.[44]

As to the words of the service, Lewis believed that if you have a liturgy in the vernacular then you must have a changing liturgy, because no living language can be timeless. He thought it best if any changes made to the liturgy, however, would be made gradually and almost imperceptibly, with only one obsolete word being changed every century.[45] He made the point that prose needs to be very good in a special way in order to stand up to repeated reading aloud. He felt it would be hard for any modern writer to beat Thomas Cranmer, the original compiler of the English prayer book, as a stylist.[46]

Yet, in favor of diversity, Lewis said that what pleased him about an Orthodox mass he once attended was that there seemed to be no prescribed behavior for the congregation. Some stood, some knelt, some sat, some walked, and one person even crawled around on the floor. The beauty of it was that no one took any notice of what anyone else was doing.[47]

Lewis believed that anything the congregation could do could also properly and profitably be offered to God in public worship, including such things as sacred dance, so long as the congregation could do it well.[48] (One can quickly see how this principle might be applied to the use of other arts in the Church.) Lewis affirmed that the most valuable thing the Psalms did for him was to express that delight in God that made David dance. He thought this spirit was so much better than the merely dutiful churchgoing and laborious "saying our prayers" to which many Christians in his day were often reduced. He wanted to see the Anglican Church recover the same joy seen in the Psalms, but for the Christian, such joy would need to be compatible with the tragic depth of the cross.[49]

Regarding music and literature, Lewis often wrote about how both books and music conveyed beauty to him. However, he urged that we must not trust in books or in music because the beauty is not in them, it only comes through them, and what comes through them is longing.[50] Lewis was a great lover of music, at least in his youth. He especially enjoyed the music of Wagner, for it communicated joy, sehnsucht, longing to his soul.[51] Certainly, Screwtape expressed the opposite of Lewis's view when he said that he detested both music and silence and that he wanted to make the whole universe one noise in the end.[52]

However, Lewis states some caveats regarding the religious importance of music. He writes that we must distinguish between the effect which music has on the musically illiterate, who get only an emotional effect, and the effect that it has on real musical scholars who perceive the structure of the music and get an intellectual satisfaction as well as an emotional one. He asserts that either of these effects is ambivalent from the religious point of view. Both emotional and intellectual satisfaction can be a preparation for or even a medium for meeting God, but these satisfactions can also be a distraction and impediment to meeting God. He goes so far as to suggest that the emotional effect of music may also be a delusion. Some people, feeling certain emotions in church, think they have had a supernatural experience when they have only had a natural one. Genuinely religious emotion is only a servant; no soul is saved by having it or damned by lacking it. The test of music is always the same. We should ask ourselves, "Does this music make me more obedient, more God-centered and neighbor-centered or more self-centered?"[53]

> Lewis found hymns to be dead wood in the English Church because he thought that the English couldn't sing well and that the art of poetry had developed for two centuries in a private and subjective direction. Yet, he felt if the hymnody could be improved then it was his duty, as a layperson, to submit to it, whether it would suit his preference or not.[54] Lewis often noted how he disliked hymns,

> but as he grew in his Christian life, he saw that saints very different from him were singing these same hymns with devotion and benefit. This, Lewis maintained, helped to peel away his pride and conceit.[55]

Lewis wrote an essay entitled "On Church Music" in which he made the following points: First of all, nothing should be done or sung or said in church which does not either glorify God or edify the people or both. Secondly, church music glorifies God by being excellent in its own kind. In the composition and highly trained execution of sacred music we offer our natural gifts, at their highest, to God. Third, as noted above, Lewis was unconvinced that the physical and emotional exhilaration produced by singing hymns had any religious relevance. He asserted that he would like to have fewer, better, and shorter hymns, especially fewer. Fourth, he thought the case for abolishing all church music was strong. (Incidentally, Lewis most regularly attended the service without music at his parish church.) However, he recognized that the main sense of Christendom would be against him and others if they tried to abolish all church music. Fifth, the High Brows and the Low Brows each assume far too easily the spiritual value of the music they like. Sixth, Lewis was confident that there are two musical situations on which God's blessing rests. One is where the High Brow priest or organist gives the people the humbler and coarser fare that they want, out of a desire to bring them closer to God. The other is where the Low Brow layperson submits humbly and patiently to the music that he cannot fully appreciate, in the belief that this somehow glorifies God. To both these groups, acting in this way, church music becomes a means of grace. Where both the choir and the congregation are on this right road, no great difficulties will occur. Discrepancies of taste and capacity provide opportunities for charity and humility. What matters most is our intention in offering our praise to God through music.[56]

Lewis believed that our present services are merely attempts at worship. When we attempt to worship God in Church, what we are really doing is tuning our instruments for heaven, where one day we shall praise God perfectly, with total delight.[57]

THE ART OF WRITING

How did Lewis go about the art of writing? Lewis says that in an author's mind there bubbles up, every now and then, the material for a story. For Lewis himself this process invariably began with him seeing pictures in his mind. The bubbling process leads to nothing, unless there is also a form in which to write the story: verse or prose, short story, novel, play, etc. When these two aspects: the content and the form come together then the author's impulse is complete.

However, Lewis says, it is at this point that the human being as a whole, not just the author, must get involved. The author's desire is very much like an itch, and the whole human is the one who must decide if this particular itch will be scratched or not. The human being must ask if the writing of this story will fit in with everything else the writer needs to do or be. Perhaps the whole idea is too frivolous to warrant the time needed to write the story. Perhaps the story would not be edifying to other people. All of these questions must be asked and answered. When the work looks like it will be good all around, not just in a literary sense, then the writing can really begin in earnest.

Lewis goes on to tell us how this whole process applied to the writing of his fairy stories. First, he notes that he did not begin by asking himself how he could say something about Christianity to children, then fixing on the fairy story as an instrument. Rather, once again, the whole process began with a picture, in this case with the picture of a faun carrying an umbrella in a snowy wood, a picture that had been in Lewis's mind since he was sixteen. Finally, when he was in his forties he wrote a story about it. At first there wasn't anything Christian about the story.

Next came the form. The images he had in his mind: a faun, a queen on a sledge, a magnificent lion, all of these images sorted themselves into events. (He was having nightmares about lions around that time.) It seemed that the form that would work best to convey this story was the fairy tale.

After the content and form came together, Lewis says the man in him began to see how these stories might steal past certain inhibitions that had paralyzed his own religion in childhood. Why was it so hard to feel the way you were supposed to feel about Christ? It was because you were told you must feel a certain way about him. However, suppose you put a Christ-like figure into an imaginary world. Could the author then make the person behind Christianity appear in his real potency and thus steal past watchful dragons? Lewis felt it could be done.

The Christian bit was Lewis's human contribution. However, that cognitive part of Lewis could have done nothing if it were not for the bubbling process in his imagination. This is how Lewis came to write *The Chronicles of Narnia*.[58]

What advice does Lewis the author have for other budding authors about writing? First, he says, you must know what you want to say and then say exactly that.[59] There are no right and wrong answers about language as there are in arithmetic. Good English is whatever educated English people speak, and that varies from place to place. Lewis recommends not taking any advice from teachers or textbooks in this regard. What really matters is the following:

1. Always use language in such a way to make quite clear what you mean.
2. Always prefer the plain, direct word to the long vague one.
3. Never use abstract nouns when concrete ones will do. If you mean 'more people died', don't say: 'mortality rose'.
4. Don't use adjectives that merely tell your reader what you want him or her to feel. Instead of telling the reader a thing is terrible, describe the thing so that the reader will be terrified.

5. Don't use words too big for the subject. Don't say 'infinitely' when you mean 'very'; otherwise you won't have any word left when you want to talk about something that is truly infinite.[60]

In an early letter to his life-long friend, Arthur Greeves, Lewis urged him to write something, anything, but at any rate to write.[61] For Lewis, writing was an itch. However, it was also a trained habit. It was something he did every day. Not everything he wrote was worth publishing. However, by putting ink to paper every day he eventually came up with a lot that was worth sharing with others.

CONCLUSION

Finally, I believe Lewis would say to all Christian writers today that we need more books by Christian authors on a wide variety of subjects. Lewis says,

> The difficulty we are up against is this. We can make people (often) attend to the Christian point of view for half an hour or so; but the moment they have gone away from our lecture or laid down our article, they are plunged back into a world where the opposite position is taken for granted. As long as that situation exists, widespread success is simply impossible. We must attack the enemy's line of communication. What we want is not more little books about Christianity, but more little books by Christians on other subjects—with their Christianity latent.[62]

I think we can take Lewis's statement and apply it to the arts in general. We need more sculpture, more painting, more dance, more drama, as well as more literature by Christians. That is, we need more art that is well done to the glory of God, regardless of the immediate subject of the work of art or literature.

ENDNOTES

1 "Niebuhr's *Christ and Culture* Reexamined," accessed February 27, 2013, http://www.mtio.com/articles/bissar26.htm.

2 C.S. Lewis, *Mere Christianity* (London: Geoffrey Bles, 1952), 65.

3 Ibid., 66.

4 C.S. Lewis, *The Problem of Pain* (London: Geoffrey Bles, 1946), 138.

5 Hooper, Walter, ed., *The Collected Letters of C.S. Lewis*, Volume 2 (New York: HarperCollins, 2004), 390-391.

6 Lewis, *The Problem of Pain*, 30-31.

7 John Wain, *Sprightly Running: Part of an Autobiography* (New York: St. Martin's Press, 1963), 182.

8 C.S. Lewis, *Letters to Malcolm: Chiefly on Prayer* (London: Geoffrey Bles, 1964), 98.

9 C.S. Lewis, *Miracles*, (London: Geoffrey Bles, 1947), 42.

10 Hooper, *Collected Letters*, Volume 2, 555.

11 Lewis, *Mere Christianity*, 177.

12 Lewis, *The Problem of Pain*, 90.

13 C.S. Lewis, *Christian Reflections* (London: Geoffrey Bles, 1967), 6.
14 Ibid., 10.
15 Hooper, Walter, ed., *The Collected Letters of C.S. Lewis*, Volume 3 (New York: HarperCollins, 2007), 449.
16 C.S. Lewis, *Reflections on the Psalms* (London: Geoffrey Bles, 1958), 128.
17 C.S. Lewis, *The World's Last Night and Other Essays* (San Diego: Harcourt Brace and Company, 1987), 78-79.
18 Ibid., 80.
19 C.S. Lewis, *God in the Dock*, (Grand Rapids: Eerdmans, 1994), 279-280.
20 C.S. Lewis, *The Screwtape Letters* (London: Geoffrey Bles, 1942), 128.
21 Lewis, *Christian Reflections*, 12-13.
22 Ibid., 13. See also Hooper, ed., *Collected Letters*, Volume 3, 69.
23 Lewis, *Christian Reflections*, 13.
24 Ibid., 14.
25 Matthew 5:29; 12:48; 19:12; Luke 14:26.
26 Philippians 3:8.
27 Matthew 18:3.
28 Matthew 23:8.
29 Luke 7:26.
30 1 Corinthians 1:26.
31 1 Corinthians 3:18.
32 Romans 1:20.
33 1 Thessalonians 4:11; 2 Thessalonians 3:11; Ephesians 4:28.
34 Lewis's view at this point is very close to the Gregorian view of culture as a weapon.
35 Lewis, *Christian Reflections*, 23.
36 Lewis, *The World's Last Night*, 33-34.
37 Ibid., 39.
38 C.S. Lewis, *Transposition and other Addresses* (London: Geoffrey Bles, 1949), 49.
39 Ibid., 51.
40 Hooper, ed., *Collected Letters*, Volume 2, 918-919.
41 Lewis, *Letters to Malcolm*, 14.
42 Ibid., 46.
43 Ibid., 130.
44 Lewis, *God in the Dock*, 336.
45 Lewis, *Letters to Malcolm*, 14-15.
46 Ibid., 17.
47 Ibid., 19-20.
48 Lewis, *God in the Dock*, 331.
49 Lewis, *Reflections on the Psalms*, 45-46, 50, 52.
50 Lewis, *Transposition*, 24.
51 C.S. Lewis, *Surprised by Joy* (London: Geoffrey Bles, 1955), 75-77.
52 Lewis, *The Screwtape Letters*, 113-114.
53 Hooper, ed., *Collected Letters*, Volume 3, 731-732.
54 Lewis, *God in the Dock*, 331. See also Lewis, *Reflections on the Psalms*, 94 and Lewis, *Christian Reflections*, 13.
55 Lewis, *God in the Dock*, 61-62.

56 Lewis, *Christian Reflections*, 94-99.

57 Lewis, *Reflections on the Psalms*, 96-97.

58 C.S. Lewis, *On Stories* (San Diego: Harcourt Brace & Company, 1982), 45-47.

59 Lewis, *God in the Dock*, 263.

60 Hooper, ed., *Collected Letters*, Volume 2, 766.

61 Walter Hooper, ed., *The Collected Letters of C.S. Lewis*, Volume 1 (London: HarperCollins, 2000), 186.

62 Lewis, *God in the Dock*, 93. See also Hooper, ed., *Collected Letters*, Volume 2, 683.

OTHER SQUARE HALO BOOKS

It Was Good: Making Art to the Glory of God

"*It Was Good* is one of the best examples I know of the new day that is dawning in Christian conversation on the arts. What we have needed is a thick description both of Christianity and of art making. And both are here in abundance, along with generous displays of great art motivated by faith both from the present and the past. This will definitely be a part of my course syllabus."
—William Dyrness, Fuller Theological Seminary

It Was Good: Making Music to the Glory of God

"Lively, engaging and eminently readable—this book shows that it is still possible to write about music in a way that enriches our experience of it. Above all, it will renew your gratitude to God for making such an art possible."
—Jeremy Begbie, Duke University

The Beginning: A Second Look at the First Sin

"Bauer's work demonstrates a strong commitment to the authority of Scripture as well as a creative approach to the theology of the fall into sin. His efforts will stimulate much helpful discussion about the nature of good and evil on very practical levels."
—Richard Pratt, Reformed Theological Seminary

Objects of Grace: Conversations on Creativity and Faith

"[A] colorful and concise collection of interviews and art from some of America's most intriguing Christian artists. [James] Romaine interviews ten artists, presenting color reproductions of the artists' work along with the text of the interviews. Each artist dialogues on what it means for a Christian to engage in the creating process."
—*Image: A Journal of the Arts & Religion*

Beauty Given by Grace: The Biblical Prints of Sadao Watanabe

". . . a much needed book on a significant Christian artist who is known all over the world and, rare though it may be, it is vast in its importance. Not only are the evocative, Japanese-styled prints beautiful to behold, cover many Biblical texts in Biblical order, the well-crafted essays are very informative and strangely poignant."
—Hearts & Minds Bookstore